VOICES
IN
THE DARK

VOICES IN THE DARK

The Narrative Patterns
of *Film Noir*

J. P. Telotte

University of Illinois Press
Urbana and Chicago

Publication of this work was supported in part by a grant from
the Georgia Tech Foundation, Inc.

First paperback edition, 1989

⊗This book is printed on acid-free paper.

Library of Congress Cataloging-in-Publication Data

Telotte, J. P., 1949–
    Voices in the dark : the narrative patterns of film noir / J.P.
Telotte.
        p.   cm.
    Filmography: p.
    Bibliography: p.
    Includes index.
ISBN 0-252-06056-3 (alk. paper) / ISBN 978-0-252-06056-4 (alk. paper)
    1. Films noirs. I. Title.
PN1995.9.F54T44   1989
791.43'09'09355—dc19   88-17525
                                           CIP

Portions of this work have appeared earlier in the following journal articles:

"Effacement and Subjectivity: *Murder, My Sweet*'s Problematic Vision,"
    Literature/Film Quarterly 14.4 (1987): 227–36.
"*Film Noir* and the Dangers of Discourse," *Quarterly Review of Film Studies* 9.2
    (1934): 101–12.
"*Film Noir* and the Double Indemnity of Discourse," *Genre* 18.1 (1985):
    57–73.
"Narration, Desire, and a *Lady from Shanghai*," *South Atlantic Review* 49.1
    (1984): 56–71.
"Outside the System: The Documentary Voice of *Film Noir*," *New Orleans
    Review* 14.2 (1987): 55–63.
"Seeing in a *Dark Passage*," *Film Criticism* 9.2 (1985): 15–27.
"Talk and Trouble: *Kiss Me Deadly*'s Apocalyptic Discourse," *Journal of
    Popular Film and Television* 13.2 (1985): 69–79.
"Tangled Networks and Wrong Numbers," *Film Criticism* 10.3 (1986): 36–48.

Contents

Acknowledgments   vii

1   *Noir* Narration   1

2   The Double Indemnity of *Noir* Discourse   40

3   Narration, Desire, and *The Lady from Shanghai*   57

4   Tangled Networks and Wrong Numbers   74

5   Effacement and Subjectivity: *Murder, My Sweet*'s Troubled Vision   88

6   "The Real Thing Is Something Else": Truth and Subjectivity in *The Lady in the Lake*   103

7   Seeing in a *Dark Passage*   120

8   The Transparent Reality of the Documentary *Noir*   134

9   The Evolving Truth of the Documentary *Noir*   154

10   *Film Noir* and the Dangers of Discourse   179

11   Talk and Trouble: *Kiss Me Deadly*'s Apocalyptic Discourse   198

12   Conclusion: *Noir*'s Dark Voice   216

Appendix: A *Noir* Filmography   224

Bibliography   236

Index   243

Acknowledgments

Many people contributed to the successful completion of this work and are due some thanks.

I appreciate the help of many colleagues and friends who have read, listened to, and commented upon this work in its various stages, among them Bob Wood, Gerald Duchovnay, and Lloyd Michaels. I owe a special thanks to Bill Nichols and Bruce Kawin for their sensitive evaluations of the work and helpful, in many cases formative, suggestions.

The Department of English at Georgia Tech and its Head, Elizabeth Evans, provided me with release time at a crucial point in this work. And my students at Tech not only humored my enthusiasm for dark tales of crime and corruption but also asked the sort of questions about these films that prompted thought.

My wife Leigh also deserves much credit, partly for putting up with far more *films noir* than one should, in a short period, be exposed to, and also for acting as chief consultant and troubleshooter on all matters related to the computer, software, and printer needed for this project.

Finally, I want to thank the editorial staff at the University of Illinois Press for their interest in and patience with this work. Senior Editor Ann Lowry Weir has, as in the past, provided needed support, good judgment, and reassurance, and Patricia Hollahan contributed an eye for detail and unfelicitous phrasings of the sort to which I am prone.

CHAPTER 1

Noir Narration

The deep of night is crept upon our talk,
And nature must obey necessity.
—Shakespeare

In the darkened movie theater, it is understood, we are supposed to be silent. Sometimes reminders appear on the screen to prompt us, and there are always the irritated looks of fellow filmgoers to reinforce the custom. If for some reason we have to speak, we know not to raise our voices above a whisper, for here it is the *movie's* role to talk and ours to listen. Most popular American films seem to take this injunction a bit further; that is, they seldom appear to speak above a whisper about the problems that weigh most heavily upon us. Instead, they usually talk in what we might term a *conventional* way: encoding our concerns within patterns of generic conventions, reducing them to a kind of sign language, and thereby resolving them for us in an imaginary, almost silent way. Such quiet "speech," however, has generally proved quite useful for a culture like ours, propelled as it is by such varied and contradictory dreams that their unmuffled or shrill expression might well create problems rather than resolve them.

Violations, of course, always occur; in the theater someone invariably talks and spoils our concentration. The same thing happens in our film. For from time to time, despite a possibility of disturbing viewers, our films will speak directly and even forcefully about our cultural and human problems. They do so not only because, as Walker Percy warns, "silence prolonged can induce terror," but also because talk, even when it addresses those "unspeakable feelings" that "nobody wants to hear about," can serve a therapeutic function of sorts.[1] "Through its re-presenting," Percy explains, our alienation, fear, or cultural anxiety can undergo "an aesthetic reversal," producing a measure of comfort in the very "speakability" of our problems.[2] Seen in this context, the violation of a customary silence, or the raising of popular film's narrative voice, seems a natural response to a kind of need. It is a need whose satisfaction points up the basic contradictions that, in the modern world, seem to structure both our speech and our silences.

When we look at the group of films we call *film noir*, we find both a notable instance of such violation and a revealing articulation of the sort of tensions that shape our film narratives. This large body of films, flourishing in America in the period 1941–58,[3] generally focuses on urban crime and corruption, and on sudden upwellings of violence in a culture whose fabric seems to be unraveling. Because of these typical concerns, the *film noir* seems fundamentally *about* violations: vice, corruption, unrestrained desire, and, most fundamental of all, abrogation of the American dream's most basic promises—of hope, prosperity, and safety from persecution. Taken as a whole, the *noir* films are noteworthy neither for their subtlety of expression nor their muting of our cultural problems; to the contrary, they deploy the darkest imagery to sketch starkly disconcerting assessments of the human and social condition. In their vision, crime and corruption seem almost a matter of decor, dark trappings of a world suddenly shown in a new and most revealing light.

Admittedly, American films have periodically focused on such violations. D. W. Griffith's *Musketeers of Pig Alley* (1912), for example, with its naturalistic detailing of urban crime, already looks toward the gangster cycle of the 1930s, as well as to such typical *films noir* as *Kiss of Death* (1947), *Cry of the City* (1948), and *The Asphalt Jungle* (1950). But what makes the *noir* voice so distinctive is that the patterns of violation it speaks of also appear to be the patterns of our cultural and human order. That identity, of course, forestalls any easy or conventional imaginary resolution. Moreover, it adds a special inflection to the narrative voice that drives these films, which talks not simply about crime and corruption but about how we understand and give formulation to self and society; it asks how we see ourselves, individually and culturally. If that voice at times seems a bit loud, even coarse, directly addressing us in ways we are not accustomed to in the cinema, it is also generally a therapeutic voice. For by speaking forthrightly, it helps us to recognize, understand, and perhaps better cope with the problems it so starkly describes.

To continue in what might seem an uncinematic analogy, I would suggest that what makes *noir*'s social commentary both possible and distinctive is this different manner of speech, the form's narrative voice. One aspect of that difference is the form's ambiguous posture on the borders of genre. As critics have often noted, at times the films seem to adopt what we might term a generic voice, following the conventions and stylistic characteristics that usually mark our popular narrative formulas; yet at other times they defy formula and even capitalize on the disrupting of our narrative expectations.[4] Is *noir,* then, simply a cycle of films that flourished in the backwash of World War II and the early cold war days, borrowing its markings from a variety of established genres; or is it a genre in its own right, simply appearing, disappearing, and then reappearing, in keeping with the usual principles of audience popularity and *need?* Those who see it as a unique and time-bound phenomenon argue the former, while those who find the *noir* spirit repeatedly resurfacing, notably in such more recent films as *Chinatown* (1974), *Body Heat* (1981), *Blood Simple* (1985), and *D.O.A.* (1988), hold to the latter. It is an argument that finally has as much to do with criticism itself, especially with the varying ways that we define film genres, as it does with the *film noir,* and thus one that we probably cannot fully resolve here.

What we can quickly note, though, is that a similar ambiguity marks the *film noir*'s relationship to the dominant style of its period, what we term classical film narrative. This conventional voice is characterized by a seemingly objective point of view, adherence to a cause-effect logic, use of goal-oriented characters to direct our attention and elicit our sympathies, and a progression toward narrative closure.[5] In the *noir* family we find many films that seem by turns to contravene and to support these classical conventions. In fact, this form may be most remarkable not just for the subjects it addresses but for its efforts at finding an adequate voice for those subjects, as if the normal manner of film narrative had come to be perceived as unsuitable, inadequate, or, like the various structures of daily life it examines, even suspect. It is, after all, the *film noir* that, energized by some singular literary models of the pre- and postwar era, popularized the voice-over and flashback devices which implicitly challenge conventionally linear narratives, while it also developed the extended subjective camera sequence and brought into vogue a variety of documentary techniques that influenced our whole sense of film realism.

Ultimately, I want to argue, these are not just isolated violations of conventional styles but telling indicators of a curious phenomenon: when viewed as a group, these films demonstrate a remarkable pattern of narrative experimentation, certainly one that is unique for a particular cycle or, if you will, genre of films. In fact, not since the days of film pioneers like Griffith, Thomas Ince, and William DeMille had the American cinema experienced such a fascination with the mechanics and the *possibilities* of storytelling. In this consistent pattern of narrative experimentation, violation, and development, then, we can see both one of the form's most distinctive characteristics (one that could argue for its generic status), and the extent of its departure from a tradition of American films depicting cultural violation.

The *film noir's* historical context, that is, its appearance in the closing years of World War II and its flourishing in the immediate postwar era, obviously has much to do with this curious mixture of violations. For example, one of the war's immediate effects was to radically curtail the export market for American films, even as home attendance saw a steady rise. Reacting to this shift in audience, Hollywood apparently intensified its focus on the specific concerns of American moviegoers. Of course, this focus was partly prompted by government calls to support the war effort and avoid any potentially divisive subject matter. But as Colin Shindler notes, it was also generally true that "What Hollywood feared above all else was deep division in the country that would cloud the image of America that the majority of film-makers tried to reflect."[6] As the war began to wind down and those governmental and ideological pressures eased, however, the culture gradually came into a more critical focus. American life was viewed not simply as the subject of some outrageous violation by an outside force—Japanese or Germans—but as the very locus of various long disguised, almost invisible violations of our individual and cultural dreams. And in the unsatisfying return to normalcy that the war's conclusion brought to America—a return punctuated by rampant inflation, unemployment, labor strife, shifting social patterns, and the rapidly growing anxieties of the cold war[7]—this pattern of self-examination and self-critique seemed increasingly justified.

As if inspiring a voice of violation, then, the calamitous troubles that had convulsed the world became internalized by postwar American culture and, as we might expect, were reflected in its films. Fittingly, it is the German critic Siegfried Kracauer who, recalling his experience of Nazi Germany, noted this trend, observing an almost obsessive concern with crime and the criminal mind in our postwar films. In them he saw an image of "the weird, veiled insecurity of life under the Nazis," now "transferred to the American scene. Sinister conspiracies incubate next door, within the world considered normal—any trusted neighbor may turn into a demon."[8] But why this transference and the almost ritualistic mirroring of the world's violations it implies? Kracauer believes these films reflect both a cultural and human failing that the American cinema had, intentionally or not, previously overlooked. On the one hand, he felt, they show the "uncertainties" Americans had begun to feel about their own system and its ability to cope with problems the war had uncovered; on the other, they evoke a larger sense of fear and anxiety that increasingly seemed to be "accepted as inevitable and almost inscrutable."[9]

While he is mainly trying to describe Fascism's destructive lure of order and simplicity, laying bare its potential attraction for a disillusioned America, Kracauer also points to a deeper, almost semantic significance in these films. Drawing on his interpretation, we might see them as signs of a disturbing lack of adequate models or terms for dealing with a broken, seemingly deranged world: as emblems of a failure not just in our culture but in its conventional genres, in its narrative techniques—by which we try to make imaginary sense of our world—in effect, in the very voice with which it spoke. Seen in this context, the *film noir* seems most remarkable for the various ways in which it copes with and casts into relief these different failings. What I want to suggest is that these films served a significant liberating function for the American cinema that merits more careful examination. For not only did they manage to voice violation, to articulate what the classical cinema might normally have muted or stifled, but they also called attention—and at times fell prey—to the very power of our cultural discourse to permit speech and to impose silence.

That same function had already been taken up by our literature—or at least by a significant subset of the literary canon, the hard-boiled and mystery fiction of the 1930s. And that example not only helped clear the narrative ground for the *film noir*, through the work of writers like Dashiell Hammett, Raymond Chandler, Cornell Woolrich, and James M. Cain, but it also continued in the vein of the cinema, developing into a kind of *noir* literary genre in the works of such novelists as Jim Thompson, David Goodis, and Dorothy B. Hughes, among others. In fact, the strongest argument for *noir* as a genre might ultimately be based on this point, that it is a narrative form with specific conventions and concerns which bulk beyond the cinema's limited confines, in much the way that, say, the melodrama does.

In their pioneering overview of *noir*, the French critics Raymond Borde and Etienne Chaumeton made much of this literary influence. The *film noir*'s "immediate source," they asserted, "is clearly the American or English detective thriller novel," exemplified by the work of Hammett, Chandler, Cain, W. R. Burnett, and Graham Greene, and they noted that early *noirs* seem marked by "a total submission by the cinema to literature" as a source.[10] Alain Silver and Elizabeth Ward's "encyclopedic reference" book on the *film noir* largely bears out that assessment. For of thirty-six *noirs* listed from the early period of 1940–

45, twenty-seven are based on previously published works—novels, short stories, or plays—while seven derive from unpublished stories, and only two are original film scripts.[11]

Hammett and Chandler are the two figures who most often surface in discussions of these literary origins, in part because of the kind of characters and world they depicted, but also because of their approach to those depictions. Hammett's protagonists, such as the anonymous Continental Op of what may be the prototype *noir* story, *Red Harvest*, and the more well known Sam Spade of *The Maltese Falcon*, move through a dark and corrupt world (Poisonville, the nickname for the city in *Red Harvest*, would fit any of Hammett's locales). Whether his protagonist narrates the tale or is only its focal point, though, he provides a kind of measure of that world through his ability to remain apart from its corruption; as Terry Curtis Fox notes, "The Op's voice is never neutral . . . every descriptive sentence carries an emotional and moral judgment on the matter at hand."[12] What results is a constant tension between the lure of that corrupt world and his characters' stance—one that at times seems nearly pointless, given the pervasive criminality, and at other times self-destructive, because of the dangers it involves. But that stance is finally crucial to the attraction of these tales, for the moral center it fashions reassures us that, individually, man can cling to some human values, even as he is faced by corruption on all sides.

Raymond Chandler's oft-quoted prescription for the detective, "down these mean streets a man must go,"[13] clearly suggests his link to Hammett. His characters, especially the detective Philip Marlowe, move through a world with which they are odds. They are like knights in a realm where, as Marlowe notes in *The Big Sleep*, "knights had no meaning."[14] But that figure with no "meaning" controls both our perspective and our sympathies for, thanks to Chandler's first-person narration, all that we see in the Marlowe novels is what the detective himself sees; his experiences—and his thoughts—are ours. This outer-directedness ultimately proves just as important as Marlowe's moral stance (style an equivalent of theme), since it equally defines our relationship to the world he inhabits. Through Marlowe we become different from, and in many ways stronger than, that world. We perceive its truth, understand its ways, and avoid its pitfalls as no one else in the novels can. What this singular experience produces, in effect, is a new vantage on the relation of psyche and surface, as *how* we perceive becomes our one sure proof against *what* awaits on those "mean streets."

For James Cain, author of such *noir* source novels as *Double Indem-*

nity, Mildred Pierce, and *The Postman Always Rings Twice,* the question of narrative technique was a fundamental issue, and his solution was akin to Chandler's. He has confessed that he initially found the novel form "hopeless," because "I didn't seem to have the least idea where I was going with it, or even which paragraph should follow which. But my short stories, which were put into the mouth of some character, marched right along, for if I in the third person faltered and stumbled, my characters in the first person knew perfectly well what they had to say. . . . I began to wonder if *that* wouldn't be the medium I could use to write novels."[15] Of course, the first-person, pointedly retrospective format became the key to Cain's best work, providing him with both a narrative pattern and a way of organizing all that occurs in the narrative. Cain's characters look back at a series of events that have led up to their present situation, like the impending execution of Frank Chambers in *The Postman Always Rings Twice,* and what they recollect is just what they could have seen, experienced, or heard about. It is, moreover, constantly being weighed, often for ironic effect, against all that they know *now.*

More than simply a narrative formula, then, that retrospective approach, which was retained for the screen versions of the novels mentioned above, contributed to a complex vision of the individual in modern society. Like Chandler's, Cain's approach clearly foregrounds the consciousness, gives center stage to reason as it attempts to sort out a welter of past events. But Cain's protagonists hardly rival Marlowe in the ability to puzzle out their world; as one critic puts it, "reason doesn't stand a chance" in his novels.[16] Whether his characters are trying to manipulate others or simply hoping to figure out how their plans went wrong, they invariably find that things do not make sense, or that, as Frank Chambers bluntly puts it, "When I start to figure, it all goes blooey."[17] What Cain has done is to fashion a disturbing dialectic between the passions that led his characters to their current pass and a mind that, in the present, must sort out and make sense of all that has transpired. While his first-person narrators thus give order and reason to their narratives, much as Chandler's do, the very things of which they speak—the passions and pathological acts that defy all reason—give us pause, call into question their ability ever to sort out or explain their lives.

That paradox becomes the driving force behind the fiction of Jim Thompson, whose work appears at the height of the *film noir*'s popularity and continues beyond its day, and who contributed to the script of Stanley Kubrick's *noir* film, *The Killing* (1956). Besides a reporter's eye for detail—at various times he wrote for the *New York Daily News* and *Los Angeles Times Mirror*—that ranks his work alongside Chandler's and Hammett's for effective and telling description, Thompson also brought to the hard-boiled/crime novel a fascination with exploring various narrative approaches that gives his work a distinctly modernist stamp. In addition to straightforward first-person narratives much in the Chandler and Cain mold, we find in his works multiple-narrator novels like *The Criminal;* narratives that break into alternate versions, like *A Hell of a Woman*'s final chapter, which tells two stories in alternate lines of type, one the story the narrator consciously wishes to relate and the other the truth which he simply cannot escape or ignore any longer; and narrators who seem to be dying or, in the pattern of one of the most famous *noir* films, *Sunset Boulevard* (1950), already dead as they speak (*Savage Night*'s narrator describes his reactions as his girl hacks him to death with an axe). In such a character, who is being physically reduced even as he recounts events, Thompson seems to be playing at the very margins of narration, exploring, in much the way that the *film noir* as a form did, the limits of conventional storytelling practice.

In describing *Savage Night*'s conclusion, Geoffrey O'Brien notes how "being itself erodes, right in front of us."[18] It is, though, not just being but Thompson's narrative that typically "erodes" or, perhaps, deconstructs itself, reminding us that we have simply been attending to a voice in a void that has sought to construct its own version of reality, and thereby to stay a tendency for erosion, for the gradual eating away of whatever we fashion. What Thompson does, in the best *film noir* fashion, is lure us into a seemingly unified narrative, only to violate our expectations, revealing finally how illusory that unity is. Having drawn us into a human consciousness—or several consciousnesses—he then springs a narrative trap of sorts that leaves us in a hallucinatory realm—the realm of the human psyche deprived of all the customary supports that normal experience leads us to expect.

In this pattern, I believe, Thompson models or reflects the narrative developments found in the *films noir* more than he influences them. While several of his novels have been successfully adapted to the screen—and we might particularly note *The Getaway* (1972) and the later *Coupe de Torchon* (1981), based on Thompson's *Pop. 1280*—most of those adaptations appeared long after the period of *film noir*'s greatest appeal.[19] His importance for this study, though, lies in the way his fiction mirrors the patterns we find repeatedly worked out in the *noir* mainstream, as his narrators set about providing us privileged access to a world, only to find that the path they have staked out is full of obstacles and pitfalls, in fact that, like truth itself, it seems virtually to disappear before us. Thus even as he narrates his fast-eroding situation, *Savage Night*'s Charlie Bigger notes how language itself has become almost empty and meaningless: "after a while everything was said that we could say and it would have been like talking to yourself. So we talked less and less, and pretty soon we were hardly talking at all. And then we *weren't* talking at all. Just grunting and gesturing and pointing at things. It was like we'd never known how to talk."[20] Not only is the fragile order of his life rapidly disappearing, but even the means of describing that situation, of accounting for the mystery, seems to have vanished. Still, he goes on speaking, the narrative itself a kind of straw at which he clutches, as a last desperate hope or human gesture against a world marked by an inhuman violence and cruelty.

Most other studies of the *film noir* examine this literary background in far more depth than the brief sketch offered here. And in doing so they follow the lead of the French critic Nino Frank, who in 1946 drew the very term *film noir* from the similarity of these works to the novels then being published in Gallimard's *Serie Noire*.[21] But that linkage never answers the real question, never tells us what the *film noir* is, only what it is *like*. It resembles, in both themes and narrative patterns, a variety of popular literature that appears prior to the *film noir* and that continues beyond its heyday. This material helps cast into relief several of *noir*'s most distinctive narrative developments, but that literary perspective alone does not let us see the form's larger scheme. To do so, we have to turn to the films themselves.

The primary difficulty facing most inquiries into the *film noir* is its very amorphous nature. It simply does not sit still for an accurate or conventional portrait. While many historians describe it as a discrete genre with its own conventions, others see it as nothing more than a limited cycle, a strange outgrowth of various social factors at a special time in our history. Certainly, *noir* seems to push at the normal bounds of genre designation, its varied settings, subjects, and actions confounding the sort of easy classification that samples of the Western, musical, or science fiction genres allow. More often, a *noir* film seems related to other, established genres, for example, to the gangster or detective formulas,[22] or to straddle generic lines, drawing simultaneously on a variety of conventions and expectations. The historical limits often cited for the form, the period from 1941 to 1958, further block thinking of *noir* as we do of other, seemingly longer-lived genres with their implicitly mythic appeal. For such reasons, Paul Schrader flatly asserts that "*film noir* is not a genre": "It is not defined, as are the western and gangster genres, by conventions of setting and conflict, but rather by the most subtle qualities of tone and mood."[23] And following this lead, J. A. Place and L. S. Peterson argue that "visual style" alone proves the "consistent thread that unites the very diverse films that together comprise this phenomenon," as they then attempt to describe precisely what constitutes this peculiar "*film noir* style."[24]

The question of style, however, only broadens the debate about what the *film noir* is. After all, a number of distinct "looks," as well as various combinations of them, mark the *noir* canon. Thus we might take *style* to mean the baroque play of light and dark, of line and volume that *noir* drew from its roots in German expressionist films of the 1920s. But it could also refer to the stark realism and urban locations that Schrader and others link to the influence of Italian neorealist films in the postwar period. Then too the documentary look of films like *Boomerang* (1947), *The Naked City* (1948), and *Panic in the Streets* (1950) owes much to the impact of war documentaries and newsreels on American audiences, as well as to various technical advances that made location shooting commonplace. Seldom, though, do we find the documentary style combined with the surrealistic imagery and distorted perspectives of yet another, more fantastic offshoot of the *noir* style, glimpsed in the Dali-designed dream sequences of *Spellbound* (1945), as well as those of *Murder, My Sweet* (1944) or *The Dark Past* (1949). The *noir* "style," I would suggest, ultimately seems as curiously diverse as its subject matter, and equally as inadequate for accurately defining the form.

The very disagreement underlying practically every discussion of *film noir* is significant, though. For despite a lack of consensus, critics generally agree on which films merit a *noir* classification. The *noir* filmographies published by John S. Whitney, Foster Hirsch, and Alain Silver and Elizabeth Ward,[25] for example, differ mainly in two respects. First, they disagree about which *modern* films to put in their groupings as inheritors of the *noir* tradition. And we might read into this a hint of their common bias toward seeing the form not as a singular, time-bound cycle but as a true genre, recurring through time as cultural conditions dictate. Second, they differ in terms of the minor or "B" films which, because of their elusiveness and limited distribution, may have been seen by one compiler and not by another. As James Damico suggests, therefore, it might seem "self-evident that the foremost task of any inquiry into the category ought to be the identification of exactly what it is that causes films intuitively classed as FN [*film noir*] to appear to share affinities."[26] In effect, we must consider how to account for the general agreement in classifying these films when the definitions that might justify such classification seem so elusive.

In exploring Western culture's changing perceptions of "madness," Michel Foucault faced a similar difficulty. Judging from the "multiplicity of objects" that supposedly constituted madness and the variety of commentaries that made up "a discourse, concerning madness,"[27] he found coming to any universally acceptable definition of the condition almost impossible. As a result, he adopted a broadly inclusive strategy, concluding that "mental illness" has been "constituted by all that was said in all the statements that named it, divided it up, described it, explained it, traced its developments, indicated its various correlations, judged it, and possibly gave it speech by articulating, in its name, discourses that were to be taken as its own."[28] One approach he initially entertained recalls that of Schrader, Place, and Peterson, namely an effort to examine his subject from a vantage determined "not so much by its objects or concepts as by a certain *style,* a certain constant manner of statement."[29] However, aware that such "descriptions could not, in any case, be abstracted from the hypotheses" about his subject, in effect that "style" depended upon a prior select group, he rejected such a stance.[30] In its place, he tried to isolate certain "discursive formations" or regularities that marked our identification of the objects and events of madness, as well as the various ways in which we speak of them. With this approach, he began to isolate and analyze "small islands of coherence,"[31] and then examine the various strategies that embrace the disparate objects, shifting styles of description, and changing contexts of his study.

This approach might well serve our thinking about the *film noir,* since it lets us account for both the play of difference noted by most commentaries on the form and the "intuitive" perception of unifying factors Damico describes. By trying to describe *noir*'s primary discursive formations, we might obviate—or at least postpone—the question of its generic status, while also avoiding the simplistic notion of "style" as the determining factor—especially since it only hides an unexplained predetermination of what films are truly *noir.* This study thus takes a broadly inclusive focus, accepting for the purposes of a discursive description all that is usually grouped within the time-bound or traditional *noir* canon. Thereafter, regardless of whether we think of *noir* as a discrete genre (with an unnaturally restricted life span or irregular cycle of recurrence), or as a congealing of forces and attitudes operating in various genres in a specific era, our vantage on those formations can remain stable, our analysis securely anchored in the works themselves.

When viewed from this perspective, the *film noir* seems to mirror both the large cultural forces and the immediate human impulses that shape our lives and that seem to generate their own discourse. On the one hand, then, we shall see *noir* in a *reactive* context, as a response or resistance to the dominations of power in society, and thus as a generic effort at revealing, examining, and, as far as possible, gaining some freedom from the forces that both structure and violate our daily lives. In this sense it is a social myth, one evoked by the particular conditions of postwar America. On the other hand, we shall see it as a symptom, a distortion that cuts across generic lines and that is caused by the same desires and powers that propel our culture and our lives. But whether viewed as a response to distortion or as itself a stylistic and thematic distortion that infects our prevailing cultural myths—thereby producing, for example, *noir* Westerns like *Rancho Notorious* (1952) and *Johnny Guitar* (1954)—the *film noir* can designate a field of deviation that mirrors the problems of modern America in particular and modern man in general. And this field is characterized by a remarkable variety of discursive formations, as Foucault would term them, through which the form manages to articulate a rising awareness of the limitations and paradoxes that shape our culture, our lives, and the stories we tell of them both.

A survey of the large body of films usually classed as *noir* suggests that one of its most distinctive yet often overlooked features is its singular concern with or awareness of the nature of narration. For more than any other body of popular films, and certainly more so than its near relative, the gangster genre, *film noir* pushes at the very boundaries of classical narrative, particularly with its frequent use of voice-over narrators, flashbacks (even flashbacks within flashbacks, as in *Sorry, Wrong Number* [1948] and *The Enforcer* [1951]), convoluted time schemes, and subjective camera techniques. Schrader and others basically pass these varied approaches off as further examples of *noir* stylistics, seeing them as evidence of "a love of romantic narration" that mainly serves to establish "a mood of *temps perdu:* an irretrievable past, a predetermined fate and an all-enveloping hopelessness."[32] Foster Hirsch, however, distinguishes between two complementary elements of the typical *noir* narrative, noting that "*noir* tells its stories in a particular way, and in a particular visual style."[33] While he neither explores nor identifies this range of *noir* narrative patterns, he does point us in a valuable direction by recognizing that the form's curious rhetoric is as remarkable as its look and tone. This observation is, I believe, crucial to understanding the *film noir.*

My survey of the *noir* form, based on a sampling of more than 130 films,[34] isolates four dominant narrative strategies or discursive formations: (1) the classical, third-person narrative, (2) the voice-over/ flashback style, (3) the subjective camera technique, and (4) the documentary mode. Because they emerge from an industry dominated by the classical pattern, we should expect that a majority of *noir* films largely follow this first approach, with its linear unfolding of events from a third-person or "objective" vantage. Certainly some of the best-known *noirs*, such as *The Maltese Falcon* (1941), *In a Lonely Place* (1950), and *Kiss Me Deadly* (1955), work in this way, using a traditional narrative approach to counterbalance the disturbing or unconventional events they depict. Most *noir* critics, though, find the combination of voice-over and flashback, with its implicit suggestion that the viewer has privileged access to a mind meditating on the past, to be more symptomatic of the form. In describing the typical *noir* film, Robert Porfirio, for instance, takes this view, noting that "instead of writing his story, the hero tells it to us directly, and the combined techniques of first person narration and flashback enhance the aura of doom. It is almost as if the narrator takes a perverse pleasure in relating the events leading up to his current crisis."[35] While not quite the "typical" style critics would have it, this basically subjective approach surfaces often, and it occurs in one of the earlier and most influential of *films noir, Double Indemnity* (1944). Following its successful application in this film, more than forty other *noirs* would use the same narrative approach.

It remained for a third strategy to explore more fully the possibility of subjective narration. A subjective camera, used either with a voice-over or as a separate narrative device, promised viewers a far more radical sense of shared consciousness, by literally giving them a character's vantage on events for large portions of the narrative. Robert Montgomery's experiment with almost completely subjective narration, *The Lady in the Lake* (1947), is the most famous instance of this briefly popular style. A fourth discursive formation, that of the documentary-style *noir*, worked a compromise between the first two strategies we have described. Films like *Boomerang* and *The Naked City* use the camera as an objective recorder of events, but they also yoke it to a voice-over commentary that guides our point of view and testifies to the truth of what we see. Transported into the streets, among the people and locales where the factually based events occurred, we were supposed to gain in these films a new view of reality, of our world stripped of its veneer of custom and habit. Of course, we were also supposed to overlook the irony implicit in this approach: the notion that through the natural, by evoking film's mimetic capacity, these documentary-style works sought much the same sort of revisioning of the commonplace that other *films noir* pursued in more fantastic ways, through expressionistic imagery, distorted camera angles, and chiaroscuro lighting.

What this variety of discursive formations quickly points up is the extent to which the *film noir* reflects a new openness toward narrative experimentation and development. That this exploration occurs in a period still dominated by the practices of classical film narrative and, for the most part, in an industry that was historically reluctant to alter or challenge any proven profitable procedure, seems equally significant. Certainly it suggests the sort of tensions and contradictions that we typically find in *noir* narratives—tensions that, Foucault would offer, ultimately mark all forms of discourse. Even more significantly, though, this exploration points to a deeper identifying characteristic of the form: a compelling urge to understand, formulate, and articulate the human situation at a time when our old formulations, as well as the means of expression underlying them, no longer seemed adequate. That urge, I feel, drives the *film noir,* and gives reason to the basic commitment to expression it evidences even in the face of the obvious limitations and conventions that condition all cinematic speech. The following overview of *noir*'s primary discursive formations will sketch the shape of this narrative thrust and describe some of those tensions that inform it.

The Voice-Over/Flashback

The voice-over, usually introducing and accompanying a flashback to some prior action or event, is often seen as the most characteristic *noir* narrative strategy. One reason for this assumption is that this approach seems only to have reached its real potential in *noir,* as if the form's themes and concerns, especially its fascination with the workings of the human psyche, naturally complemented such a narrative. Of course, the voice-over and flashback were both established cinematic techniques prior to *noir*'s heyday. The former traces its ancestry back to the commentative "voice-of-god" narration of the newsreels, while the latter finds its origins in the earliest manipulations of narrative time. While popular films like *The Power and the Glory* (1933), *Judge Priest* (1934), and *Rebecca* (1940) had already employed the voice-over/flashback combination with great effect, it is *Citizen Kane* (1941), itself often seen as one of *noir*'s sires,[36] that seems to bring this strategy to full development and to anticipate the *noir* usage. As the later discussion of *Sorry, Wrong Number* will show, Orson Welles's use of multiple voices and vantages on the life of his subject, Charles Foster Kane, illuminates a fundamental variance and tension between the individual point of view and reality that would prove a *noir* hallmark. In essence, Welles's approach calls attention to the relativity of perspective that characterizes all cinematic seeing, as well as to the limitations that attend such relativity, marking every point of view as potentially detached, distanced, alienated.

As the *film noir* canon shows, the voice-over/flashback strategy lent itself to a variety of uses. Most commonly, a voice in present time introduces and then comments on a scene from the past, so that we see as if through the narrator's mind's eye.[37] In this way, the narrative can insert some significant information from the past or set up a context for present events, as in the case of *Double Indemnity, Out of the Past* (1947), and *The Big Clock* (1948). Embedded within a larger narrative structure, such sequences invariably seem to violate diegetic normalcy, to suggest an eruption of the subjective in a world that we initially see in a conventional, objective manner. However, as a kind of partially glimpsed truth, that eruption qualifies and even raises questions about the larger narrative context, in the process suggesting other possibilities for truth and a sense of this world's complexity.

Following *Kane*'s lead, a number of *noir* films compound this pattern with a variety of narrators and flashbacks. Films like *The Killers* (1946) and *Sorry, Wrong Number* use so many subjective viewpoints that they ultimately seem to abandon all notion of an objective vantage or the possibility of ever synthesizing their multiple perspectives. Christine Gledhill's description of "the plot of the typical film noir . . . as a struggle between different voices for control over the telling of the story"[38] seems especially fitting for these films. For in their often contradictory multiplicity, those narrative voices seem to fight for the right to speak. And in so doing, they point up not only truth's elusiveness but also the very contentiousness of what often passes for truth, how much it depends on its own ability to argue for its acceptance.

In contrast to this disturbing multiplicity is the all-embracing voice-over of films like *The Postman Always Rings Twice* (1946) and *Lady from Shanghai* (1948). The sole voice we hear in such films, usually beginning its tale as the very first images appear, functions as the source of all that we see, although not, as one critic suggests, because the entire film is "a sort of linguistic event, as the narrator's speech even when there is none."[39] Rather, the words we hear and the images that seem to spring from them mark our privileged access to a consciousness, to a world of memory and thought that is far more detailed and vivid—if potentially more colored by the imagination—than any simple linguistic utterance. What this technique offers, then, is telling access to a person's inner world, especially to that level of the self where desire and repression interact and seek formulation. It is the level not so much of utterance but of linguistic formation, where we try to formalize, conceptualize, and even disguise evidence of our inner turmoil.

Where these different approaches to the voice-over/flashback strategy find common ground is in their basic function. As Bruce Kawin in his analysis of first-person techniques explains, "the question of voice becomes, finally, the question of mind, and both are inseparable from the question of meaning."[40] In fact, the "question of mind" implied by this strategy is very near the meaning itself for this type of *film noir*. For whether it uses an embedded voice-over, multiple ones, or a single, all-embracing voice with the flashback, the film testifies to a subjectivity at work, an "I" whose most basic purpose is to provide us with a privileged and personal "eye" on the world. In the process, it reminds us that seeing and understanding are always someone's, and that every view comes from a single, invariably limited perspective. While classical film narrative usually tries to conceal its point of view—to cover over relativity—these films reveal theirs, and in that revelation lies their true strength. For what impels them and forges their strongest appeal is an abiding desire to assert their own view of truth, their private vision as a rival and alternative to a public, supposedly objective one.

In *noir*'s primary literary sources, as we have noted, this effect is both obvious and crucial. The fiction of Cain and Chandler, for example, typically uses a first-person, retrospective narration which, Terry Curtis Fox believes, "may be the key to Hollywood's uneasy relationship with the hard-boiled story."[41] The voice-over/flashback strategy used in the adaptations of such Cain and Chandler novels as *Double Indemnity, Mildred Pierce* (1945), *Murder, My Sweet,* and *The Brasher Doubloon* (1947) clearly seems an effort to approximate this narrative style. In these works, especially the latter two with their private eye protagonist, the narrating voices represent an alternative knowledge, an individual, nearly alienated perspective on the world that challenges, through its implicitly greater access to truth, a prevailing view of things. It is precisely this emergence of a "private I," defined by its opposition to the reality perceived by the public eye, that seems to escape the typical estimation of *noir*'s voice-over technique as a kind of "romantic narration."[42] Certainly a film like *Sunset Boulevard,* with its cynical retrospection emanating from the corpse of writer Joe Gillis, challenges this interpretation. In Gillis's voice we sense no nostalgia for the past—indeed, for a life already gone, even wasted—but a persistent, even paradoxical desire to speak when the very possibility for speech has long been denied or overlooked. Having harnessed his writer's talents to the past in the person of faded film star Norma Desmond, in effect having silenced his own voice by selling himself to a silent screen actress, Joe finally, belatedly—in the sort of black joke that increasingly marked Billy Wilder's films—has his say, as if to an audience of fellow ghosts. The resulting narrative stands witness to the self's impelling desire for a voice even in death, for a say in and about the truth of the world, despite a prevalent, even deadly power for silence or for submission to a popular discourse and its given truth.

As testimony to a growing awareness of the repressive force of mass culture in the postwar era, this technique's emergence seems especially noteworthy. For in championing the personal voice and the consciousness it denotes, in privileging such evidence of individuality, these narratives fundamentally underscore the individual's function as a mirror and measure of his culture. Through their human narrators, such films privilege the impressionistic as an alternative to the objectivity we implicitly attribute to classical narrative. And in so doing, they speak a nagging concern with the place of the self in modern American society and with the ability of the individual voice to be heard in this world. On a more optimistic level, they also suggest the self's felt need to sound out other, normally stilled voices, to test whether his is simply a solitary, dissenting voice within the cacophony of mass culture.

The Subjective Camera

With the films that use a subjective camera as a narrative device, the emphasis on a "private I"—on its longings *and* its limitations—becomes even more pronounced. Far more than the voice-over/flashback mechanism, the subjective camera emphasizes point of view, but in a radical way that challenges our normal perspective by forcibly aligning our vantage with another's. It is an approach that reminds us of the expressionist influence, since it is rooted in the aesthetic brought to Hollywood by various German directors, writers, and technicians in the 1920s and 1930s, who would eventually find a channel for their avant-garde stylistics and psychological focus in *noir*'s budget-mandated economies of expression. During the expressionist period, filmmakers like Fritz Lang, F. W. Murnau, and G. W. Pabst had sought a language of heightened expression, one that would let them give external shape and substance to inner, subjective experiences, feelings, and attitudes, in effect turning the psyche inside out.[43] The pictorial techniques used to achieve this end—foregrounded oblique objects, unbalanced compositions, irregular spatial arrangements, chiaroscuro lighting with a heavy play of shadows, an emphasis on oblique and vertical lines over the horizontal, and a fascination with reflection and reflective surfaces—eventually contributed to a *noir* style that suggests far more than just an atmosphere of instability and confusion. It punches a hole in the conventional picture we have of reality, at least of reality as classical film narrative typically portrays it, and challenges us to see our world, as it is presented on screen and encountered outside the theater, in a radically different manner.

While a subjective camera narration seems a logical extension of this aesthetic, its full development could only come with specific technical advances made during the war years. For example, the appearance of lightweight, highly mobile cameras, like the German Arriflex and American Cunningham Combat Camera, gave cinematographers a new range of motion and an ability to shoot from what before would have been considered impossible positions.[44] Similarly, the development of the "crab dolly," a device that, as Barry Salt explains, could "instantaneously be turned from a straight forwards track to a sideways movement . . . at 90 degrees to the original path,"[45] increased camera mobility and made possible the longer takes that would be necessary to approximate the normal human experience of movement. By permitting the camera more accurately to imitate natural human movements in space and time, these and other technological developments transformed what had been largely a narrative punctuation—the subjective shot—into a viable narrative device—a sequence shot.

Also favoring this technique was a calculated promise of commercial viability. The increasing popularity of the detective genre, for instance, marked by an economic shift at the major studios from producing series of B-films in this vein—such as the Falcon and Saint series—to big-budget productions like *The Maltese Falcon, Laura* (1944), and *Murder, My Sweet,* spurred an interest in finding a cinematic correlative for the detective novel's style, as well as for the very nature of the detective experience. The subjective camera could address both concerns, since its vantage could approximate the prying eye of the private eye, particularly as it had come to be formulated in Chandler's first-person narratives. Moreover, letting the audience see as the detective does might produce a new level of narrative engagement, involving viewers in a pattern of discovery and solution similar to that enjoyed in the most successful popular fiction. Thus *Lady in the Lake* begins with its detective protagonist telling us that we shall visually relive his own experience: "You'll meet the people; you'll find the clues—and maybe you'll solve it quick and maybe you won't." He is inviting us, just as in popular detective fiction, to join in a game of detection, the subjective vantage promising to give us equal access to the clues and a chance to compete, with the detective and with each other, in solving the mystery. As we shall see, the success of the limited application of such techniques in *Murder, My Sweet,* an adaptation of Chandler's *Farewell, My Lovely,* seemed to bear out this potential.

The technique's vogue proved to be short-lived, however. Closely following on *Lady in the Lake*'s experiment with an almost totally subjective narration, *Possessed* and *Dark Passage,* both using the technique in lengthy but isolated sequences, and *The High Wall,* which employed it several times to suggest a drugged state (as in *Murder, My Sweet*) all appeared in quick succession in 1947. But thereafter the extended subjective narrative practically disappeared from *film noir,* making one of its few appearances years later to add a surrealist effect to *The Dark Past*'s dream sequences. The brief popularity of the extended subjective sequence does leave its mark, though, in the way it affected filmmakers' notions of what point-of-view shots might do. For example, when point-of-view scenes are used in Hitchcock's later work, like *Psycho* (1960) and *Frenzy* (1972), they are more than just extensions of the subjective shot as punctuation that we often encounter in his earlier British films; rather, they are usually linked to a voyeuristically tracking camera that implicates the audience in on-screen events in much the way that the *film noir*'s extended subjective sequences do. That combination has become a kind of *noir* legacy—one that today finds major application in the horror/slasher films of the *Halloween* (1978) and *Friday the Thirteenth* (1980) ilk.

While this technique's relatively short life suggests a lukewarm box-office reception and a faddish vogue at best—particularly with so many of its appearances clustered in a single year—it also speaks to the device's implications for film narrative in general, and for the classical style in particular. In letting viewers see as the film's protagonist does, whether for an isolated sequence, as in *Possessed*'s catatonic scenes, or for nearly the entire story, as in *Lady in the Lake,* the individual or private perspective becomes privileged as an alternative to classical narrative's cultural vantage. How we usually perceive our world, and at least the way it was normally seen through the window of conventional narrative, was radically challenged. By distorting our perspective, or rather by channeling it unexpectedly through a specific character's point of view, this technique forcefully calls attention to the fact that the film image is always a product of directed attention.

In making us aware of point of view in this way, the subjective camera has a doubly subversive effect. One of the fictions fostered by classical narrative, after all, is its illusion of objectivity, which implies that what we see represents a kind of privileged vantage on truth itself. But as Julio Moreno explains, the subjective camera shatters this illusion by revealing "the only reality which is truly real: the living reality of perception"; and through this awareness it vanquishes "the dictatorship of impersonal vision—false because it is impersonal— which has been up to now the vision of the camera."[46] With this shift in perspective there also potentially comes a new and more truthful vision for the viewer, who is no longer, as Nick Browne describes the normal spectator situation, "entrapped in an ideological (social) machine in order to insure the reproduction of the social order."[47] Rather, he gains a perspective on the cinematic mechanism itself, in the process being transformed from a simple consumer to an evaluator of the images that our culture provides us with.

This approach also undermines classical narrative's reliance on character and with equally disturbing effect. Traditionally, character provides the narrative with a kind of social construct with which we are encouraged to identify; it securely "places" us in the narrative world, which becomes an extension of our own world. While the subjective camera may have been perceived by some as a radical and innovative way of fostering such identification, as what might be termed a "special effects" method of achieving classical narrative's usual end, that spectator projection or identification never quite comes off. As a reviewer remarked about *Lady in the Lake,* the effect was as if "the spectator was standing beside the hero rather than existing within him."[48]

The problem, of course, was not simply a technical one, that the subjective camera could not actually put us in the character's place. Rather, it results from the very nature of cinematic narrative which, as Pascal Bonitzer explains, involves a constant "dialectic" between "two fields": "on-screen space and off-screen space; we could say, between specular space and blind space."[49] Because it places the character who is the source of our perspective in a kind of blind space, the subjective camera has, as we shall see, a mystifying residue: it "can only make enigmatic a character who, in the story, is not enigmatic."[50] And with this problem of identification, there also comes an unsettling effect that undercuts the usual stabilizing influence of character, with its psychological motivations and goal-oriented actions. For it is not just the figure in the narrative, but our spectator position, our inscribed *characterization*, that comes to seem enigmatic, more a cultural construct or the product of an apparatus than a given entity, having a unique, inherent, and self-determining nature. In effect, our sense of self seems to slip into this "labyrinth," as Bonitzer so accurately styles it. By implication, the place from which we are to see and understand, our consciousness, comes to seem estranged and foreign, our very identity undermined by that *other* identity which we are supposed to embrace.

Such effects might well prod us to question how both our culture and the narratives we normally tell of it are structured. But we should note that even the darkest *noir* visions of American culture usually reserve a stable position from which to speak. Even when it seems to strike at the very foundation of popular film, to lay bare its ideological operations, the *film noir* typically exempted the *spectator's* position from direct scrutiny. After all, in pointing out that what we see is always subjectively, not objectively, given and that the individual himself is partly fashioned by the movies' discourse, working through what Stephen Heath terms a process of "subject address,"[51] the subjective technique could jeopardize a profitable practice and a traditionally comforting experience, inserting a wedge of distrust or suspicion between Hollywood and its audience.

Moreover, besides this increased awareness of how film fashions a cultural identity for its viewers, this technique also produces an ancillary sense of instability that strikes not just at classical narrative but at the whole fictional film experience. The unanchored, vaguely identified subjective view, after all, potentially speaks in a most disturbing way about our own identities, suggesting a level on which we too are enigmatic, unknowns who wear the mask of culture as solace and a way of forestalling a darker confrontation—with the disturbing questions that nag at us, not just about our place in society, but about our very natures. In opening up the problem of the self as a cultural—or cinematic—construct, subjective narration risks posing these more unsettling questions, positing a possibility of the self as *unconstructed,* unthought, perhaps even meaningless. Any effort to tell a truth about the individual in society, therefore, implicitly risks speaking a larger and more debilitating truth, in the face of which both film as a project of entertainment and film as an ideological reassessment pale in significance.

In reaching for a new way of seeing, the subjective narration of films like *Lady in the Lake* and *Dark Passage* indeed privileged the spectator in an unprecedented way. On the one hand, it offered viewers a new cinematic experience, even a kind of thrill, while promising some freedom from classical narrative's usual manipulations of the spectator position. But on the other hand, that new perspective opened up a potentially disturbing vision. It revealed how much of our lives always remains unseen, particularly how much of the self persistently eludes our vantage or understanding, remaining elusively within the "blind space" of life itself.

The Documentary Style

Those efforts to see more clearly and in ways normally closed off to Hollywood narrative met with more critical and popular success in the films that turned to the strategies of documentary film in a kind of end run around conventional narrative. In the cultural and techno-logical climate surrounding World War II, the semidocumentary *noir* finds its roots. For during this period the documentary itself gained a new degree of sophistication and popular acceptance, mainly because it proved so important to every aspect of the war effort, especially its home-front publicity. As Lewis Jacobs explains, "not since the docu-mentary form was developed had it been used on such a gigantic scale, or employed so deliberately to serve a single purpose."[52] That pur-pose was the effort by every warring nation to record the war's events and, more important, to *interpret* them effectively for the home audi-ence.

In this effort, Hollywood proved a particularly valuable resource, providing both patriotic narratives for home consumption and skilled technicians to support the armed forces' own efforts at documenta-tion, information, and propaganda. In fact, many of the industry's most skilled storytellers—Frank Capra, John Ford, John Huston, Wil-liam Wyler—signed up for the duration. While with the exception of Huston none of these figures is usually associated with the *noir* form, the narrative approach and fictionalizing techniques they successfully married to the documentary during the war years would have an immediate and lasting impact. In fact, a number of directors who had, during the war, worked largely in conventional popular forms found a new impetus in this stylistic turn. We might note Henry Hathaway in particular, who had been known mainly for his romances and formu-laic adventure films—such as *Trail of the Lonesome Pine* (1936), *The Shepherd of the Hills* (1941), or *A Wing and a Prayer* (1944). After the war, his career took a marked upswing, as he embraced the documentary-style narrative and, in films like *The House on 92nd Street* (1945), *13 Rue Madeleine* (1946), and *Call Northside 777* (1948), helped develop a new brand of film realism.

I do not want to suggest, though, that Hathaway and others like him were simply pursuing a new aesthetic. Whatever formal possibilities they saw were certainly matched by commercial considerations. They were, after all, also catering to an audience of millions of Americans who, by the war's end, were used to seeing both the news of the conflict and its stark ideological issues—see especially Capra's "Why We Fight" series—set forth in an informative and entertaining style that owed far less to the social problem documentaries of the 1930s than to classical narrative traditions. Together with the period's popular newsreels, particularly Fox's pacesetter *The March of Time*, with its mix of documentary footage, archival material, and reenactments of key events, the war documentaries helped create an audience for a new kind of fictional film, one that Hollywood readily supplied in the postwar period.

Besides the creation of an audience and certain narrative expectations, the semidocumentary *noir*'s emergence owes much to technological developments in this era. Writing in the period, Parker Tyler noted that "the infiltration of documentary into film fiction, whatever the artistic worth of its results, must be gauged as part of the overpowering forces of a technological era."[53] As we have already noted, a major result of the war and the unprecedented efforts by all sides to document its events visually was a series of significant technical developments. Besides the lightweight cameras previously mentioned, the conditions of combat and nonstudio shooting led to the introduction of safety-base film stock for use in 16mm combat cameras, faster stocks for shooting in limited or uncontrolled light, portable lighting equipment for such conditions, and magnetic sound for higher fidelity recording. The developments in cameras and lenses in this period also brought the introduction in 1947 of the zoom lens. By allowing filmmakers to vary their vantage on a subject while at some distance and without actually moving the camera, it offered not only a new kind of observational technique but also the potential for more economic shooting by limiting the need for tracking shots and multiple camera setups.[54] Technology was simply moving in the direction of reality, toward devising more effective—and economical—ways of telling the story of actuality.

Ensuring that these developments would play a shaping role in postwar film narrative was a series of equally important economic factors that undercut traditional studio-shooting practices. The war's end had brought price decontrols and, as an immediate result, soaring studio production costs, especially those involving film stocks and labor. In 1946, for example, the two major film suppliers, DuPont and Eastman Kodak, raised their prices to the studios by 13 and 18 percent respectively. As a consequence of growing union power and a series of labor disputes that followed, the costs of set construction and decoration followed suit with their own drastic gains.[55] Such rapid cost

increases, along with the appearance of numerous independent production companies rapidly formed to take advantage of income tax
laws, led to more and more films being shot beyond the confines—and
thus away from the supervision—of the Hollywood studios. Given the
proper technology, filmmakers simply found the streets of America's
cities and the nonunion labor available outside of Hollywood economically advantageous and invitingly free from interference. As William
Lafferty sums up these factors, "Rather than a stylistic attribute of the
semi-documentary alone, the emphasis upon location shooting of
features seems to have arisen out of economic necessity during the
mid- to late-1940s."[56]

The narrative technique that emerged from these various cultural,
economic, and technological influences, though, shows a basic kinship
to other *films noir.* Basically, the semidocumentary is concerned with
perspective—with how we see our world and how we tell of it. Its
documentary-style footage, location shooting, use of non-actors, and
traditional narrative sequences conspire to create the sense of an
objective reality, dramatized and attested to by the sort of certifying
voice-over audiences had become accustomed to hearing in *The March
of Time* and similar news series—a voice-of-god narrator, as it was
known.[57] In films of this sort, most notably *The House on 92nd Street,
Boomerang, The Naked City, T-Men* (1947), and *Call Northside 777,* the
main concern seems to be not just telling an interesting tale but
fashioning a realistic context for the narrative, so as to suggest its
relevance to the spectators and to assure them that they are indeed
gaining a new and revealing perspective on the world they inhabit.

This trend is hardly surprising, though, for as Paul Schrader notes,
in the immediate postwar era "every film-producing country had a
resurgence of realism."[58] It almost seems as if the war had wiped away
much of our susceptibility to illusion, and with it our ability to sustain
the aesthetic world of classical narrative. One of the most influential
shapes this trend took was Italian neorealism, exemplified by films like
Open City (1945) and *Paisan* (1946). These films, with their mix of non-
actors, location shooting, real stories, high-grain film stock, and concern with capturing what André Bazin termed "the *continuum* of
reality,"[59] impressed American audiences and critics alike. What they
suggested was an immediately unfolding reality, a world not bound by
traditional narrative conventions or filtered through the elaborate
apparatus of Hollywood technology—in sum, life directly and truth-
fully perceived.

Of course, that impression was itself a kind of cinematic illusion,
crafted from a compromise between reality and aesthetics. As Bazin

explains, neorealism's realistic look could "only be achieved in one way—through artifice,"[60] that is, through selection, organization, and careful staging. And the documentary *noirs* followed much the same tactics. While they tried to shape a realistic context for their actions through location shooting, while they sought to evoke a sense of real human rhythms by enlisting non-actors, even people involved in the true events on which the films were often based, and while they employed a stentorian, authoritative voice to certify the truth they offered for public consumption, these films still basically catered to what Schrader describes as "the public's desire for a more honest and harsh view of America"[61] with a calculated artifice. If it was one that at times disarmed viewers by admitting even the reality of its mechanism—*The Naked City*'s voice-of-god narrator, after all, is its producer, Mark Hellinger, who tells us as much as the film opens—that artifice nonetheless hints of a level of control and unreality, of directed perceptions, allowed insights, and melodramatic shaping, that continued to characterize our film experience. As a result, these films, with their alternate vision of American culture put in a narrative context, may be the ones that most clearly point up the rhetorical bind that seems to mark the entire *noir* project.

What eventually eludes and in part confounds this impulse is the cinematic mechanism itself, both insofar as it partakes of the double nature of all discourse and as it functions ideologically. As we noted in discussing the voice-over/flashback mechanism, which is often part of the semidocumentary technique, a pattern of contradiction or paradox marks all human discourse. As Foucault explains it, all "relationships of communication . . . produce effects of power," which work to disguise or deny the power they wield.[62] We might be tempted to think of the truths the semidocumentaries offered—of hidden corruption in *House on 92nd Street*, of the judicial system's failure in *Call Northside 777*, of a harsh economic determinism in *City across the River* (1949)—as affording a kind of release from the sway of these powerful cultural forces, a release because they have been rendered visible and spoken of. But Foucault asks the disturbing and often overlooked question of "whether critical discourse about repression" serves as a "block" to these powers "or a part of the power mechanism it denounced."[63] In this context, we should recall the film industry's implicit function as an ideological voice. In this capacity it is always partly powered by the desire, as Bill Nichols puts it, "to persuade us that how things are is how they ought to be and that the place provided for us is the place we ought to have."[64] Then, too, the film industry has a prior interest in affirming the apparent truth of what it offers, in suggesting its privileged position as a reliable access to actuality, even when the world it depicts is admittedly a fabric of fictions. So a pattern of contradiction seems invariably woven into the texture of truth these films produced.

This pattern may help explain why the semidocumentary's popularity lasts only from 1945 to the early 1950s. I hesitate to cite a specific end point, though, since the form never quite disappears; it simply goes through a kind of transformation enabling it to merge with the *noir* mainstream and even become a primary tributary for its realistic developments. After jettisoning its most obtrusive documentary trappings, especially the prologue and the voice-of-god narrator, while continuing to emphasize location shooting and objective camera style, the semidocumentary became a stylistic model for realistic examinations of American urban culture. Elia Kazan's *Panic in the Streets* (1950), for example, shot on the streets and docks of New Orleans with several local officials in supporting roles, seems directly descended from his earlier film *Boomerang,* and it might be viewed as a kind of watershed film in this development of the *noir* style. Contrary to Foster Hirsch's belief that the emphasis on "documentation" in the semi-documentary *noirs* "leads to a dramatic dead end,"[65] this film and others like it show how this technique opens onto a successful synthesis of reality and artifice that marks later *noirs*. In fact, once the documentary style's more obvious elements begin to drop out or, through custom, to become almost invisible, the dramatic potential of locale clearly becomes apparent, as evidence the evocative use of urban landscapes in films like *Night and the City* (1950), *The Asphalt Jungle* (1950), and *Kiss Me Deadly* (1955). In that environment a more naturalistic acting style, as well as a more realistic sense of the individuals inhabiting the modern American cityscape, was not only possible but narratively necessary.

The Classical Narrative

As we have noted, a majority of *films noir* generally follow the classical narrative model. But that adherence too holds a potential for paradox, for while traditional narrative implies a kind of common cultural discourse, a conventional manner of seeing and understanding, the *film noir,* because of its disconcerting look and equally disturbing events, plunges viewers into a world that seems anything but conventional. Uncontrolled passions, corruption, murder, and plottings of every sort are woven into its fabric, suggesting threatening eruptions in the normal, or what we might term the larger cultural narrative: the "story" society typically tells about itself through its various channels of speech. Of course, given such perceived disruptions and challenges to the way we usually see our world and talk about—or narrate—it, we might expect classical narrative to remain dominant, even as it at times embraced *noir*'s darker "look." The reason is not just that familiar conventions can serve, as Stephen Heath offers, "as an obliteration or covering over of divisions" in the culture, but that they can balance the disturbing, and in the process even help us to see that problem as a function, or to be more precise, a *mal*function, of the norm. Furthermore, the classical perspective can hold the *noir* world's disturbing elements at an aesthetic distance and thus place them in a context that ultimately seems far less threatening or subversive.

Even the many *films noir* that adhere to classical narrative conventions, though, betray a fundamental dis-ease with the nature of discourse in the modern world. And this anxiety links these more conventional films to those we have been discussing, echoes the impulse behind the various narrative developments outlined here, and points up what may be the *noir* film's most consistent generic marking. For even as this large body of films works mainly within a traditional discursive form, it also reveals a preoccupation with the conditions and problems of discourse—including that of the movies. A brief survey shows that *noir* works focus on and examine practically every mode of public and private discourse: newspapers (*The Big Carnival* [1951], *Beyond a Reasonable Doubt* [1956]), radio (*Nightmare Alley* [1947]), popular magazines (*The Big Clock* [1948]), the postal system (*Appointment with Danger* [1950]), the telephone system (*The Blue Gardenia* [1952]), the Broadway stage (*Sweet Smell of Success* [1957]), television (*The Glass Web* [1953]), and, of course, the movies themselves (*In a Lonely Place* [1950], *The Big Knife* [1955]). And even when such mediated discourse slips far into the background, we find a focus on the various contrived and crippling stories we commonly tell of each other and all too eagerly embrace (*Notorious* [1946], *Framed* [1947]). Despite a more conventional narrative styling, then, these films show no less concern with how we see and speak, with how our culture can be accurately viewed and its truth might be conveyed, than do the less conventional *noirs* we have previously described.

As a narrative backdrop, these films usually sketch a world that seems keyed to the various forms of our media and the patterns of human discourse. Given this context, they then explore not only the flaws and falsehoods pervading that discourse but also the state of human isolation that has almost paradoxically followed. While inhabiting a society that seems practically wired together by multiple media forms, a world in which every manner of discourse is readily available, the characters in these films seem singularly distanced from each other and unable to achieve any kind of intimate or meaningful communication. As a result, this world seems largely populated by isolates, and the ability to reverse that situation or to communicate any vital truths at all appears increasingly unlikely.

Seen in this light, the more conventional *films noir* become almost case studies in the mechanism of repression. For while they speak in a manner that asks us to accept their own form of discourse, their commentary on the conditions that shape our discourse reflexively points to the limitations under which they too work. Jacques Lacan's notion that "the unconscious of the subject is the discourse of the other"[66] reflects tellingly here on how these films mirror the modern psyche. Although their stories proceed in a largely conventional manner that suggests a certain perspective of normalcy, they also betray a widespread distrust of the prevailing channels of public discourse, register a level of anxiety that attaches to all discourse, including the film industry's, and signal a sense of *other*-ness that weighs upon us, individually and collectively. In sum, this "discourse of the other," this sense of the problematic or conditioned nature of human communication that seems to render us strangers even from ourselves, reflects a nagging anxiety over how much we are controlled, spoken, or simply reduced to silence, in effect, by the "other" disturbingly glimpsed in us. This fundamental concern with the very conditions of our discourse might be said to constitute the secret structure and distinctive narrative pattern of these more conventional *films noir*.

What this deep structure speaks of, in the films cited above and in many other works, is more than just an awareness of cultural limitation or repression, though. Rather, it is a sense of the paradox that inhabits our discourse and, through it, ourselves. Speech, as I have suggested, can by turns mark a violation of the status quo—an eruption in a realm of silence—or its affirmation; it can be a call for help or a way of disguising a desperate situation. As Foucault explains, though, this paradox traces the trajectory of cultural discourse, which is "the path from one contradiction to another: if it gives rise to those that can be seen, it is because it obeys that which it hides."[67]

The movement along a path "from one contradiction to another" describes a pattern easily observable in the *film noir*. Repeatedly, these films detail the power and pervasiveness of our various patterns of cultural discourse, even describing characters who seem well versed in these powers and who, at the urging of their culture or self, try to turn that knowledge to profit. But while exercising that seemingly privileged knowledge or ability, these figures, like the protagonists of ancient Greek drama, eventually find themselves trapped in the realm of which they thought themselves master. Caught in a labyrinth of discourse, they wander its mazelike paths of contradictions and falsehoods, of mysteries and lies, until exhausted and destroyed by the powers they hoped to control or turn to profit. In following out such a pattern, these films effectively lead from one level of contradiction to another, while they also model the cultural conditions that give their analyses immediacy. What they thereby show most clearly is how the individual in modern society, even as he tries to forge a meaningful link to others or to society as a whole—or to what the public discourse of radio, newspaper, television, and film seems to view society as—constantly finds the self denied and isolated, reduced to a permanent other in a world of others.

The more disturbing portent, and perhaps the greater value of these films, lies in this resulting perspective, one that goes beyond a simple ideological reassessment. For more than just a vision of American culture, these works depict *cultured* man, the modern individual bound by the world he inhabits and the sense of self he has constructed for that world. In fact, the self-image that the *film noir* describes is of an individual perpetually bound by his own desires. What these films emphasize is how those desires seem to gain a new and forbidding force in the moment of their articulation, as they are translated into the common stock of discourse. Not only do our most threatening impulses thus reveal an origin in the self, but their patterns of operation show up as self-ordained too.

In its reporter protagonist Tom Garrett, Fritz Lang's *Beyond a Reasonable Doubt* provides a clear paradigm of this dark design. Garrett and his newspaper's editor contrive to frame the reporter for a murder, have him convicted, and then reveal the frame—all in order to get a sensational story on the weaknesses of the justice system. But when his editor suddenly dies, Garrett finds himself without an alibi and condemned by his own carefully contrived circumstantial evidence. In a subsequent doubling of the film's ironic thrust—and weak denial of its darker implications—he is eventually shown to be guilty, having cleverly planned to use the "story" stratagem to cover up a murder he intended all along to commit. However, this twist dispels little of the narrative's larger paradoxical thrust; it only doubly underscores the incessant play of contradiction that characterizes our discourse and repeatedly mocks our dreams of sovereignty and control.

While it has mainly an ironic effect in *Beyond a Reasonable Doubt*, this play of contradiction more often traces the strangely asocial dimension of much modern discourse. What we repeatedly find in the *film noir* is a concern with our compelling desire, even a felt need to communicate to others, as if only by talking to another could we deter an impending threat or maintain what we have come to recognize as a most fragile sense of order and of self. Thus Christina in *Kiss Me Deadly* warns detective Mike Hammer, "When people are in trouble, they need to talk." But like many other *noir* protagonists, Hammer pays little attention to this desperate "talk," dismissing it as the ramblings of a "loony"; as a result, numerous deaths and a cultural calamity follow. Such missed connections, though, are common in the *noir* world, as are communications that have quite the opposite of their intention, distancing people all the more from each other rather than bringing them together, reinforcing a sense of otherness instead of community. The *noir* world, consequently, always seems pulled in two contrary directions, to talk and to silence, toward community—like the war-era community of common cause and united will—and toward the isolation of a universal otherness—another war legacy, along with widespread feelings of disillusionment and alienation. Of course, this is hardly a specifically American dichotomy, but a modern *human* predicament that simply shows all the more glaringly in the wake of the war and the disappearance of the sense of community it had so easily generated in our far-from-homogeneous culture.

In those films that bring a conventional style to an analysis of the modes and conditions of modern discourse, we thus see almost a paradigm of the *noir* form. While not looking for a narrative voice free from the traps and entanglements to which the classical form seemed prey, they too, often in more subtle ways—see, for example, *The Big Sleep*'s concern with pornography and IOUs, *Phantom Lady*'s (1944) series of perjured testimonies that wrongly condemn a man, or *Fallen Angel*'s (1945) phony spiritualist who taps the voices of the dead— explore the conditions and consequences of discourse in modern society. In these films how we talk *to* each other and *about* our cultural situations becomes the central concern, and that manner points to what Sylvia Harvey terms "a series of radical and irresolvable contradictions buried deep within the total system of economic and social interaction that constitute the known world."[68] Through a thematic focus on our discourse, these films show how fundamentally our communications, even the movies themselves, carry a certain estranging force, one that renders all discourse precarious and every effort at human communication a risky wager against misunderstanding and alienation.

This overview of *film noir*'s main narrative techniques should come with a warning: like the films themselves, this taxonomy provides but a partial, although valuable, view of their workings, while it points toward, if it never quite satisfactorily resolves, the question of *noir*'s generic status. As I have tried to suggest, the *film noir* is a remarkably large, varied, and complex body of films. Due to the size of the canon, the ensuing discussion invariably omits films that some readers might see as paradigmatic. In some cases, it is because those films are so frequently discussed; in others, it is because a "classic" film is not always the best example of a particular narrative style—hence, *Double Indemnity* rather than, say, *Out of the Past* (1947). Then too, because of their variety and narrative complexity, *noir* films trouble easy classification, their narratives often mixing the various practices discussed here. So as much as possible, I have tried to pick out "pure" or highly representative types of films.

These same characteristics join with the knotty question of precisely what constitutes a *film* genre to leave that question, I am afraid, still unresolved.[69] An argument for *noir*'s generic status based on its discursive focus does begin to resolve the problem seen by Schrader and others by showing that it is marked by far more than just "subtle qualities of tone and mood."[70] By noting that these films are fundamentally about the problems of seeing and speaking truth, about perceiving and conveying a sense of our culture's and our own reality, we might at least clarify the debate, shifting it from whether the *film noir* represents a cycle or a genre to whether it is generically distinct from the melodrama, with which it shares so many characteristics. The problem, finally, is with our concept of film genre, which remains a rather loose and convenient, yet certainly telling, means of classification. It is for this reason, though, that Schrader can, as Barry Grant observes, begin his stylistic description of the *film noir* "by asserting that film noir is actually not a genre," only to have his analysis suggest "that it may indeed be considered one."[71]

At least I hope to bring together what have proven to be the two major approaches to the form. Previous analyses have generally focused on either questions of style, that is, the characteristic *noir* "look" and manner, or, ideologically, its level of "truth," that is, how it mirrors our culture's darker elements. But we often simplify or even overlook how closely these two perspectives are linked. To assert simply that our films were dark because a dark and despairing sense had crept upon the land seems reductive and simply stops discussion. It does not shed much light, at any rate, on the continued popularity of these films into the more prosperous 1950s.[72] An examination of *noir*'s efforts at locating an appropriate and satisfying narrative voice, though, adds a revealing perspective. As a complement to its visual estrangements— the unbalanced compositions, strange angles, and shadowy images that represent its expressionist heritage—*noir*'s varied narrative techniques seem especially appropriate, as if an outgrowth of visual style. And for viewers accustomed to the patterns of classical narrative, *noir*'s structural manipulations might have just as subversive an effect as its dark, expressionistic look. But besides scandalizing our normal point of view, the narrative forms discussed here suggest an unusual awareness of film rhetoric at this time, a mindfulness of the nature of film storytelling that underscores the form's paradoxical manner.

Again Walker Percy, novelist and language theorist, offers a useful touchstone, describing the existential predicament of modern man: "In the very age when communication theory and technique reached its peak," he offers, it has become increasingly apparent "that men were in fact isolated and no longer communicated with each other."[73] While our ability to transfer information has increased, real communication seems far more problematic, as if our symbols simply carried less meaning or bore an increasing level of ambiguity about what was said or meant. Usually we look for new ways of expression either as a rhetorical flourish or out of need; either we want to show our mastery of language and its richness, or we recognize that the old expressions are no longer adequate to convey our meanings or to account for what we perceive. In its exploring of new narrative forms and its concern with the very nature of modern discourse, the *film noir* hints of both impulses, but predominantly the second. While no *film noir* seems impelled by purely aesthetic concerns, the talent that gravitated to the form, led by such German émigrés as Fritz Lang, Robert Siodmak, and Otto Preminger, possessed a remarkable level of technical and artistic ability. At the same time, it must be clear that neither the expressionist look nor the frequent voice-over/flashback narratives are just a stylistic flourish. The *film noir* shows a singular awareness of a general failing in our discourse and of a particular inadequacy in our received cinematic language that would frustrate efforts to accurately describe the reality of modern life.

Of course no narrative form, no special language ever truly overcomes the basic limitations of our discourse. A paradox always haunts even our efforts at revealing paradox. In fact, it may be for this reason that a majority of *noir* films retain classical narrative's broad outlines. They simply accept a frame of limitation, mirror its workings thematically, and thereby produce a reflective surface in which we can more clearly see the mechanisms of individual and cultural limitation at work. In the protagonist of one of the most famous *noirs, Out of the Past's* Jeff Bailey, this pattern has a clear model. Before walking into a situation he knows is a trap, Bailey tells a friend, "I think I'm in a frame [but] all I can see is the frame. I'm going in there now to look at the picture." For the *film noir* the operant "frame" is in part the system of film production itself, that of Hollywood and its customary narrative forms. Sensing this frame, as well as its analogous bounds of discourse and culture, the *film noir* seems to take a stance akin to Bailey's. It points to the picture contained therein, offering us a vision of the individual and his world equally constrained by forces beyond their control or full understanding.

It is in this context that the ideological question of "truth" usually surfaces in *noir* discussions. Working from Althusser's explanation of how ideological structures represent "the imaginary relationship of individuals to their real conditions of existence,"[74] critics have profitably looked at these films as articulations of our culture's powerful voice, as it tries to reconcile our real situation with the "imaginary" conditions of existence in society. Such analyses try to reveal those contradictions that ideology normally works to disguise. The recurring image of the "black widow," the treacherous and destructive female who figures in so many *films noir,* well illustrates this approach. As Janey Place explains, this figure might be read as a "male fantasy," springing from a pervasive anxiety about the changing roles of women in postwar society.[75] In the repeated, almost ritualistic punishment and destruction of this figure, she sees reflected a male "need to control women's sexuality in order not to be destroyed by it."[76] This critique of woman's place in the *noir* world, explaining how she must suffer because she threatens or has usurped male dominance, typifies how *film noir* has been deconstructed to reveal a significant and previously repressed cultural truth.

However, this perspective is limited, as is evident when we consider how these films already carry out a persistent and even sweeping cultural critique, in effect how they often already deconstruct our cultural images. Ultimately, no institution or set of human relationships—not the government, the family, or the movies—is immune to their questioning. Nor do they usually settle for a cultural scapegoat of some sort, such as corruption in office, delinquency, or poverty, to bear the full burden of our various afflictions, while the larger social structure remains inviolate, as was the case in the social problem films of the 1930s, like *Wild Boys of the Road* (1933). Rather, in the *noir* world the criminals and the law usually seem equally culpable, both the self and society at fault. For this reason, Robert Porfirio describes its typical character as one who finds himself "set down in a violent and incoherent world" that he must deal with "in the best way he can, attempting to create some order out of chaos, to make some sense of his world."[77] Such conditions are not the stuff that ideal or even very effective "imaginary relations" are usually built of; rather, they would seem to leave audiences feeling less assured that right and justice would prevail than disturbed and challenged in a most fundamental way—in terms of their individual desires and interests, the cultural order, even the human condition.

Basically, the *film noir* advances a sort of ideological criticism in itself, laying bare the systemic contradictions that our films usually cover up. In this way, it *reverses* how ideological structures like the genre film usually work, by embracing rather than disguising paradoxes, even talking about them structurally and thematically. This principle shows most clearly in *noir* discussions of the manipulative and destructive powers of the film industry, for example, in *Sunset Boulevard, In a Lonely Place,* and *The Big Knife.* Part of the *film noir*'s coloring could even derive from its focus on the seams or cultural contradictions that our genre narratives normally cancel out. In this singular capacity for turning a critical eye on both the self and the culture that engenders it, Marc Vernet sees a paradoxical play of narrative patterns at work, which he describes as a Freudian effort "to overturn and reinforce defensive structures at one and the same time."[78] If this characteristic helps explain why the form's "truth" often seems so elusive, it also seems a natural outgrowth of *noir*'s deep fascination with our equally paradoxical discursive practices.

While these stylistic and ideological approaches have both proved quite valuable, then, they also lead back to our concern here with the problems and potentials of discourse. Even as they point beyond the everyday world of appearances, *noir*'s expressionist stylizations, for example, suggest that to live an authentic life we need to see beyond the simple surfaces of reality. And a similar attitude propels the ideological vantage, as Bill Nichols offers: "how we see ourselves and the world around us is often how we believe ourselves and the world to be. Images generally present views; films present particular kinds of views . . . and how we see them has everything to do with how we see ourselves."[79] But what these films say about ourselves and our world depends not only on their ability to point beyond; it is implicit in their impulse, indeed, in their *struggle* to point, reveal, and articulate. Their basic truth, I would argue, resides in that desire to speak despite the limitations on our speech and to lay bare the rules of silence and concealment. In fact, what makes *noir* films *noir* or truly disconcerting, even today, is how they strike to this fundamental level, revealing the disturbing contradictions that mark the modern human experience.

Of course, the *film noir*'s subjects are disturbing enough, but the fact that their focus on crime, corruption, psychosis, and desire channels into an unprecedented concern with *how* we see, understand, and describe our world doubly imprints the anxiety, leaving viewers to wonder if there is any reliable posture from which to gauge truth. In this respect, *noir* might most accurately be described as being about our cultural stories: about the apprehension of reality, about its fabulation, and about our too-easy or too-frequent embrace of that fabulation simply to suit our desires or needs. *Noir,* after all, not only confronts us with the images and events that possess us as cultural beings, that weave us into their narrative; in the process, it also casts in relief the discursive practices that lead us to see ourselves as the creators, possessors, and narrators of these things. One result is that it reveals us as figures within the very fabric—of self and society—that we commonly weave. Another, more important one is that it warns us to take better care in that weaving, giving thought to the limitations of our loom.

What we should also see in these effects is a trace of the positive force that energizes even the darkest *films noir*. The moment of darkness or misfortune, Foucault theorizes, "marks the point where language begins," for it is at this juncture that man usually turns to his discursive powers as a last resort against his troubles: "The gods send disasters to mortals so that they can tell of them, but men speak of them so that misfortunes will never be fully realized, so that their fulfillment will be averted in the negation of their nature."[80] Even *noir*'s dire articulations of personal and cultural decay thus show a paradoxical side, its disturbing images hinting of an effort to forestall disaster. They imply that by speaking of—or filming—these things we might hold them at a safe, rational distance, perhaps even find agreement on how to cope with their threat. And beyond this hope there lies a kind of talismanic potential based in the form's repeated emphasis on how we speak in such circumstances. For discourse can grant a temporary sanctuary from disaster, hollow out a safe place from which to think and plan. As Foucault notes, it can turn "back upon itself" where "it encounters something like a mirror; and to stop this death which would stop it, it possesses but a single power: that of giving birth to its own image in a play of mirrors that has no limits."[81]

If the *film noir*, in its emphasis on modes of human discourse, often generates what seems like an image of its own operation, it is as a version of this mirror play Foucault describes. For in this way *noir* turns discourse's paradoxical nature to its own ends in a manner unequaled by prior American films. It finds in our narrative practices a way to hollow out in the present a shelter against corruption, manipulation, and destruction—to create a mirror that might reflect light into the darkness of our *noir* world. So long as we gaze steadily at those dark images, the individual and cultural forces stand at bay, their chaotic potential halted by our narratives' ordering force. Thus, even as the *film noir* reveals discourse's nature, and particularly the manner in which it often frustrates our desires for truth and understanding, it also speaks about our communications in a way that reminds us of our human longing and even need for an effective language—filmic and otherwise. As eminently effective cinematic communications, the best of these films manage to turn life's *noir* aspect against itself, thereby reminding us how necessary it is to look into and speak against the darkness.

NOTES

1. See Percy's novel *Love in the Ruins*, p. 184, and his essay "The Delta Factor," in *Message in the Bottle*, p. 26.
2. Percy, "Man on the Train," in *Message in the Bottle*, p. 83.
3. If pressed to name bracketing films for the genre/cycle, I would choose such titles as *The Maltese Falcon* (1941) and Orson Welles's *Touch of Evil* (1958).
4. For opposite positions in this debate, see Damico's "Film Noir: A Modest Proposal," pp. 48–57, and Schrader's "Notes on *Film Noir*," pp. 278–90.
5. For a discussion of classical film narrative and its distinction from modernist styles and structures, see Bordwell, "Art Cinema as a Mode of Film Practice," and Bordwell, Staiger, and Thompson, *Classical Hollywood Cinema*.
6. Shindler, *Hollywood Goes to War*, p. 10.
7. For background on the changing social patterns and production practices in this period, see Cook, *History of Narrative Film*, pp. 398–411, Hirsch, *Dark Side of the Screen*, and Lafferty, "Reappraisal of the Semi-Documentary in Hollywood."
8. Kracauer, "Hollywood's Terror Films," p. 132.
9. Ibid., p. 133.
10. Borde and Chaumeton, "Sources of Film Noir," pp. 58, 59. This selection is excerpted from their *Panorama du Film Noir Americain*.
11. Silver and Ward, *Film Noir*, pp. 333–34.
12. Fox, "City Knights," p. 30.
13. Chandler, "Simple Art of Murder," from *Simple Art of Murder*, p. 15.
14. Chandler, *Big Sleep*, p. 146.

15. Cain, *Three of a Kind,* p. viii.
16. Fox, "City Knights," p. 34.
17. Cain, *Postman Always Rings Twice,* p. 119.
18. O'Brien, "Afterword: Jim Thompson, Dimestore Dostoevsky," in Jim Thompson, *Savage Night,* p. 152.
19. In addition to the two adaptations mentioned, we might also note Burt Kennedy's *The Killer inside Me* (1975), and Alain Corneau's *Serie Noir* (1979), taken from Thompson's *Hell of a Woman.*
20. Thompson, *Savage Night,* p. 144.
21. See Frank's "Un Nouveau Genre 'Policier': L'aventure Criminelle."
22. As examples of this approach, see Shadoian, *Dreams and Dead-Ends,* and McArthur, *Underworld USA.* Both of these scholarly works treat the *film noir* as simply a variant of a larger genre of gangster or crime films.
23. Schrader, "Notes on *Film Noir,*" p. 279.
24. Place and Peterson, "Some Visual Motifs of *Film Noir,*" p. 30.
25. See Whitney, "Filmography of Film Noir"; Hirsch in his *Dark Side of the Screen;* and Silver and Ward's *Film Noir.*
26. Damico, "Film Noir: A Modest Proposal," p. 50. Damico calls for "a complete restructuring of critical approach and methodology" for thinking about *film noir:* "a new attack on the subject which would be specific rather than general, inductive rather than deductive, and investigatory rather than conclusive; in short, an examination of FN which is interested in working from the objects of study outward rather than in imposing assumptions upon those which suit such assumptions" (p. 51). This study is intended generally to follow these guidelines.
27. See Foucault's *Madness and Civilization* and his *Archeology of Knowledge,* p. 32.
28. Foucault, *Archeology of Knowledge,* p. 32.
29. Ibid., p. 33.
30. Ibid., p. 33.
31. Ibid., p. 37.
32. Schrader, "Notes on *Film Noir,*" p. 284.
33. Hirsch, *Dark Side of the Screen,* p. 72.
34. See the Appendix for a title list of the films consulted for this study.
35. Porfirio, "No Way Out: Existential Motifs in the Film Noir," p. 216.
36. See, for example, Whitney's "Filmography of Film Noir," which includes an entry on *Kane.*
37. Bruce Kawin has introduced a term that seems particularly applicable to this sort of *noir* narrative. He terms all such visualizations of a character's perspective "mindscreens." See his *Mindscreen.*
38. Gledhill, "*Klute* 1: A Contemporary Film Noir and Feminist Criticism," in Kaplan, *Women in Film Noir,* p. 16.
39. See Smoodin's discussion of voice-over narration in "Image and the Voice in the Film with Spoken Narration," p. 29.
40. Kawin, *Mindscreen,* p. 22.

41. Fox, "City Knights," p. 30.
42. Schrader, "Notes on *Film Noir*," p. 284.
43. For a discussion of the expressionist film style, see Eisner, *Haunted Screen*. For background on the expressionist aesthetic, I have also relied on Furness, *Expressionism*.
44. Kerr's "Out of What Past? Notes on the B Film Noir" describes the effects of the technological advances made during the war years on the development of *noir* style. The most detailed discussion of these technological developments and their influence on film style can be found in Salt, *Film Style and Technology*.
45. Salt, *Film Style and Technology*, p. 292.
46. Moreno, "Subjective Camera: And the Problem of Film in the First Person," pp. 351–52.
47. Browne, "Introduction: Point of View," p. 106.
48. Brinton, "Subjective Camera or Subjective Audience?" p. 360.
49. Bonitzer, "Partial Vision: Film and the Labyrinth," p. 58.
50. Ibid., p. 58.
51. See Heath's *Questions of Cinema*, p. 94. According to Heath, the subject is in a constant state of "address" in film, for "the subject is an effect of the signifier in which it is represented, stood in for, taken place (the signifier is the narration of the subject)" (p. 52).
52. Jacobs, "Military Experience and After," in Jacobs, *Documentary Tradition*, p. 184.
53. Tyler, "Documentary Technique in Film Fiction," in Jacobs, *Documentary Tradition*, p. 265.
54. See Lafferty's "Reappraisal of the Semi-Documentary in Hollywood."
55. Ibid., p. 24.
56. Ibid., p. 24.
57. This technique was described as voice-of-god because of the seemingly divine sense of detachment, distance, and omniscience that attached to the narrator. For a discussion of the characteristics of this narrative device, see Kozloff, "Humanizing 'The Voice of God.'"
58. Schrader, "Notes on *Film Noir*," p. 281.
59. Bazin, *What Is Cinema?* I.37.
60. Ibid., II.26.
61. Schrader, "Notes on *Film Noir*," p. 281.
62. Foucault, "The Subject and Power," Afterword to Dreyfus and Rabinow, *Michel Foucault*, p. 218.
63. This is a point paraphrased by Dreyfus and Rabinow in *Michel Foucault*, p. 142, drawing on Foucault's *History of Sexuality*. In that work he notes the sort of paradox I have tried to trace out in the *noir* films, "the paradox of a society which . . . has created so many technologies of power that are foreign to the concept of the law: it fears the effects and proliferations of those technologies and attempts to recode them in forms of law" (p. 109).

64. Nichols, *Ideology and the Image,* p. 1.
65. Hirsch, *Dark Side of the Screen,* p. 173.
66. Lacan, *Ecrits,* p. 55.
67. Foucault, *Archeology of Knowledge,* p. 151.
68. Harvey, "Woman's Place: The Absent Family of Film Noir," in Kaplan, *Women in Film Noir,* p. 22.
69. See Williams's review of recent genre criticism, "Is a Radical Genre Criticism Possible?" Asserting that genre criticism has so far produced only "loose groupings of works"—groupings that are, to his thinking, of questionable value—he suggests that we might see the various formula films "more profitably as subcategories of one type," and that perhaps "film narrative" in itself "is the real genre" (p. 120).
70. Schrader, "Notes on *Film Noir,*" p. 279.
71. Grant, Introduction to *Film Genre Reader,* p. xv.
72. According to Silver and Ward's *Film Noir,* the peak of *noir* production occurs in 1950, when they identify thirty-one such releases.
73. Percy, *Message in the Bottle,* p. 25.
74. Althusser, *Lenin and Philosophy and Other Essays,* p. 53.
75. Place, "Women in Film Noir," in Kaplan, *Women in Film Noir,* p. 35.
76. Ibid., p. 36.
77. Porfirio, "No Way Out: Existential Motifs in the Film Noir," p. 217.
78. Vernet, "Filmic Transaction," p. 8. With this pattern, Vernet suggests, the *film noir* essentially carries out a "fictional destruction" of our normal cinematic expectations, although it then "hastens to reestablish its structuring oppositions, to straighten out its situations, to reinstate, as it were, the cinematic institution which it threatens" (p. 9). In this way, the *film noir* comes to represent a kind of "limit-text" that speaks of the very boundaries of longing and repression that describe the human state.
79. Nichols, *Ideology and the Image,* p. 5.
80. Foucault, *Language, Counter-Memory, Practice,* p. 54.
81. Ibid., p. 55.

2

The Double Indemnity of *Noir* Discourse

Upon seeing *Double Indemnity* (1944), producer Jerry Wald, who would later make such classic *films noir* as *Mildred Pierce* (1945), *Dark Passage* (1947), and *Key Largo* (1948), remarked that "from now on, every picture I make will be done in flashback."[1] While he eventually set aside that vow, Wald had quickly and accurately gauged both the popularity and potential of a narrative mechanism that would become fundamentally associated with the *film noir* form. In fact, today we would typically begin any list of the basic *noir* conventions with that narrative combination of voice-over and flashback.[2]

Why did this approach become so popular, appearing in a variety of forms and in major studio productions like *Mildred Pierce* and *The Postman Always Rings Twice* (1946), as well as in numerous B-films such as *Detour* (1945) and *Killer's Kiss* (1955)? A film like *Double Indemnity* offers a clue, for it demonstrates a complex relationship between the narrator and his narrative, between discourse and its subjects, that is crucial to this technique, as well as to the thrust of the *film noir*. In his study of the form, Foster Hirsch notes a curious "distance" that the voice-over/flashback mechanism produces, the narrator's voice creating "a frame in which the characters enact a drama that he knows the outcome of."[3] With this distance comes a certain tension between the speaker's present situation and those scenes of the past that seem to come flooding from his memory, as if overbrimming from the unconscious. The narrator, we gather, is trying to sort out, order, and locate some meaning in these prior events, although as he does so they seem to display a life of their own, as if possessing his voice and consciousness even as he seems to be, at this temporal remove, the source of their continued existence. In this paradox we begin to see the fundamental plight of the *noir* protagonist, who longs to possess and order the confusing pattern of his existence but who invariably finds himself possessed and determined by all manner of forces. It is also a model that describes both the psychological pattern such figures usually project and an ideological pattern at work in these films, as the characters seem simultaneously to stand outside of familiar culture and to find themselves immersed within a cultural discourse that determines much of their action.

To trace out the implications of this approach, we need to consider a salient trait that underlies even its complex mingling of past and present. The voice-over/flashback technique tacitly attributes a special importance to language. As Eric Smoodin explains, "Once the presence of the voice-over narrator has been established, the entire film serves as a sort of linguistic event, as the narrator's speech even when there is none."[4] The narration consists of a voice, but it indicates an individual's presence and consciousness, which together motivate all that we see, move our vantage freely about in time and space. That voice, though, stands "over" all else, signaling its proprietary nature. Even if the voice disappears after introducing or moving us into the flashback, it maintains proprietary control over the narrative. For this reason, we are not surprised, our narrative expectations are not violated, when, from time to time, it reappears. Having already announced its "possession" of all that we see, proved that *it* is the key to this other realm, the voice assumes a kind of liberty to come and go.

Beyond all other motivation, then, the narrator's speech assumes a kind of causal posture, accounting for all that happens, and even for the speaker's existence. It serves as a point of demarcation, gesturing in one direction toward a consciousness that stands outside of the images we view, distanced from them by the flow of words, and in another direction toward the world those words vividly conjure up. Thus Bruce Kawin notes that when a "narrator *tells*" us something in film, it is doubly important: it implies that the accompanying images are "the result, and the indicator, of directed attention."[5] Indirectly, they remind us of what Kawin calls a "mindscreen"—"the field of the mind's eye" or narrator's consciousness[6]—which is in the process of sorting through events and sifting some meaning from their imaginary persistence. With language as a signpost or kind of central processor through which all information is passed and conditioned, the voice-over narration thus directs our attention first toward a mind intent on finding an order or significant shape in the welter of past events, and second toward a world that is already possessed and shaped by the patterns of language and implicitly capable of exerting its own possessive power.

This doubly directional characteristic of the voice-over assumes added significance in the *film noir*, which typically develops a tension between a dark, puzzling world, usually the nightmarish maze of the city, and a protagonist who seems trapped by the urban jungle he inhabits or the destructive passions he has unleashed but who, through his discourse, looks to gain some mastery over his situation. Like a nightmare, the film's shadowy, enigmatic images seem simultaneously to claim an independent existence and to signify the protagonist's anxiety-ridden state of mind. The resulting tension only amplifies the questions of control and meaning that become the unspoken message in the narrator's voice. The *noir* narrative, consequently, almost seems to take on the shape of its subjects—or the shape of discourse itself—projecting the sense, as Hirsch offers, that "the film is a maze, as circuitous and convoluted as the most devious *noir* liar."[7]

To achieve such a *mise en abime*, wherein narrative and character seem to become infinite mirror images of each other, the genre at times emphasizes the act of narration in an extreme, in some cases illogical, way—as in *Sunset Boulevard*'s (1950) narration by a corpse. While a focus on the past seems constant, this discourse, as we have noted, can take various shapes. For example, it may be the voice of a single narrator spinning out his life story, or it may be several narrating voices, each offering a different, ultimately confusing version of events, after the model of *Citizen Kane* (1941). Moreover, it may frame and constitute the entire story, or be only partial and embedded within the larger narrative. Regardless of the shape and combination, though, the narration effectively molds our experience of the film's dark events, while also evoking a correlative darkness or depth in the consciousness from which this telling ensues. Rather than permitting us to perceive and impose judgment upon a pattern of causality, then, the narrative tension brackets cause, motivation, and human behavior and prompts us to reassess them. The typical assumption that this form is concerned with the consequences of unleashing the passions, we might note, overlooks the implications of this emphasis on narration.

Double Indemnity well illustrates this pattern and its effects, especially since, as one of the earlier and most influential *noirs*, it established a formula that other films would follow. Although "told" by insurance agent Walter Neff, the film is not a pure first-person narrative, with everything we see filtering through his consciousness. While much of the narrative is first-person, the film actually frames or embeds most of its diegesis in a ground of present-time, non-narrated events. In a series of images that stresses the individual's isolation in the city and the dark menace of the urban environment, we see the dying Neff return to his place of business, the Pacific All Risk Insurance Company, to leave a record of his deeds before fleeing from the police. Subsequently, the confessional narration of the James M. Cain novel on which the film is based translates into a series of lengthy flashbacks introduced by Neff's voice, as he talks into claims investigator Barton Keyes' dictaphone. What he recounts is the story of his involvement with Phyllis Dietrichson and their complicity in murdering her husband to collect his insurance. In fact, Neff's story pointedly emphasizes both a shift from the novel's confessional style and a specific quality of the film's narrative voice: "Dear Keyes, I suppose you'll call this a confession when you hear it. Well, I don't like the word 'confession.' I just want to set you straight about something you couldn't see because it was right smack up against your nose." More than simply rumination or a mind unburdening itself, this narration clearly has a purpose in mind and a sense of self. Its purpose is pointedly corrective: a desire to reveal what could not be seen, to render the puzzling "straight," and thus to find some way out, even if only through words, from an imprisoning predicament. At the same time, the speaker understands how he must sound, and how his speech might be classified—"a confession"—perhaps because he has already experienced the ease with which words become bonds, and so he tries to liberate his speech from that binding power right from the start.

The key signifier of this directed discourse, as well as the agent of its "straightening," is the dictaphone itself—which becomes the central focus of the framing third-person scenes. Whenever we see it, we know we have returned to present time, temporarily rescued from the dark events of the past. In its function here, as a mechanical agent of narration and a demarcation point, therefore, it suggests how the film itself works. In the classical narrative tradition, the film's point of view is implicitly identified with objectivity and truth. However, since the dictaphone serves to mediate or channel discourse, particularly to translate a personal history into a businesslike communication, or what Neff terms an "office memorandum," it also hints of an ideological aspect to our perspective, and analogously, of film's role within an industry that sets it the task of covering over any troubling truths. Thus the dictaphone takes on a problematic status; it seems hardly likely to clarify a situation at such a remove or to straighten anyone out, the grooves on its recording cylinders suggesting how, in the original speaker's absence, the testimony it contains might spiral around and back upon itself to no sure effect. In sum, we might interpret these ground scenes as a self-contained narrative voice that "speaks" of the very nature of discourse—its dual capacity for the straight/truth and the spiral/obfuscation—and of the human relationships, especially of Neff and the absent Keyes, that it here defines.

The addition of these bracketing scenes and subsequent embedding of the subjective, Frank Krutnik argues, weakens *Double Indemnity*'s narrative. Due to the "intermittence" of the third-person ground and to the general "dominance of the image in filmic representation," he suggests, "the voice-over does not have the same authoritative hold in the channeling of the discourse of Truth" as does the novel's simple first-person account.[8] As a result, "a dislocation emerges between the voice-over and the image, the former failing to contain the latter. This leads to a structural confusion in regard to the control over the discourse of Truth." In other words, despite the sense of authority a voice-over almost inevitably projects, here its partial and embedded character casts a shadow of doubt on Neff's narration. And that shadow reasserts a dual potential here, for both the straight and the spiraling trajectory of discourse. When combined with the seductive images of Phyllis Dietrichson as the typical erotic, threatening female of *film noir*, this dislocation, in Krutnik's view, emasculates the narrative's dominant masculine voice.

While granting an element of the sexual subversion Krutnik identifies—and which he links to the threatening aspect of woman in the *film noir*—we should not overlook the more significant side effect of this compromising of the narrative voice and its mindscreen. By being embedded in this way, the voice-over becomes part of a chain of discourse, consisting of the third-person framing scenes, Neff's narrating consciousness identified by his first-person commentary, and the images of his former desires which, as his voice fades away, come to seem as objective, truthful, and present as the film's framing scenes. It is a chain that injects a sense of interdependence to replace the illusion of autonomy that first-person narratives usually evoke. At the same time, the undercutting of a masculine "Truth" also aligns Neff's discourse with Phyllis Dietrichson's—which consists of the lies she freely tells to others, the half-truths with which she manipulates Neff, and the deeper desires she seems unable to articulate even for herself—and thereby suggests the need for a similar questioning of her "Truth." The result is a pervasive anxiety that attends every level of testimony in this film, and that echoes Michel Foucault's explanation of the angst with which human discourse is typically freighted: "anxiety as to just what discourse is, when it is manifested materially, as a written or spoken object; but also, uncertainty faced with a transitory existence, destined for oblivion . . . uncertainty at the suggestion of barely imaginable powers and dangers behind this activity, however humdrum and grey it may seem; uncertainty when we suspect the conflicts, triumphs, injuries, dominations and enslavements that lie behind these words, even when long use has chipped away their rough edges."[9] *Double Indemnity*'s narrative structure traces out this problematic, even threatening, aspect of human discourse. And in so doing, it reflects an anxiety fundamental to the *film noir* over who or what controls man's life and over what, if any, truths might lurk behind every appearance, in any assertion, within all discourse.

Despite its slightly different narrative style, the Cain novel had established the potential for this focus, although it subordinates a concern with discourse to the threatening power of desire itself. What inspires the film's voice-over narration and its added complications, though, is the novel's structure as a written statement, a notarized confession of murder by its protagonist, Walter Huff. It is a curiously double-edged document he produces, since his admission of guilt results from a bargain struck with Keyes, allowing Huff to flee the country in return for his confession. Moreover, this strange bargain of guilt and freedom only hides another disturbing paradox, that of an insurance agent's murder of his client to collect the very insurance he has sold him. That arrangement saves face for the company; but more important, it saves faith in the system, which otherwise would be clearly seen to contain the most dangerous contradictions in its workings. Together with the substantial portion of dialogue that Raymond Chandler lifted from the novel in adapting it to the screen, this narrative motivation suggests Cain's implicit interest in the doubleness of discourse and further emphasizes how much the *film noir* owes to the work of hard-boiled writers like Cain, Chandler, and Hammett.[10]

The film builds on this concern, as the various ways in which people talk or communicate within the narrative reflect the same uncertainty and hesitation that mark Neff's recorded statement to Keyes. In fact, we might see the recurrent image of the dictaphone that introduces most of the third-person scenes, as emblematic of a pervasive inability or unwillingness to speak directly here. Of course, as this study suggests, that is the very territory of *film noir:* a narrative world in which individuals constantly lie to or trick each other, where they always find communication difficult or simply irrelevant.

Double Indemnity is such an exemplary *noir* because practically every incident turns upon or points up this pattern. Walter's desire to see Mr. Dietrichson, for example, requires a subterfuge, as he tries to get into the Dietrichson residence without revealing his purpose.[11] But the deflections that meet his efforts begin to suggest how discourse can double back on its user: first, the maid guesses he is a salesman and tries to turn him away; and then, Phyllis Dietrichson rebuffs him before engaging Neff in an exchange of thinly veiled sexual assays that almost reverse their roles, rendering him less a salesman than a potential consumer of her allure. Their next meeting, supposedly to discuss her husband's insurance needs, further develops this situation, as it quickly becomes a multilayered discussion weighted with what Foucault would term the "powers and dangers" of discourse; as Neff recalls it, "we were talking about automobile insurance, only you were thinking about murder, and I was thinking about that anklet you were wearing." This barely submerged discourse of death and desire leads the two to agree to arrange a fatal "accident" for Phyllis's husband to gain his insurance money. But as a result of their compact, the ensuing conversation in which Walter "sells" Dietrichson insurance models the sort of anxieties that can infuse even "humdrum and grey" discourse. While Walter explains the terms of his car insurance and tries to trick Dietrichson into signing an accident policy as well, Phyllis deflects her husband's concentration, ironically by arguing that he needs no insurance. The surface features of the resulting discussion are totally at odds with Phyllis's true desires—a situation that already hints at her familiarity with the circular or spiral capacity of discourse.

The most effective image of this tension occurs after the subsequent murder, as Keyes drops in unexpectedly just before Phyllis arrives. Poised in an open hallway, Walter carries on a maddening conversation with Keyes, who reveals that he suspects Phyllis and is keeping her under supervision to discover her accomplice. She, meanwhile, stands in the same hall, only barely concealed by the door that Walter awkwardly yet desperately holds open. Like a scene from a French farce gone wrong, this encounter points up the layering of discourse that operates here and the anxieties which mark—and nearly mock—man's efforts to control it.

More than just anxiety, though, this duplicity generates a very real sense of alienation—from both others and the self—that is also suggested by the dictaphone Neff substitutes for Keyes, who is his only friend. Neff is already alienated in one way, for after killing Dietrichson he must masquerade as his victim, speaking and acting just as he would. But this sort of role playing hardly stops with the murder, since to avoid discovery, as Neff's dictaphone monologue notes, "we couldn't let anybody see us together. We couldn't even talk to each other over the telephone." What seemed to begin as a crime of passion thus becomes an act that cancels out passion, a love affair, as Phyllis complains, in which the lovers can never come together: "We did it so we could be together, but instead it's pulling us apart."[12]

Given a situation in which they can only talk surreptitiously across the aisles at a local market or, infrequently, on the phone from random booths, given a circumstance in which every conversation carries the anxiety of discovery and every public meeting becomes an instance of disguised feelings, both seek to replace their displaced identities and establish a new, less-troubled relationship. In effect, each tries to locate a true self by abandoning that other with whom he shares in a most dangerous and frustrating discourse. So Walter begins seeing Lola, Phyllis's stepdaughter, while she turns to Nino Zachette, Lola's disreputable boyfriend. Significantly, their stated reasons for looking to these surrogates recall their original purpose in killing Dietrichson—to remove any possible obstacles to their own relationship. Walter starts seeing the younger girl, he explains, only to stifle a potentially damaging revelation; she wants to tell the police of her suspicions that Phyllis had murdered her mother some years before. Phyllis, in turn, contends that she just plans to use Nino, framing him for her husband's murder to deflect attention from Walter and herself. But those stated rationales ring hollow, suggesting instead their own uncertain motivations and the "enslavements that lie behind" their words—enslavements to the powers and uncertainties, in fact to the power *of* uncertainty, within their own discourse.

The mutual self-deceptions that follow combine with the central deceptive discourse here—the murder Walter and Phyllis try to pass off as an accident—to produce a chain of such discourses within the story that parallels the structure of *Double Indemnity*'s narrative. As the film's central event, Dietrichson's murder breeds a line of deceptive actions and testimonies, including Phyllis's indignant reaction to the president of Pacific All Risk, Walter's feigned consternation for Keyes, and Walter and Phyllis's eventual plottings against each other. From Lola's account of her mother's death, Walter becomes increasingly suspicious of Phyllis and, as he says, begins "to think about her in that way, dead, I mean." Even as he "saw a way to get clear of the whole mess," though, Phyllis arranges "plans of her own" for him, as the dangers inherent in their individual plottings simultaneously surface. In fact, she plans to use Nino to kill Walter or to take the blame for his death if she must do the deed herself. Clearly modeled on her use of Walter to eliminate her husband, this new plot points to a long chain of deception and murder that we now see reaches back at least as far as the original Mrs. Dietrichson's mysterious death.

What cloaks this continuity is Phyllis's ability to fashion a narrative about herself as a neglected and confined wife, forced into a life with no possibility of human communication; as she tells Walter, "sometimes we sit here all evening and never say a word to each other." However, in a later scene that comments on this pose, as well as on her generally cynical attitude, Phyllis easily reverses her complaint, telling Walter how wonderful it would be to have "just strangers beside you; you don't know them and you don't hate them." In this chain of deceitful, unreliable, and clearly dangerous discourses—their full menace revealed in the string of murders plotted and carried out, almost without detection—we find a parallel to the film's narrative pattern, as what is shown, recounted by Neff, and enacted in his flashbacks reflects on how much remains to be revealed or spoken, and thereby gives reason to the anxiety that pervades the larger narrative.

Between the different possibilities for truth and duplicity here moves the figure of Walter Neff who, in his desire to "set" Keyes "straight" and in his narrated attempt at the perfect crime, initially seems to assert some freedom from discourse's "uncertainty." It is Walter's way with words, after all, that makes him Pacific All Risk's top salesman, gains him access to the Dietrichson home, and helps him counter Phyllis's initially naive pose ("I wonder if I know what you mean?" she responds to one of Walter's own double entendres) with a line that suggests a fine understanding of what "dominations and enslavements" lie behind words ("I wonder if you wonder," he replies). This understanding also lets him see through Keyes' gruff posturing, especially his treatment of one of Walter's clients who puts in a phony claim; as Neff observes, "You never fooled me with your song and dance, not for a second. I kind of always knew that beneath the cigar ashes on your vest you had a heart as big as a house." More significantly, this insight leads him to review whether or not he is suspected in the Dietrichson case by listening to Keyes' dictaphone recordings. In his ability to tap this tool of mediated communication for its truth, Walter clearly shows an ability to recognize and traffic in a world of uncertain and qualified communications. In sum, he seems almost a master of discourse's spiraling trajectory, and as his occupation hints, nearly *insured* against its hazards.

However, the power of discourse is seductive, at least as much so as a beautiful woman, and it can lead to a carelessness about its dangers. In fact, it is Walter's understanding of the insurance industry and how its policies operate that leads him to give free reign to his desires and to believe that his murder and insurance collection scheme could "be perfect." As one of the framing scenes of Walter's narration makes clear, Phyllis's attractions and the promise of easy money simply opened onto a dark realm of anxieties and desires already in place. As Neff explains, the roots of his plotting ironically reach back into his immersion in the insurance business' own discourse, with which he has been so successful:

> It was all tied up with something I'd been thinking about for years, since long before I ever ran into Phyllis Dietrichson. Because . . . in this business you can't sleep for trying to figure out all the tricks they could pull on you. You're like the guy behind the roulette wheel, watching the customers to make sure they don't crook the house. And then one night you get to thinking how you could crook the house yourself and do it smart, because you've got that wheel right smack under your hands. You know every notch in it by heart. And you figure all you need is a plant out front, a shill to put down the bet. Suddenly the doorbell rings and the whole set-up is right there in the room with you.[13]

The notion that one can indeed "do it smart" originates in the very anxiety that his work produces, as if that uncertainty were so seductive as to suggest its opposite's possibility, an illusion of certainty and human control. Apparently, even as it asserts a fallibility or a potential for deception, discourse also plays upon the desire for truth that motivates it. Or as Jacques Lacan explains, "even if it is intended to deceive," a particular text still "speculates on faith in testimony" and implicitly argues "that speech constitutes truth."[14] It is this characteristic that here allows for both belief and deception, for trust in and manipulation of another, and consequently for Walter's paradoxical stance, as he is effectively seduced by a system into believing that he might master its possibilities for belief and deception.

In this situation, discourse seems both desire's source and—as evidence Walter's narration—its logical end. This perspective should shed light on what Krutnik terms the "difficulties" of adapting any of Cain's novels to the screen. In these works, he suggests, woman usually functions as "a fundamental enigma," while the *film noir* is often concerned with "the definition and delimitation of desire."[15] Of course, *Double Indemnity* does more than simply trace out the consequences of an impulse that finds its source in a mysterious, unknowable force: desire impelled by an alluring enigma. Phyllis eventually proves no more enigmatic than Walter, and even less able to deceive Keyes; meanwhile, Walter's voice-over makes him seem less mysterious, and argues for our ability to understand his motivations by seeing them as a discourse of the other—the lure of money, the attractions of Phyllis, a desire for an exciting alternative to his hum-

drum life. This marriage of the enigmatic with an impulse for definition makes good sense if we see the generating force of *Double Indemnity* as not just the erotic female image but a larger context of repression, caution, and calculation that both defines and marks the limits of
human desire. What is *defined* here, in fact, *is* the enigmatic, the
ineffable. It is given temporary embodiment in the treacherous female, but ultimately finds its source in a most basic cultural discourse
of desire that speaks through these characters and surfaces most
forthrightly in Walter's voice-over narration.

The displacement of the erotic and its mystery by the determining
power of discourse also marks the relationship between Keyes and
Neff. In fact, a major change from the novel is the expansion of Keyes'
character for this purpose.[16] The scenes between the two emphasize
their mutual respect, offer a certain balance to the heterosexual pairing of Walter and Phyllis, and hint of their basic similarity. Just as
Walter "can't sleep" at times, wondering what "tricks" a client is con-
templating, so too is Keyes bothered by indigestion whenever a claim
seems irregular. As he explains, this discomfort takes the form of an
internal discourse, as a "little man" inside tells him to be suspicious, to
look for hidden complexities and possibilities even in seemingly transparent testimony. Consequently, he views the various claims and papers he processes as "not just forms and statistics and claims for
compensation; they're alive. They're packed with twisted hopes and
crooked dreams." Because they are "alive," though, they cannot be
reliably manipulated, he realizes. While Walter seems to understand
these complexities just as well, his consuming belief that he can still
manage to "do it right" and pull off the perfect murder ultimately
runs counter to Keyes' recognition that "murder's never perfect,"
especially "when two people are involved." In his abiding suspicion we
thus find a clue as to why Keyes has remained a bachelor and has spent
much of his life sifting through a discourse of claims and forms,
searching out the falsehoods and uncertainties their words almost
inevitably conceal. That realm clearly has the same sort of enigmatic
allure for him as does the woman in Cain's novel, and it holds Keyes in
its grip just as strongly as Phyllis Dietrichson does Walter.

In light of their shared understanding of the devious potential of
discourse, we can better comprehend the bond between Walter and
Keyes—a bond of mutual respect, trust, and shared knowledge. It is
also a bond that sharply contrasts the skewed relationship of desire
that links Walter and Phyllis, who ultimately seem to lack any respect
or trust for each other. In fact, they never describe their attraction as
"love." When Phyllis comes to him with the proposal to murder her

husband, Walter confesses, in a telling choice of words, "I'm crazy about you, baby," and she answers similarly, that she is "crazy" for him too. After shooting Walter and being shot herself—the result of their dual "craziness"—Phyllis points up what was missing from that earlier avowal, confessing what the narrative has already made plain: "I never loved you."

However, the notion of love does surface several times in the easy banter that Walter and Keyes repeatedly fall into. Following one of Neff's acerbic comments, Keyes half-jokingly replies, "I love you too, Walter," and with a hint more seriousness, Walter admits in his narration to similar feelings for his colleague. The value judgment suggested here is more important than the sexual reversal implied by these comments—a reversal that several critics have read simply as homosexual compensation for the threatening female figure so common to *film noir*.[17] While sexual desire is labeled "crazy," Keyes and Neff's relationship, defined by their mutual sense of discourse's problematic nature and given symbolic presence through their shared use of the dictaphone as a conduit of truth—which we should contrast with Walter and Phyllis's shared *twisting* of discourse in the form of the insurance contract—assumes a more privileged status. It is not just a case of the dependable male being elevated over a treacherous female, and thus what Krutnik terms a "delimited 'truth' of sexuality"[18]; rather, discourse itself has been privileged over sexuality and revealed as the true route of desire.

In developing this connection between Neff and Keyes, Wilder and screenwriter Raymond Chandler qualified the novel's main focus on a destructive sexual desire—the Cain-text's assertion "that the hero is a *victim* to desire"[19]—by emphasizing the determining aspect of discourse itself. Lacan's speculations on the source of desire help explain this qualification. He suggests that "desire exists" because there is a level of language "which escapes the subject in its structure and effects, and because there is always, on the level of language, something which is beyond consciousness, and it is there that the function of desire is to be located."[20] Read in this context, the transformation of Walter and Phyllis's sexual desires into a compelling concern with beating the system by manipulating its discursive rules represents not a narrative inconsistency, nor a simple laundering of the tale's sexual content to appease the film industry's Production Code, but a sign of its deeper consistency. What it points up is the film's abiding concern with the powerful and ultimately dangerous ways in which discourse plays in and upon the unconscious, making one susceptible to a variety of immediate or superficial lures, including the sexual. Because he serves as both Walter's best friend and, as investigator, his chief nemesis, Keyes provides a most logical ground for this focus by embodying discourse's double potential.

As the film repeatedly shows, discourse can, with its alternately straight and spiraling trajectories, reveal or obscure, communicate or undermine communication, and thus bind together or rend asunder. This is, in fact, its double bind and the real "double indemnity" about which this film and similar *noir* voice-over narratives speak. Even as Neff recounts his deterioration and destruction—given visual measure by the bloodstain that grows noticeably as he speaks into the dictaphone—his narration suggests a measure of recompense in a manner noted by Lacan, who theorizes that "in its symbolizing function speech is moving towards nothing less than a transformation of the subject to whom it is addressed by means of the link that it establishes with the one who emits it—in other words, by introducing the effect of a signifier."[21] The film's final scenes twice develop such transforming links. First, as Neff ends his narration, he turns to look directly into the camera and says "Hello, Keyes." As he acknowledges the previously unseen presence of the subject to whom his monologue is addressed, we realize that Keyes has been silently watching for some time, letting Neff spin his tale without interruption. This brief look of outward regard reverses the narrative's earlier "mindscreen" pattern, momentarily transforming Keyes—an object of Neff's narration, a figure in the visual field fashioned by his discourse—into the camera's eye, putting him in a narrator's position. He thus becomes the "key" to our own access to a visual field that includes Neff.[22] What Neff has described as "a crazy story with a crazy twist to it" effectively twists or spirals round to link the two men, placing them alternately in the roles of narrator and narrated.

This narrative development heralds a thematic shift here as well, with Keyes displaying a skill, the ability to strike a match on his nail, that has previously identified Neff and differentiated him from his supervisor. Such dexterity has suggested the street wisdom that characterizes Neff and separates him from Keyes, who at one point wistfully comments that he "never could do that." But as Neff lies dying and Keyes offhandedly lights a cigarette for him in this way, we glimpse the sort of transformation Lacan describes. That act signals a limited wisdom these two have come to share—a sense perhaps of the flickering light of truth that marks all discourse. It is the same light that flickers in the voice-over narration of a film like *Double Indemnity,* as it briefly, intermittently, and unpredictably dispels the larger darkness to which the individual in *film noir* always seems consigned.

These shifts effectively conclude the film by suggesting, on the one hand, the intricate pattern of causalities and relationships here, as the narrative's various levels seem alternately to plot out events and to be engendered by them. On the other, they also emphasize what lies beyond the realm described by discourse, outside of Walter's narration. Despite his plea to Keyes for a head start to escape the police, it is obvious that Walter will never reach the "border" (the margins of this discursively-bound world) he seeks, and that death, not escape, awaits. In this predicament Robert Porfirio sees modeled the basic existential thrust of all *film noir*, as the genre works another variation on its primary theme that there is "no way out" from the problems of alienation, meaninglessness, and impending doom. He also interprets the voice-over/flashback mechanism from this perspective, as a technique whose purpose is to "enhance the aura of doom. It is almost as if the narrator takes a perverse pleasure in relating the events leading up to his current crisis, his romanticisation of it heightened by his particular surroundings."[23]

In truth, there is a kind of romanticizing effect in *Double Indemnity*'s narration, although it is far less pronounced than in Cain's novel. And it is far less the case than in a later Cain adaptation, *The Postman Always Rings Twice* (1946). Its narrator, Frank Chambers, tells his story from a cell on death row, as he tries to understand how "it all works out" in the end. While there is no hope for his future, he can at least pray that he and his girl Cora can be together in the next life. In both of these films the sense of an isolated consciousness, standing against society, even against the power of death, is central to their attraction. However, the existential import of their voice-over/flashback narrations is even more significant. What Frank Chambers and Walter Neff look forward to are later *noir* narrators like *Dead Reckoning*'s (1947) Rip Murdoch. Beaten and bloody as the film begins, he desperately confides his tale to a priest, although he has no expectations that he will even live through the night, only the hope that someone might believe his story, which will clear the name of his best friend. The discourse represented by such narrators reaches out to a world of listeners who, in another sort of narrative transformation, as enthralled auditors become rhetorical accomplices in the protagonist's predicament, rather than simply distanced perceivers of an action. In this way discourse leaps the bounds of isolation and extends the narrator's existence beyond the web of affairs in which he is fatally enmeshed. And in the process, he gains a last say over the events that have led up to his situation. Having learned—the hard way—of discourse's double potential, he attempts an almost absurd affirmation, trying to spiral that duality back upon itself, to locate an advantage in it, to find in the causal chain contributing to his predicament a lexical "way out," a way, at least, of getting beyond the apparent boundaries of determined action and foreclosed time.

The approach of death, though, usually provokes speech, a last effort to suspend the final individual disaster. Thus Foucault describes how, "headed toward death," language invariably "turns back upon itself" to exercise its "single power: that of giving birth to its own image in a play of mirrors that has no limits."[24] At this point too the desire for life and the desire that inhabits discourse reveal their affinity, mutually generating an image against dissolution: an image of the self *within* and *fashioned by* a world of language. In such typical *noir* voice-over narrations as Neff's or *D.O.A.*'s Frank Bigelow, who has been poisoned and, as his narration begins, has only a short time to live and make sense of his fate, the self effectively surrenders to the power of discourse. He does so, though, because as death looms—as it always does in the *film noir*—it seems to bring a realization that only in this way can the individual buy time and gain some control over circumstance. By riding the spiral of discourse, as it were, the speaking individual gains an important if brief placement, as the narrator of what has always been, after a fashion, a *narrated* life.

This "double indemnity" feature of the voice-over/flashback formula—its inevitable risk and possible payoff—may best explain why it occurs in so many *films noir.* When combined with the disturbing events that typify the *noir* world, this technique develops an effective narrative dualism. It shapes a consciousness that, albeit too late, seeks some perspective on the actions it almost compulsively replays on its dark "mindscreen," and in the process reaches for a new sense of self. In an extreme case like *The Postman Always Rings Twice,* this approach can be jarring, since it involves a nearly simultaneous accession to sexual desire—a wish fulfillment fueled by the erotic image of Lana Turner—and a rational repentance for the actions described. The contorted morality of this strategy, of an erotic fulfillment accompanied by confession and contrition, speaks to the problematic posture of the *film noir,* which operates within the traditions of Hollywood narrative even as it questions those traditions. At the same time, this paradoxical posture hints at a broader perspective of truth, demonstrated so effectively by *Double Indemnity*'s narrative mechanism. As an exemplary model of the many *films noir* that would use this strategy, it speaks about the very nature of human communication, as well as the increasingly complex forms that communication was taking in midforties America. It thereby reveals, with a characteristically dark irony, how discourse becomes both a cause of and a compensation for the individual predicament this form would repeatedly and disconcertingly describe for a culture that, in perhaps an equivalent irony, increasingly looked to film discourse for some release from its abiding anxieties.

NOTES

1. Wald's comment is quoted in LaValley's "Introduction: A Troublesome Property to Script," in his edition of *Mildred Pierce,* p. 29.
2. See Porfirio, "No Way Out: Existential Motifs in the Film Noir," p. 213.
3. Hirsch, *Dark Side of the Screen,* p. 75.
4. Smoodin, "Image and the Voice in the Film with Spoken Narration," p. 19.
5. Kawin, *Mindscreen,* p. 13.
6. Ibid., p. 10.
7. Hirsch, *Dark Side of the Screen,* p. 169.
8. Krutnik, "Desire, Transgression and James M. Cain," p. 39.
9. Foucault, "Discourse on Language," in *Archeology of Knowledge,* p. 216.
10. For a discussion of this influence, see Hirsch, *Dark Side of the Screen;* Schrader, "Notes on *Film Noir*"; and especially Fox, "City Knights."
11. This pattern of verbal subterfuge is even more marked in the novel than in the film, although it is one of the few instances in which this theme is more emphasized in the book than in the cinematic adaptation.
12. In developing the distancing effect of their discourse of deception, the film differs considerably from the novel. While the film emphasizes a desire to communicate that is constantly frustrated by the dangers of communicating, the novel downplays this problem. Neff and Phyllis Dietrichson simply do not meet and do not even seem to desire to come together following the murder of her husband, at least not until they begin plotting to kill each other.
13. This passage, which speaks plainly of the paradoxical play of discourse, derives from a speech in the novel, wherein Walter explains how the very impulse for wrongdoing can originate in the discourse of proscription. In Cain's book Walter offers the following explanation: "All right, I'm an agent. I'm a croupier in that game. I know all their tricks, I lie awake nights thinking up tricks, so I'll be ready for them when they come at me. And then one night I think up a trick, and get to thinking I could crook the wheel myself if I could only put a plant out there to put down my bet. That's all. When I met Phyllis I met my plant." See Cain, *Double Indemnity,* pp. 29–30.
14. Lacan, *Ecrits,* p. 43.

15. Krutnik, "Desire, Transgression and James M. Cain," pp. 36–37.
16. See Jensen's discussion of the changes from novel to film in his essay, "Raymond Chandler and the World You Live In," p. 21.
17. The most detailed discussion of this rather obvious motif occurs in Claire Johnston's "*Double Indemnity*," in Kaplan, *Women in Film Noir*, pp. 100–111.
18. Krutnik, "Desire, Transgression and James M. Cain," p. 37.
19. Ibid., p. 39.
20. This passage is translated and quoted by Jameson in *Prison-House of Language*, p. 138.
21. Lacan, *Ecrits*, p. 39.
22. Jonathan Culler (*Pursuit of Signs*, p. 183) describes this sort of inversion as a typical "effect of self-deconstruction." It is a "demonstration" or, put in the context of narrative, an ironic revelation "that a hierarchical opposition, in which one term is said to be dependent upon another conceived as prior, is in fact a metaphysical imposition and that the hierarchy could well be reversed." This abiding potential for reversal, of course, questions the authority with which we usually invest the voice-over and thus suggests another level of anxiety informing this type of *film noir*.
23. Porfirio, "No Way Out: Existential Motifs in the Film Noir," p. 216.
24. Foucault, *Language, Counter-Memory, Practice*, p. 54.

CHAPTER 3

Narration, Desire, and *The Lady from Shanghai*

If the embedded voice-over/flashback technique brought a valuable subjective element to the *film noir*, it fell somewhat short of suggesting a true interior human discourse. It remained for films like *The Postman Always Rings Twice* (1946) and *The Lady from Shanghai* (1948) to turn this mechanism into something more than just a partial effect. A voice accompanies the very first images in these films and continues until the final fade-out, and that all-embracing narration essentially changes how we approach the films. For this technique implies that all we view is the past, or at least a narrator's *sense* of his past; thus, for the film's duration we move within a recollected, subjective world, propelled on a "stream of consciousness" without even the minimal objective anchoring that a film like *Double Indemnity* offers. One of the more unsettling consequences is that we find ourselves placed not in a world *within* which disturbing events occur, but in a world *of* disturbance—a realm conjured up precisely because a mind is troubled. And that subjective immersion challenges our usual narrative experience, for it ultimately points up how much our ability to narrate—to give shape or order to, even to *know* our world—depends on our own uncertain and inconstant character.

In trying to discern a pattern to *noir* narrative, Marc Vernet noticed a three-part movement that reflects on this effect. The "classical" *film noir*, he offers, starts with a "set-up," introduces an "enigma" or "black hole" in the narrative, and then resolves the threat the enigma posed.[1] We find pleasure in these films, he suggests, through the pattern of reversals such movements involve, as a first premise gives way to a series of unsettling events that "interrupt and disconnect the narrative, hollowing out the fiction and shooting it full of holes."[2] On one level, the total voice-over narrative works in this way, for its flashback narration establishes a coherent world, threatens its coherence, and then, while maintaining a "structure of suspense," vanquishes the threat to coherence.

However, with a narrative that is fully narration, I would suggest, the fiction is actually "full of holes" from the start, threatened, as our experience becomes one of constant suspense or tension. Some *films noir*, for example, seem to "advance in a rectilinear fashion,"[3] after the pattern of most classical narratives, but they actually describe a circular pattern, as if they represented but one more variation in an endless round of speculations about the past. And while they might also suggest a rational effort at containing, shaping, and controlling unsettling memories—those words and images surfacing from the narrator's psyche—they also hint at a force of desire, driving the psyche, in a Freudian repetition mechanism, to dwell on the pains and pleasures of the past. What we have, in effect, is a problem of excess, of *too much* subjectivity, at least for the classical narrative experience, with its implicitly objective vantage, to contain easily. That problem recurs throughout the *noir* form, though, and it is symptomatic of the impulse for individual articulation we have already noted in these films. It simply points toward a pattern of frustration that seems built into the efforts at communication or personal articulation which these films repeatedly describe.

Lady from Shanghai well illustrates both these difficulties and the potential of an embracing voice-over/flashback. Its voice-over accompanies the initial and final images, motivating the entire narrative and clearly identifying its subjectivity. In the process, it follows a narrative pattern that seems by turns rectilinear and cyclical, goal-directed like other classical narratives but also bound to the circular trajectory of desire. Of course, since it was written and directed by Orson Welles, *Lady from Shanghai* recalls another film that operates both within and outside of traditional narrative expectations, probably the most important and influential voice-over/flashback narrative, *Citizen Kane*.

Prior to *Lady from Shanghai*, Welles had repeatedly experimented with voice-over/flashback techniques. Perhaps his experience with the Mercury Theatre of the Air, his radio program of the 1930s, made him appreciate the value of a narrating voice—and implicitly a consciousness—to guide the audience through a sequence of events, while bridging and disguising any gaps in the narrative.[4] Certainly, he would have had to use a variation of the voice-over on his abortive subjective camera adaptation of *Heart of Darkness*, and his *Magnificent Ambersons* (1942) relies heavily on its detached voice-over narrator to sketch the manners of a bygone era in which the Ambersons ruled society, as well as to guide us through the various personal and cultural changes that signal their fall from prominence.

But *Citizen Kane* provides the most telling introduction to *Lady from Shanghai,* for while it uses several voice-over narrators whose narrations are joined in an objective frame of sorts, they form a springboard for exploring the same problems that the later film does with its single narrator. These are the basic problems of subjectivity and desire, which invariably limit our ability to make sense of or to narrate the individual experience. *Kane* is fundamentally concerned with its egocentric title character's all-consuming desires—desires that ultimately become *self*-consuming, leading him to exchange the human realm for one of things, the acquisitions of wealth that crowd out the human. Motivating the narration of Kane's desires is the reporter Thompson's effort to organize the fragments of Kane's life into some meaningful form; and his effort is, in turn, driven by his boss's desire for an "angle" on Kane's life, one that will help their newsreel "sell." However, the secret that seems to be the key to this intricate binding of desire within desire—the meaning of "Rosebud," Kane's last word— consistently eludes discovery, at least by those within the story, and when we make the connection to the boy Kane's sled through a privileged shot, it seems almost a pointless discovery, one that suggests a variety of ambiguous constructions rather than a single truth and that remains cut off from the world in which that truth is so eagerly sought. Thus the narrative becomes a story of frustration, desire's natural coeval—a story in which, Robert Carringer explains, the "search for a clear-cut, simple explanation continually works against the possibility of ever finding one."[5]

For Carringer, the film's central image is a decorative glass ball in which we glimpse Kane's reflection at the film's opening. This curio prompts his "Rosebud" remark, before it drops to the floor and shatters as Kane dies. Describing the ball as "an intact world in miniature, a microcosm,"[6] Carringer sees it as a model of the perfectly ordered realm Kane has, throughout his life, tried to fashion for himself. Such an interpretation suggests that Kane is essentially consumed by his own desires, particularly his fascination with creating a full and ordered microcosm that might mirror his personality. It is a useful vantage, for from it we can see Kane's desire reflected in the larger narrative that is similarly driven by a longing for completion and explication, and that also seems destined to frustration and fragmentation because of the absence of a single, coherent perspective on events.

With its single voice-over/flashback, *Lady from Shanghai* pursues the same phantoms of desire as its famous predecessor and comments equally on the problems of narration. Of course, its protagonist, the sailor Michael O'Hara, is different—more innocent and obviously less powerful than Kane—and his narration affords a more stable, because singular, point of view. But the result is a similar analysis of the circular, almost self-consuming pattern of desire, accompanied by a similar shattering of the microcosm—or narrative—it tries to project in compensation. If less complex than *Kane,* then, *Lady from Shanghai* still points up a tension lodged in the very conditions of its narrative unfolding, as it both describes and demonstrates the impact of desire on our ability to "narrate" our lives in the largest sense—that is, to organize, direct, and find achievement in our most fundamental actions. More than just an interesting companion piece to *Kane* and *Ambersons, Lady from Shanghai* clearly demonstrates how intricately intertwined the impulses of desire and narration are, and how together they shape *noir*'s use of the voice-over/flashback.

Just as we usually direct our efforts to some goal, so classical narrative and desire are equally concerned with ends; that is, both are goal-directed in a way that reflects the connection between the self and satisfaction, as it also does between narration and its drive toward closure or conclusion. In fact, *Lady from Shanghai* repeatedly talks about its concern with conclusion, and especially the end of all human endeavors—death. For example, as Michael's narration—and the film—begins, he confesses, "If I'd known where it would end, I'd never have let anything start." Later, when the lawyer George Grisby asks if he thinks the world may be coming to an end, Michael offers a logical reply that repeats this motif: "There was a start to the world someplace, so I guess there'll be a stop." And later, when his employers, Arthur and Elsa Bannister, ask what he thinks of them, Michael hints at another dimension to this concern with ends, as he notes, "I never make up my mind about anything at all until it's over and done with." Just as these comments suggest Michael's tendency to think in terms of resolution and a rectilinear development, they also prime us to expect a linear plot, a movement toward a goal contained within the tale—the film—that Michael's narration unfolds. And in this suggestion of a gradual progress toward denouement, the narrative promises an eventual revelation of meaning, hinting at the sort of satisfying unraveling that mystery or thriller films—which this work consistently recalls—typically provide viewers.

As one critic notes, though, this promise of linearity, wherein a recounting of the past leads up to the present, operates within another, "circular structure, which involves a doubling back of present to past."[7] All of Michael's narration, for instance, signals a kind of turning back; in it, a consciousness, prodded by confusion and fascination, once more tries to sift some meaning or pattern from the prior, unsettling encounter with the Bannisters who, like Charles Foster Kane, have upset the narrator's usual expectations. But that encounter resists both understanding and formulation, and only returns Michael to his present, past-haunted, and bewildered situation. In this regard especially the film recalls *Kane*, whose structure similarly turns back upon itself, as if it were attempting to take its own measure and thus resolve a frustrating circularity into a linear narrative. *Lady from Shanghai* simply varies this formula by identifying that circular impulse with the film's narrating consciousness, thereby suggesting that it springs from within the self, sourced in our basic human desires.

Despite its multiple narrators, *Kane* too locates a frustratingly circular pattern in the common human desire to know, to formulate, and to dispel our anxieties at ambiguity. Thompson's search for an "angle" on Kane's life is an effort to make sense of a life and a death for an information-hungry movie audience, and thus to turn the latter event to economic account for his studio. As he interviews those closest to Kane, though, it is a *series* of lives that gradually emerge, each one diverging from the others just enough so that the larger narrative perspective on Kane becomes doubled and redoubled, twisted like a Möbius strip through these varied, almost contradictory views. At the same time, the narrative moves toward the destruction of the one object promising to lend some coherence to these multiple vantages— Kane's sled "Rosebud." Consequently, the film ends where its search really begins, with this image of Kane's childhood, consumed in flames after his death, so that we seem to have traveled a frustratingly circular path, on a quest taking us no nearer our ultimate goal of understanding this figure. In fact, even the "angle" offered by the sled is privileged beyond the narrative voices and Thompson's searching gaze, eluding all comment here by its fleeting and unremarked appearance for the viewers who, thus teased, are then pulled back from the narrative by a series of dissolves and tracking shots, moving away from Kane's enigmatic estate and merging with the darkness that ends the film. This ironic twist not only frustrates our own desire for completion and closure; it also hints of a link between that desire and the others that have driven the narrative.

If no *single* account adequately explains Kane's life, so too no "story" accurately measures Michael's experiences in *Lady from Shanghai:* his chance meeting in Central Park with Elsa Bannister, wife of "the world's most famous criminal lawyer"; his taking a job on the Bannisters' yacht, the *Circe;* his unwitting involvement in a plot with Grisby to kill Arthur; and his being framed for Grisby's murder when the plot founders. Michael's voice-over, though, frames the entire narrative, identifies all that we see as flashback, and quickly establishes the storytelling impulse at work here. In effect, it emphasizes Michael's desire to arrange these strange events into a story for himself, to make a narrative of the jumble of his past, especially his obsession with Elsa, in order to render it all meaningful in some way.

The opening voice-over points up this frame of mind, suggesting a memory constantly replaying events, reevaluating something that happened in his past. With the water whose blank but agitated surface fills these first shots, as if it were that narrating voice's source, the film hints at the realm of the unconscious wherein these events are stored and from which they insistently resurface to demand attention and reconsideration. In fact, as Michael speaks, his desire to formulate rushes to the fore. Thus he begins recounting his rescue of Elsa from some hoodlums in the park by noting that we are seeing a fiction of sorts, as Michael notes how "I start out in this story a little bit like a hero, which I most certainly am not." With his tale's fictional quality established, the first-person voice-over gradually recedes from attention, as it usually does in this narrative mode, blending into a seemingly conventional third-person narration, wherein reminders of the fictionalizing process again surface, as when the Bannisters' maid Bessie disdainfully calls Michael "Mr. Poet" by way of chastising his aloofness. Mr. Bannister too comments on Michael's authorship, remarking on his novel-writing ambition and noting how his search for material for that novel has left him "traveling around the world too much to find out anything about it." Such remarks and the early scene in which we view Michael typing a manuscript remind us of that narratizing process which is the film itself, while also hinting at a divergence from lived experience that it might well involve.

Of course, Michael is supposedly trying to *account for* experience, to locate a meaning or pattern in its variety and ambiguity. Included in that material are numerous scenes which he could not logically have observed, like Bannister's discussion with Goldie and Jake in the Seamen's Hall, Grisby's spying on Elsa with his telescope, and the picnic conversation among Arthur, Elsa, and Grisby. If the inclusion of these scenes does not trouble us, it is because we assume that they represent Michael's efforts at filling in the gaps, disguising what cannot be known by extrapolating from what can: the typical actions and attitudes of the characters involved. Such scenes might also imply that all we see derives from Michael's imaginative reconstruction of the past. But whether that narratizing is satisfactory, successfully stilling his desire for Elsa, which it seems to have superseded, or simply gives another shape to frustration is another matter.

What is clear is that a concern with storytelling pervades the film and points to an almost infinite recession of fabulation at work here. Early on we hear that Michael "has a lot of blarney about him," and when glimpsed in the hiring hall he is seated at a typewriter, working on his novel—which the film may or may not be a version of. This image of the storyteller nested within his own story resurfaces several times, but especially when Arthur, Elsa, and Grisby ask Michael to join their picnic. He responds by spinning an elaborate tale that binds his hosts within a metaphor. Beginning with an image of the sea that recalls the film's opening shot, Michael recounts a story of animal nature and self-destruction that links the patterns of desire and circularity here in a way that forms almost a microcosm of the film itself:

> Once off the hump of Brazil, I saw the ocean so darkened with blood it was black. A few of us had lines out for a bit of idle fishin'. It was me had the first strike. A shark it was, and then there was another, and another shark again, till all about the sea was made of sharks, and more sharks still, and the water tall. My shark had torn himself away from the hook, and the scent, or maybe the stain it was, and him bleedin' his life away, drove the rest of them mad. Then the beasts took to eatin' each other; in their frenzy, they *ate at themselves*. You could feel the lust of murder like a wind stingin' your eyes, and you could smell the death, reekin' up out of the sea. I never saw anything worse, until this little picnic tonight. And you know, there wasn't one of them sharks in the whole crazy pack that survived?

As the intercut medium and close-up shots of Michael's listeners and his own careful manipulation of rhythm and climax suggest, he has deliberately shaped his tale as a sort of fable, chastising the Bannisters and Grisby for their actions. Whether or not it is based on fact, Michael's tale forms another story-within-a-story here, but one whose central image, of the sharks turning back and feeding upon themselves, Ouroboros-like, comments doubly. Most obviously it describes the self-destructiveness Michael recognizes in these people, the consumptive nature of their desires. But at the same time, it signals a circularity to the entire narrative, as his narration opens onto other narratives that, reflexively, recall the original narratizing process and thus suggest a level on which his narration is also a consumptive act: a tale that consumes other tale-tellings and ultimately itself in moving toward some moral or significance for the teller and his audience, while also hoping to defy the element of frustration that seems to haunt all narratives.

In developing these concerns with doubling and self-destructiveness, and grounding them in his first-person narrator's involved perceptions, Welles probably drew heavily on his earlier effort at adapting *Heart of Darkness* to the screen. But Michael's shark tale suggests an additional source that sheds an important light on the consumptive pattern described here. In seeking an analogy for Welles's narrative style, Mark Graham suggests *Moby Dick*'s Ishmael, whose first-person narration similarly seems to shift into an omniscient, third-person commentary for much of the novel.[8] Supporting this analogy is the fact that Michael's shark story clearly echoes Melville. Ishmael describes how, when a whale is caught, great care is taken to keep the carcass from being stripped by sharks before it can be cut up and rendered down by the whalers, and he recounts an incident in which a group of sharks became maddened and, "in the foamy confusion of their mixed and struggling hosts, . . . viciously snapped, not only at each other's disembowelments, but like flexible bows, bent round, and bit their own; till those entrails seemed swallowed over and over again by the same mouth, to be oppositely voided by the gaping wound."[9] This "shocking sharkish business," as Melville puts it, is just part of a larger cosmological system *Moby Dick* describes, another instance of "the universal cannibalism of the sea," that Melville qualifies by phrasing a complementary question: "Cannibals? Who is not a cannibal?"[10] If Welles omits that obvious qualifier from his version of the shark story, it seems implicit in the rest of the narrative, which demonstrates just what a universal round of consumption our desires frequently lead to, and analogously, how even our narrative practices can describe such a pattern.

What the similarity to *Moby Dick* points up in *Lady from Shanghai* is a connection between a circular impulse in the film's narrative and the pattern of consumption operating here—both grounded in human desire. The picnic sequence that introduces the shark story underscores this connection. It begins with a canoe trip through a swamp full of various predators, and intercut with shots of the excursionists are a snake and a bird, natural antagonists that suggest both the sort of company Michael is in, and the metaphorizing tendency that marks his narration. An almost comic shot sequence occurs as well, as Grisby spots an approaching alligator, jaws open in anticipation of having *him* for *its* picnic lunch. Shot and reaction shot show the lawyer's response, a furious paddling to avoid being eaten. When Michael later describes Grisby and the Bannisters as similarly predatory, part of the cosmic round of eaters and eaten, Arthur readily accepts the title of shark and even tells Grisby that, "if you were a good lawyer, you'd be flattered." The sharklike nature of these characters—each feeding on the others and ultimately on himself—then resurfaces as they hint at stories they know, tales they could tell on their companions that would destroy them. It is a promise subsequently acted out when George and Elsa plot to kill Arthur, he schemes with the detective Broome to counter their machinations, and she shoots George and frames Michael when the plan goes awry. The film's mirror maze conclusion, wherein Arthur and Elsa shoot each other, while the former remarks that, "Of course, killing you is killing myself," only recasts the circular, consumptive image and prepares for Michael's final reprise of his metaphor, as he recalls his shark story: "Like the sharks, mad with their own blood, chewing away on themselves."

Neither his ability to transform others into tropes nor his own survival excludes Michael from this consumptive round, as his narration makes clear. Like Melville's Ishmael, he has been forced to look into "the subtleness of the sea,"[11] finding it both beautiful and terrifying—or as he describes Acapulco, where the Bannister yacht harbors and he agrees to "kill" Grisby, "a bright, guilty world." We might recall that the film began with repeated shots of the sea: opaque, agitated, and, as the image of crashing waves hints, potentially violent. Fittingly, the tale ends with Michael walking away from the amusement park where the Bannisters have shot each other and toward the sea in the background. If the setting sun in the background threatens to reduce this conclusion to the trite, the high camera angle effectively diminishes Michael and dispels any romantic connotations. Michael is, finally, a small man in a large and complex world. A sailor, he has proved little able to cope with life ashore, especially the ambiguities of this world and the desires that seem stirred there. This conclusion, moreover, reasserts the narrative's circularity, while the repeated associations of the Bannisters and Grisby with various predatory sea creatures—sharks, alligators, and the octopus and barracuda of the aquarium sequence[12]—recall a dual potential that has been developed here: how water might either sustain one or suck him into its depths, there to be consumed by its dangerous denizens.

Michael has simply been trapped within a circular pattern at least partially of his own devising, as a convergence of the motifs of storytelling and appetite in the course of his narration demonstrates. To explain his accepting an offer to work for the Bannisters, despite his forebodings, Michael tells how he created a low-grade fiction for himself: "To be a real prize fathead, you've got to swallow whole all the lies you can think to tell yourself." Consuming one's own stories, though, seems to spur an appetite that only more of the same can satisfy. Because he desires Elsa but lacks the money to take her away from Arthur, then, Michael readily listens to Grisby's almost farcical proposition about feigning his murder so that he might go off to the South Seas unmolested. It is a story full of holes, of inconsistencies that Michael overlooks; and thinking back on it, Michael recognizes that, "even without an appetite, it's amazing how much a fool like me can swallow." But he keeps on "swallowing" those stories and fashioning others, because fictions, especially ones that flatter the self and feed its desires, are far more appetizing than reality, and apparently addictive.

Thus, because he desires Elsa and wants to believe that she loves him, Michael unquestioningly accepts almost all that she says. Only in retrospect does he note how such desires leave a person with "no taste for any pleasure at all except for the one that's burnin' in you." Emphasizing how appetite can turn full circle into self-consumption, this line again recalls Melville and suggests the sort of merger Welles achieves here, as in many of his other films, that of the observer Ishmael and the obsessed quester Ahab. For Michael's admission of this consumptive desire at work in him recalls Ahab's comment on "those malicious agencies which some deep men feel eating in them, till they are left living on with half a heart and half a lung."[13] It is an echo that might suggest a new understanding of how such voice-over narrations work in other *films noir,* wherein the play of appetite always seems near the narrative's surface, haunting the speaking voice. We might see such narrators as speaking almost compulsively, as if a story were simply eating away at the consciousness, compelling a narration that brings the self only momentary—and imaginary—relief.

As such a narrator, Michael recalls his immersion in a "guilty world," while still bound by its alluring images. Like many other *noir* protagonists, he has been shanghaied by a mysterious, beautiful, and manipulative woman, held spellbound by the occupant of the ship *Circe,* and her enchantment yet holds him. But each step of the way he has acceded to his entrapment, never looking beyond the attractive surface of this movie pinup come to life. When Arthur comes to hire him, Michael stays aloof, acting as if he is in command of the situation. He manipulates his prospective employer into buying drinks for his friends, so he can "amuse" himself by refusing his offer before an audience. However, he defers that refusal while returning the drunken Bannister to his yacht, where Michael again turns down a job. By the scene's end, though, he inexplicably changes his mind and joins the *Circe*'s crew. Throughout the subsequent cruise from New York to Sausalito, Michael's desire to quit is frequently *talked* about, but again he never acts on that decision. Instead, what we repeatedly see is how his efforts to write an end to this association and assert his autonomy constantly give way to the lure of Elsa Bannister and the mysterious, almost hypnotic gratification she seems to hold out. And this is the narration's pattern too, as the narrator finds himself drawn on by the residue of these same lures, compelled to spin out and embellish his account. In this way, the narrative's concerns with circularity, fiction, and consumption all join together, as a fascination with and desire for certain *things* develops in parallel to an obsession with certain *images* and a need to narrate them. Finally, both impulses describe a full circle that, in the best *noir* tradition, promises to consume the self.

Exploring the relationship between desire and narrative, René Girard observes this same circular impulse. He explains how desire, activated by others, projects a sense of absence in the self: "at the origin of a desire, there is always the spectacle of another real or illusory desire"[14] that gives it its strength and origin. In this case, the other feeding Michael's desire is multiple; Arthur and Grisby both want Elsa and demonstrate a sort of mimetic desire that spurs him on. But Elsa's image also works in a larger and more complex imaginative field here, for she is depicted as a paradigm of the Hollywood sex goddess, a vision of the collective desires that the movies themselves project. Thus in describing Rita Hayworth's portrayal of Elsa, James Naremore offers that Welles was trying to suggest "Hollywood's synthetic sexuality" by dyeing his wife's hair "a fluorescent blonde and dressing her in near parodies of calendar-girl fashion, such as her little yachtsman's suit with white shorts, clog heels, and officer's cap. He poses her rather like a figure in an advertisement—a smiling woman in a bathing suit, reclining on a rock, her toes nicely pointed and the wind blowing her hair."[15] The uncharacteristic—for Welles—soft focus close-ups of Elsa and Grisby's leering views through his telescope further develop her symbolic status here, that of the movie siren and pinup girl Rita Hayworth was in real life, the focal point of a collective male desire fanned by the movie industry. As Naremore accurately notes, that image comments on the cinema and its subtly seductive capacities, even as it sketches the basic problem of desire that Welles was exploring here and in many other films: a tendency to reduce another or even the self to an image without dimension, a consumer product of sorts, but one which, in the end, never truly satisfies.

A lack of satisfaction, though, seems implicit in the very size of the field of desire Michael has entered, a field that places him in competition with others—among a pack of sharks, we might say—and one that his narration insistently but unsuccessfully attempts to limit, frame, and organize for his own consciousness. *Lady from Shanghai* thereby points to Michael's own ambivalent nature by detailing a series of contradictory pulls. As the narrative proceeds, it measures the immediate lure of desire against his narration's distanced intellectual appropriation, and a willing surrender to the desired against the sovereignty his voice asserts.

From its start, as Michael's sea-borne voice-over introduces the alluring image of Elsa that impels the narrative, the film emphasizes the power of such images to evoke desire. However, it also shows how they play upon our weaknesses, leading us to question our basic beliefs and deny our best intentions. While Elsa's image dominates the film and, indeed, the consciousness of all these characters, she remains, like "Rosebud," largely a mystery, foreign and unfathomable despite Michael's best efforts to "make her out" or narrate her allure. But through her we do glimpse another kind of otherness, one within the self, in fact, an absence or "black hole" there whose very mark is desire. As an alluring image of desire, Elsa suggests a fundamental potential for consumption, but not simply in the manner of the usual *noir* black widow. Rather, it is a kind of self-consumption at work, as if she evoked a deep-seated longing for oblivion that seems to characterize many *noir* narrators and that surfaces here in the orgy of violence that concludes the film.

In its closing sequence, the mirror maze shootout, *Lady from Shanghai* arrays a variety of confusing and distorted images to illustrate the destructive circularity desire can unleash. Michael has, all along, shown his gullibility, his tendency to believe that appearances, in fact, represent truth: that Elsa is, as Bessie says, simply a "poor child" who needs his protection; that Arthur, because he is a cripple and, Michael feels, hardly "a man," is no real threat; and that Grisby is just an eccentric who wants to run away to the South Seas. Of course, Michael's swallowing Elsa's story of love for him and fear of her husband is the main example of his being swallowed in a deceptive realm of images, which is in turn symbolized by the mirror maze itself. In Michael's background we find further evidence of this attitude toward appearances, as we learn that during the Spanish civil war he killed a man, a Franco spy, he emphasizes. In that conflict the lines seemed clearly drawn between right and wrong, and when faced with an aberration, a spy in his camp, Michael simply destroyed it, as he assures Grisby he would do again.

However, when Elsa spirits him to a deserted carnival funhouse, Michael observes that amid its expressionist decor he was so disoriented that "for a while there I thought it was me that was crazy." And even as he begins to get his bearings, the floor gives way, plunging him on a long slide that runs through a menacing dragon's head, its jaws coming together just as he passes through. What that long plunge illustrates is how Michael has effectively been swallowed up by a world where the lines cannot be clearly drawn; he has been consumed by a realm of deceptive images that defy his normal way of seeing and judging the world. The mirror maze into which he is then deposited— the insides of this beast of deception that has swallowed and seems about to digest him—underscores how unreliable all images are here, so unreliable that one cannot tell precisely what is real and what only a reflection, or even know if a gun is aimed at the person one wishes to kill.

This loss of certainty about his world underscores an even larger problem facing Michael, a loss of certainty about the self that reflects on both his shark parable and, more significantly, his whole narration. In the mirror maze we see not only multiple images of Arthur and Elsa, superimposed and juxtaposed through split screens, as they aim their guns at each other but Michael's image as well, similarly multiplied, superimposed, and juxtaposed—as if trapped within the same confused realm. Within a world of such bewildering multiplicity, it seems, one's sense of self is easily distorted or lost; and as the shark tale reminds us, once desire blurs the boundaries between self and other, once one surrenders or loses a secure sense of self, the individual easily becomes confused with that otherness and falls prey to its own violence. Arthur's remark to Elsa here, that killing her means killing himself—"it's the same thing, but you know I'm pretty tired of both of us"—precisely states the sort of self-destruction and consumption that can follow.

The resulting paroxysm of violence inside the maze brings the linkage of desire and narration to a brilliant climax here. As they shoot at the many confusing reflections around them, Elsa and Arthur try to destroy the mirror image each represents for the other; and while only a bystander in this crossfire, Michael also is shot, as a close-up of his wounded hand reveals. That bullet hole is the symbolic residue of this confusion, a sort of stigmata he will carry with him thereafter as a reminder of his immersion in this consumptive whirl. Meanwhile, the mirror fragments and bits of glass that now litter the floor onto which Arthur and Elsa slump suggest simultaneously the shattered images of desire and the shards of narrative coherence—all that can remain of a tale that tries to take the measure of such a deceptive and confusing world. Returning to our analogy to *Citizen Kane,* we might see in those fragments a reminder of the broken crystal microcosm which starts off that narrative, a shattered realm of human desire and order. The mirror maze scene essentially replays the glass paperweight's breaking as a kind of shattering from within.

The resumption of Michael's voice-over as he leaves the mirror maze hints of a change, a return of autonomy and distance. It suggests a persona trying to re-place itself within the narrative, to find a proper perspective on the events in which it has for a time been lost. At least we know his ability to narrate remains intact, as his consciousness tries to substitute words for the lost image of desire. His final words, however, leave us in an uncertain subjective realm, in a consciousness that recognizes the emptiness behind those words, due to the absence it also senses in the self. Walking away from the maze, Michael tries to end his narrative. He muses on the fact that at least he will be proven innocent of Grisby's murder, thanks to a letter Arthur left with the district attorney, but he also recognizes that the term "innocent" ill fits him. For while that narrative might well free him from blame, it in no way satisfies, accounts for, his experience. Impelled by desire, Michael has joined that "bright guilty world" he earlier described so moralistically. He has left behind the idealism signified by his actions in the Spanish civil war, although in so doing he has probably gained an insight into his own nature. It is with this new knowledge that he sets about reviewing events, imparting to them some half-satisfactory narrative order of his own, and attempting to "forget"—or, as his last words recognize, "maybe . . . die trying." He remains burdened with the task of trying to end his story, and that task promises no easy, perhaps even no possible, conclusion.

This final emphasis on narrative frustration again recalls the end of *Kane,* especially the teasing glimpse of young Kane's sled going up in smoke, as if consumed by the many inquiries about and misbegotten efforts to find some meaning in the old man's final word. Used up by narrative, the supposed secret of the narrative finally disappears, leaving only, we assume, a record of speculation and the prospect of an infinite succession of fruitless conjectures by those who hope to unravel the secrets of Kane's life. In its conclusion *Lady from Shanghai* hints at a similar succession of narratives, a constant round of efforts at getting the story right, and with only forgetfulness or death—both dissolutions of narrative—as a foreseeable goal.

On this meditative point, Welles leaves us to consider the problem of his film's narrator. While Michael seems bound, perhaps forever, to the subjective, to a realm of ongoing self-narration, the camera slowly removes us with a high boom shot, its disembodied and distanced vantage recalling *Kane*'s dizzying, high angle shot of the jigsaw puzzle which is Xanadu's great hall. The ending thus pulls us simultaneously in two directions: into the disturbing subjective world Michael inhabits and toward a more comfortably detached view, of a sort that recalls the resolutions of classical narrative. If not as discomfiting as *Kane*, which has us watch a story unreel and then disintegrate in a cloud of smoke, taking with it what small hope of resolution or truth remains, *Lady from Shanghai* poses its own challenge through its all-embracing narrative voice. It leaves us with a narrator speaking of those gaps his story seeks to close up—ones the narrative has left open—while visually acknowledging our own desire for closure. That irresolution is a sign of the tension that marks *noir* narratives like this one, and a reminder that there always remains a concealment within, a lost fragment, a desire yet unresolved and unnarratable, simply because of the human nature from which those efforts spring.

While desire and narration similarly seem to lead toward or promise some kind of end—self-satisfaction, conclusion—*noir* films in the mold of *Lady from Shanghai* usually deny ending. Instead, they turn longing and story back upon themselves, repeating and in the process revealing a dilemma common to both the self and the narratives we use to take its measure. In this way, such films seem to act out a repetition compulsion of the sort described by Freud in his *Beyond the Pleasure Principle*. Repetition, he explains, "is clearly in itself a source of pleasure," if also, finally, a possible danger.[16] Through it, we reexperience an enjoyable state and work toward a kind of mastery over life's situations; but that way too, he notes, lies the mindless automatism and destructiveness of the death instinct. In repetition, therefore, we walk a difficult path between desire and a desire for oblivion—a path that *Lady from Shanghai*'s narrative pattern brilliantly mirrors.

The circular movement described by this film both affirms and denies the self, on the one hand demonstrating how we long for completion, and on the other revealing an incompletion, even a mystery, that marks the human. At the same time, this pattern makes us aware of and impels us to question narrative itself, by implying that it is essentially a way we have of coping with or disguising this common human incompletion; or, as J. Hillis Miller puts it, that the impression narrative usually gives of "a homogeneous sequence making an unbroken line" only hides its true nature, which is " 'complex'—knotted, repetitive, doubled, broken, phantasmal."[17] Through an embracing voice-over/flashback mechanism, a *film noir* like *Lady from Shanghai* could both mirror this inner maze and also show how it resembles the very means by which, paradoxically, we often look for some exit.

NOTES

1. See Vernet's "Filmic Transaction."
2. Ibid., p. 6.
3. Ibid., p. 5. As Vernet explains, the typical *film noir* opening establishes "a time of stability and certainty in which the spectator persuades himself that knowledge of what is important, and pleasurable, is at hand." This initial level of certainty sets up our expectations for the rest of the narrative, while also establishing a context for disturbance, for the upset of those expectations.
4. I am indebted to Professor Bruce Kawin for this suggestion. Certainly, the narrating voice must have been crucial for Welles's efforts to adapt longer works to the radio drama format, for as Barbara Leaming notes, one of his working habits was to "red pencil" passages in texts he wished to adapt, revise them slightly, and then create a narrator to bridge the various scenes to be dramatized. In effect, he used that narrating voice to structure his radio dramas. See Leaming's *Orson Welles*.
5. Carringer, "Rosebud, Dead or Alive," p. 191.
6. Ibid.
7. Graham, "Inaccessibility of *The Lady from Shanghai*," p. 23.
8. Ibid., p. 24.
9. Melville, *Moby Dick*, p. 395.
10. Ibid., pp. 364, 393.
11. Ibid., p. 364.
12. We might note in this context Welles's efforts to use the aquarium background in a metaphoric rather than strictly naturalistic manner. In order to achieve a properly commentative effect, so that the appropriate fish would fill the background at the right time, the aquarium scene was shot in part with back-projection, and the fish images were then blown up beyond their normal proportions to be juxtaposed with the Michael and Elsa characters in the foreground. For background see Higham's *Films of Orson Welles* and Naremore's *Magic World of Orson Welles*.
13. Melville, *Moby Dick*, p. 246.
14. Girard, *Deceit, Desire, and the Novel*, p. 105.

15. Naremore, *Magic World of Orson Welles*, p. 160.
16. Freud, *Beyond the Pleasure Principle*, p. 66.
17. See Miller's "Narrative Middles," p. 375, and "Ariadne's Thread," pp. 68–69.

CHAPTER 4

Tangled Networks
and Wrong Numbers

> In the tangled networks of a great city, the telephone is the
> unseen link between a million lives. . . . It is the servant of our
> common needs—the confidante of our inmost secrets . . . life and
> happiness wait upon its ring . . . and horror . . . and loneliness
> . . . and *death!*
>
> —*Sorry, Wrong Number*

Against the background of a massive switchboard and crisscrossing wires, *Sorry, Wrong Number* opens with the above epigraph.
That message quickly establishes an atmosphere of contingent communication, of discourse under pressure, that haunts the ensuing
narrative. And its key image, of the "tangled networks" of communication, models a crisscrossing of possibilities and purposes—a play of
secrecy and disclosure, isolation and relation, death and life—that
afflicts the film's characters and suggests the typical threatened and
threatening environment of the *film noir*. While hardly an atypical
opening for such films, it effectively links the pattern of fragile and
apprehensive human relations here to the anxious atmosphere that
seems to surround every effort at speaking in the *noir* world. And that
linkage is even more telling in light of *Sorry, Wrong Number*'s complex
narrative mechanism, which, like Orson Welles's landmark work *Citizen Kane,* involves a medley of characters speaking retrospectively,
their voices weaving a kind of tangled network of human hopes and
fears.

As we have noted, many critics see *Citizen Kane* as a seminal influence on the *film noir*. Its shadowy images, unbalanced compositions,
and strange camera angles clearly prefigure much of the form's visual
style, and as our discussion of *Lady from Shanghai* suggested, its analysis
of Charles Foster Kane's acquisitive instinct looks toward *noir*'s thematic interest in destructive human desire. Given the common notion
that the voice-over/flashback is almost a *noir* convention,[1] we might

also look for the influence of *Kane*'s distinctive use of multiple narrators and flashbacks. In fact, though, few *films noir* tried such a complex scheme, the most noteworthy examples being *The Mask of Dimitrios* (1944), *The Killers* (1946), and *Sorry, Wrong Number* (1948). In light of *noir*'s concern with how we normally view and understand our world, the relative neglect of this model seems puzzling. After all, its various speakers and multiple points of view challenge the classical perspective by replacing its "objective" vantage with a relative one, wherein "reality" hinges on a variety of viewpoints. *Sorry, Wrong Number*'s use of this approach may help explain its limited application, for in it the *Kane* narrative's darker potential surfaces to reveal the various personal and cultural forces that conspire in determining the individual's tenuous place in the modern world. What its many narrative voices— as the opening epigraph hints—articulate is the sort of black vision that would eventually prove too dark even for most *films noir.*

In its most common use, the voice-over/flashback generates a distinct level of anxiety. As Bruce Kawin explains, such narration represents "a character's interpretive response to his own experience,"[2] and thus, as the previous chapter notes, a subjective rendering of events that is freighted with tension. Films like *Double Indemnity* and *The Lady from Shanghai* are dominated by a consciousness speaking from the present about past events, so the voice and the images it calls up dramatize the past's continuing impact on the present. At the same time, that voice seems to assert a mastery over the past's haunting, possessive power, as if declaring its freedom from an earlier "other." With this tension in mind, Christine Gledhill has observed how the *film noir* usually lacks the single, coherent vantage we associate with classical narrative, presenting instead "a proliferation of points of view and a struggle within the text for one viewpoint to gain hegemony."[3] What she notes is a level on which even a single voice-over/flashback implies a plurality of voices and selves vying for a say. At risk in this struggle for possession of the narrative and the present it defines is all sense of objectivity or "truth" and, more important, of the self as a sovereign being, ruling its own destiny.

Multiple-narrator films like *Kane* and *Sorry, Wrong Number* amplify this possessive tension and highlight its implications. For not only do their many voices, memories, and vantages make truth seem more relative and less accessible, but the self too emerges as far more precarious, as if trapped in a field of contending voices. Welles's film, for example, involves a dead man, six reminiscences of his life—including the cultural recollection of the "News on the March" newsreel—and the controlling perspective of the reporter Thompson, whose inquiries about Kane motivate the narrative. In this scheme the usual flashback tension between past and present springs from the relationship between an enigmatic other, the dead but still influential Kane, and the various individuals who recall his impact on their lives. Because Kane is dead and already distant from the human orbit as their narratives begin, the variety of the truths that constellate around him is not very disturbing; after all, they refer not to a *living* reality, only to a kind of legend. But those conflicting appraisals point past truth's elusive nature to a natural tendency we have to define the past and the other in terms of the self, in this case to make Kane's story as much as possible each narrator's story. For this reason, Welles himself described the "point" of his film as "not so much the solution of the problem [of Kane's life] as its presentation."[4]

Further modeling this tension is Thompson's quest for an "angle" to organize his newsreel. While he anchors our point of view and in his detached perspective suggests the sort of vantage we associate with classical narrative, Thompson is essentially a shadow figure whose viewpoint never opens onto the truth he seeks. In fact, he seems little more than a function of the larger narrative, suggesting how we are often subordinate to or controlled by intangible forces, our reason paradoxically lodged in what *we* seemingly give reason to. At the same time, his efforts to possess truth, if necessary by bribing others for it, seem doomed to failure by the very multiple, contradictory, and elusive truths they uncover. Thompson's inquisitive impulse thus reveals a telling affinity to the acquisitive one that helped to destroy Kane, while it also illustrates certain limitations that always plague the self—limitations on what we might see, acquire, or know that effectively define the self in modern society.

While Anatole Litvak's *Sorry, Wrong Number* adopts much of *Kane*'s method, it also alters it in a way that brings out its more disturbing implications. The original radio script on which the film is based was essentially an extended monologue but, like *Kane*, the film employs six narrative voices, one of them belonging to the film's subject, pharmaceuticals heiress Leona Stevenson. She organizes the story by motivating and linking the other narrative voices, and it is her presence and participation, as a kind of live Kane, that adds another, disturbing level of relativity. While we understand how someone of Kane's status might be an enigma to all who "knew" him, as well as to a reporter whose knowledge comes secondhand, it is far more discomfiting for the character we identify with to seem a mystery, her story possessed in fragments by many people, wholly by no one, not even herself. Through the competing voices of Leona, her husband Henry, his secretary, Leona's college friend Sally Hunt Lord, her physician Dr. Alexander, and Henry's associate Waldo Evans, we do learn much about Leona, Henry, and their failing marriage. But at the same time, they depict the self as fundamentally mysterious, an "other" whether dead or alive, and the individual as always a stranger, even to himself. Consequently, the self appears lost in a web—or network—of voices and recollections here, or reduced to what Foucault terms "a function of discourse"[5] over which the individual has little real control or awareness.

Another effect of Leona's multiple role—as subject, narrator, and control—is to bring out a level of contention and appropriation that this sort of narrative involves. *Kane*, like *The Killers* after it, uses an investigating individual to introduce its flashbacks and anchor their subjectivity in a seemingly objective frame. Since *Sorry, Wrong Number*'s multiple flashbacks spring from the phone calls Leona makes and receives, she serves in this role too, effectively doubling as Thompson and Kane, while also contributing her own narrative. What results is a pattern especially resonant for the troubled image of woman in the films of this period, that of a struggle between an individual trying to tell her own story and various forces and figures in her world that seek to "tell" her. In the contention over her truth that ensues, the self emerges as a kind of narrative construct, just as elusive and fragmentary as the world Leona chronicles. That she must motivate these narratives only compounds the irony here by emphasizing how little true control the individual ever wields. *Sorry, Wrong Number* thereby reveals a paradox haunting such narratives. On the one hand, it shows the individual trying to order or control the events of her life, wanting to narrate her own story; but on the other, it notes how alternate visions or competing forces—from within and without—threaten to disrupt that dream by speaking and shaping her life in ways she can never fully comprehend or control.

It is this pattern that *Sorry, Wrong Number*'s opening description of the phone network so clearly articulates. In suggesting how a power we use daily to link ourselves to others, even to control them, can also bind and control us, this image casts a revealing light on the film's protagonist and main narrator. For Leona Stevenson almost lives through her telephone. An invalid, she relies on it to link her to the outside world: to stay in touch with her father in Chicago, to keep reins on her increasingly restive husband, and to project her personality, as she does by calling the police to report her fears or suspicions of others. It is, moreover, a single phone call, a "crossed connection" on which she overhears a plot to kill an unnamed woman, that initiates the various calls to and from Leona which make up the narrative. That she might herself be the intended victim never seems to enter her mind, despite a policeman's ironic remark that Leona should worry only if "you think somebody's planning to murder you." Her self-assurance and inability to see how discourse addresses and affects the self, just as it does others, suggest some alienation from the self here, but even more, a naive sense of freedom from discourse's operations that this film, like many other *noirs,* will address.

Leona's frequent use of the telephone to control others—seen in her badgering calls to the telephone company, the police, and her husband's secretary—hardly disguises her own subservience to that mechanism and those who use it. Of the film's sixteen phone calls, only half come from Leona; and the eight calls directed to her emphasize how subject she is to that device, the information it carries, and the people who use it. The first call she receives, from her father in Chicago, is exemplary. Mr. Cotterell urges Leona to "come home" from New York and move back into his mansion which, he laments, "is like a morgue without you." The riotous party glimpsed in the background belies his comments and shows that he is not above deception to get what he wants. Subsequently, the enigmatic and frightening calls Leona receives from Sally Lord and Waldo Evans, as well as her frantic efforts to answer a ringing phone, make it clear that she is as much manipulated by the phone as manipulating. Through that image, therefore, the film quickly establishes how the individual controls and is controlled, while it also suggests the self's inability to perceive the appropriative pattern in which she is enmeshed.

The phone conversations that follow and the narrative voices they introduce let us observe both an interplay of possessive forces at work here and a general blindness to this pattern. For example, in trying to locate Henry through his secretary, Leona only glimpses the extent of his waywardness, learning that he has been visited by a mysterious woman. When that woman calls and reveals she is Sally Lord, from whom Leona had stolen Henry years before, Leona immediately fears that Sally wants revenge, perhaps to take Henry away from her. Sally's enigmatic warning that Henry is "mixed up in something" sheds some light on this reasoning by revealing how little Leona really knows about her husband's activities, and thus points up a distance between the couple. With her call to Dr. Alexander, the specialist she has consulted about her heart condition, she begins to connect that appropriative impulse ruling her life to her growing sense of estrangement. As the doctor assures, Leona's heart problem—emblematic of her inability to love—is psychosomatic, the result of her efforts to manipulate her father's and Henry's sympathies. The desire to control others has, in effect, led her to surrender control over herself, over her own body, resulting in a devastating schism, a kind of mind-body split, as Leona seems estranged from her own body.

Henry's narration, filtered through Dr. Alexander in a flashback within a flashback, reveals a similar split afflicting him. He feels torn between his love for Leona and his frustration at her control of his private life and her father's control over his career. When Waldo Evans tells of helping Henry steal chemicals from Cotterell Pharmaceuticals, the destructive consequences of this possessive relationship become clear. Appropriately, Leona learns about Henry's activities and her own predicament—her identity as the "poor woman" about to be murdered—simultaneously, as if her husband's secret and her own identity were one and the same. And they essentially are, since her planned murder springs directly from her efforts to control every aspect of Henry's life and have him all for herself. Her identity as a "poor woman" whose life is fated beyond any help or hope has simply been submerged all along in the very pattern of control and possession she has shaped around Henry's existence.

More than just multiple vantages on a single life, then, these varied perspectives emphasize a certain otherness or elusiveness that seems to plague the self in this world. They generate a clear and disturbing sense of how much, even about the self, always eludes the individual simply because he is limited to and driven by his own perspective, much as Leona is bound within her lavish yet grotesque bedroom and conditioned by her privileged upbringing. With Leona as the filter for these narratives, we can better gauge the plight of an individual forced to face these limits of self-knowledge and to assess the extent to which a person's story is ever truly her own, her voice able to speak freely.

To emphasize this sense of limitation, *Sorry, Wrong Number* develops a motif of control or possession that sketches a world of human relationships defined by patterns of appropriation and power. Everyone here seems intent on appropriating or controlling others; yet every such effort only reduces the self to an object, subject to another's possessive desires. The broad pattern of appropriation and frustration that results gradually takes shape through the various narrating voices. It is as if that pattern simply objectified their "tangled" impulse. Leona's own flashback quickly establishes this pattern, as she recounts how, on their first meeting at a school dance, she immediately set about "acquiring" Henry. Feeling that her status as a wealthy heiress allowed her to target him in this way, she ignored his initial rebuff and pressed her pursuit with references to her father and his wealth and an invitation to drive her sports car. Underscoring the "purchasing power" of these lures, as well as Henry's susceptibility to their power, the following scene opens with a close-up of the trademark on Leona's car, followed by a long shot which shows Henry driving. His naive posturing in this scene, as he asks, "What does a dame like you want with a guy like me?" brings him no answer, but neither does it conceal the basis of their relationship: a mutual dedication to getting what each wants and a willingness to pay the cost, whether in money or personal freedom. In fact, viewed under the aegis of a trademark, Henry already seems marked as one of Leona's possessions.

The subsequent scenes of their wedding and honeymoon lay out the terms of this relationship. Over a montage of the wedding ceremony, there echoes Leona's portentous marriage vow, "I, Leona, take thee, Henry"; and whether it represents her voice in the present, ruminating on the past, or signals an obsession of that former time, this phrase, repeated four times, points up a possessive impulse that drives Leona. A subsequent scene of their European honeymoon illustrates the bargain she and Henry have struck. As he dresses for dinner, she takes a wad of money from her purse and puts it in his wallet, but while making this deposit she also withdraws and rips up a picture of Sally that Henry has kept. With this act she completes the appropriative effort begun when she cut in on Sally at the school dance, continued with her boast that "when I want something I fight for it—and I usually manage to get it," and climaxed in the marriage she forces her father to accept. At the same time, that act shows what Henry has surrendered in return for the money and security Leona offers: the possibility of a relationship built upon love and a future determined by the self.

As the other narrations reveal, though, this appropriative effort will eventually fail because of its human cost. Despite her efforts to direct Henry's future, or as she puts it, "to make something of him," then, the film opens with Leona alone and unable to locate her husband. We might recall that it begins with a track-in to a close-up of the ringing phone in Henry's office; unanswered, it shows his response to Leona's possessiveness and mocks her efforts at control. At the same time, it hints at how much she is herself subject to the mechanism she uses to control others. As her only link to the outside world, the phone symbolizes her reliance on others and on a human realm beyond the sound of her voice. No less than the subsequent crossed connection informing her of a fate beyond her control and understanding, the ringing phone signals more than just an inability to make the necessary link with others. It suggests how the individual is always more the possessed than the possessor, more controlled than in control.

It is also significant that Leona's predicament is hardly unique. Only her status as a filter and organizing element for the narrative obscures the fact that she is just one link in a chain of possessors and possessed here. And this chain explains why every effort at control or appropriation only results on another level in the self's subjugation. The long distance call from Leona's father illustrates this pattern. As he begs her to come home, the camera dollies around his study, focusing first on a large, formal portrait of his daughter and then on several smaller pictures of her arranged about the room. Her replicated image suggests more than a single-minded, fatherly devotion to a daughter, though, for as it moves from one picture to another the camera also registers three corresponding mounted and stuffed animals on display. Leona's later comment, "All you want is for me to stay home with you for the rest of your life," hints that she recognizes her father's desire to keep her to himself, like another trophy, and suggests a level on which his mansion indeed resembles, as he unwittingly notes, "a morgue." The tracking camera, wandering from its subject to reveal, as if by chance, this commentative information, recalls an earlier, seemingly random tracking around Leona's room, as she demands that the telephone operator do something to help the "poor woman" whose fate she has overheard, even as it foreshadows several repetitions of this visual pattern, most notably to reveal the killer entering her house and approaching her room. This pattern of movement mocks Leona's own immobility and suggests her ignorance of the forces conspiring to control and eventually destroy her.

What grants her some freedom from her father's possessiveness and even a certain power over him is the "attack" Leona suffers when he objects to her marriage plans. It is a discourse produced by the pressure on her, but also one that effectively grants her a useful pressure or power over her father. By threatening to die, she essentially promises to deprive him of a cherished possession, herself, and this strategy, later used on Henry as well, clearly demonstrates its effectiveness in the following scene. In the wedding her father had opposed, J. B. Cotterell is reduced to a background figure, a spectator and silent supporter as Leona embarks on her own proprietary career, one signaled by the repeated utterance of the phrase symbolizing her control, "I, Leona, take thee, Henry."

But if Leona could so turn the tables on her father, she might expect to be similarly subject to appropriation. Thus Henry, frustrated by his meaningless job—"Working for your father is like running in a dream. No matter how hard you try, you know you'll never get anywhere," he complains—adopts an appropriative ethic as well, stealing chemicals from Cotterell Pharmaceuticals. To aid his scheme, he uses the techniques learned from Leona and her father, playing on another's desires. In this case, it is the chemist Waldo Evans who, after fifteen years with the firm, remains far from realizing his modest dream of possession, owning a small horse farm. Henry finds a reflection of his longing in Evans and uses it to control the older man, telling him what, we might presume, he has often told himself: "What good is a dream when you're too old to enjoy it?"[6]

Just as predictable, though, is the reversal of their initial success when the fence for their stolen chemicals, the gangster Morano, decides to take over the operation—and them. So just as Leona reversed her father's power, Morano takes control through blackmail, threatening Henry and Evans with exposure and finally forcing Henry to plan Leona's death to gain access to her fortune. Her murder at the film's conclusion thus binds her within a chain of possessors and possessed here by ironically visiting her own efforts at appropriation on her. It is, after all, the psychosomatic illness she has used to manipulate Henry that turns her into a potential source of income, her supposedly fatal disease promising him an inheritance that would stave off any economic pressures—even blackmail. Her possessive impulse, then, not only succeeds in alienating her husband; it also leads to her physical deterioration and paradoxically transforms her, in Henry's eyes, into a valuable possession, an asset to be liquidated in the present financial emergency.

Reinforcing this paradoxical pattern, wherein every effort at possession eventually leaves one possessed by others, the film develops another motif that both attests to and mocks a desire for possession. As heir to her father's empire, Leona is widely known as "the Coughdrop Queen," as she proudly admits. The laughter with which Sally's son reacts to this epithet seems fitting, though, for while Leona has all the money she needs—certainly enough to buy the husband she wants—she is really a queen without a country, lacking a home of her own and still dependent on her father. Recognizing his own powerlessness, as well as his economic thralldom to Leona and her father, Henry adopts a similar if ironic title. As he bitterly tells Sally, he is the company's "Invoice King," a record keeper with no authority. Forced to live in his father-in-law's mansion, to ask his wife for spending money, and kept from taking a job that might bring some independence, he is a powerless, landless monarch, subject to his queen's whims. And even as these anachronistic "sovereigns" fight their sense of limitation by wielding power over others, as if by controlling another they might somehow reclaim their true selves and even gain a measure of sovereignty, they ironically find themselves subject to yet another power—not J. B. Cotterell and his economic might but the aptly named Mr. Lord, Sally's husband, an assistant district attorney investigating the illicit drug sales in which Henry is involved. As his name implies, Lord works in an almost *divine* way, suggesting less a cultural force than a kind of individual fate, working inexorably to determine the destinies of this king and queen and in the process underscoring an irony in the desire for mastery or possession that drives them both.

It is this ironic residue that comments so tellingly on the multiple narrator pattern of such *films noir*. As Frank Krutnik observes, the *noir* voice-over always implies a "disjunction . . . between the hero as narrative agent and as narrator," specifically between what he now knows as narrator and what had eluded him in the past.[7] Typically, though, voice-over/flashback narratives move toward a "point of unification," as if dramatizing a process whereby an individual assimilates a story and its lesson. As Krutnik further explains, the speaker is "stabilizing . . . Truth" by reappropriating past events of his life from amid a confusing welter.[8] His tale thus testifies to a kind of gain, for as the *noir* narrator speaks, he seems to achieve or assert possession of something that has possessed or haunted him—a series of enigmatic events, a haunting love relationship, a close brush with death—and in the process lexically turns the tables on the forces that have ruled his life. He is not just trying to create some order out of chaos or render a seemingly alien and disordered world intelligible, but, as we noted in *Double Indemnity*, matching its appropriative power with a like force of his own. Such a narrative simply involves a dialectic wherein the individual is simultaneously "a function of discourse" and an entity outside of discourse's deterministic play, a master of discourse as well as its symbolic creation and constant subject.

This dialectic is at the heart of the various phone calls that comprise *Sorry, Wrong Number*'s narrative and make it such a revealing example of voice-over/flashback technique. For those structuring calls speak of both Leona's imperious posture of control and her subservience to events beyond her control and to people who seem to know more about her life than she does. Through these calls, she gradually pieces together her life, resolves her own mystery: the truth of her neurotic bond to her father, of a psychosomatic illness that has left her an invalid, of her destructive efforts to control her husband's life, and finally of the self-destruction her lack of perspective has instigated. With half of the narrative coming from others, relegating her to the status of a mystified audience for much of its unfolding, though, Leona seems fundamentally enthralled—as the word implies, enslaved, possessed—by these partial stories and the possible order of a life that is held in fragments by each of those she talks to. Incapable of turning the tables, she remains, both physically and narratively, a cripple, only marginally able to assemble the parts of a story naming her as the woman soon to be murdered, and quite unable to help herself, even as a hired killer approaches. Her inability, though, underscores the ironic weight of the voice-over/flashback mechanism here. Any feeling the individual might have about being able to stand outside of discourse or to control it is finally shown to be an illusion arising from the play of discourse and the power of control or appropriation it seductively seems to place at one's command.

While the film's various narratives reveal much, then, their revelations too are ironically colored. For they ultimately point up what Bill Nichols describes as "our own place within the process of communication and exchange":[9] our place in a realm that conditions our ability to speak about ourselves and about the relations that make up our world, and our predicament as beings who long to describe a self that is self-motivated and self-determining. Despite the fact that she orchestrates the film's various voices and is, after a fashion, its true narrator, Leona is finally trapped within a story already "told." But that seems a common predicament in the *film noir* world, where every call, every speech, every effort at narration ultimately arises from and refers back to the "tangled networks" of communication that bind and define the human. This stark vision of an inevitable "tangle" describes a situation in which every narrator is potentially an object of narration and the sovereign self may prove to be a strange other.

As the previous chapters note, our more common experience of the voice-over/flashback technique is in films like *Double Indemnity* and *Lady from Shanghai*—films whose single narrators compulsively tell their own stories, untroubled by a confusing tangle of other voices. *Sorry, Wrong Number*'s serial application of this technique, though, brings into focus an important characteristic of this *noir* strategy. Through its many speakers, each telling a story partly his own and partly another's, the film reveals a disparity between the tale and its teller implicit in every voice-over/flashback: a difference in nature and knowledge between past and present selves. We witness a narrator's effort at gauging that difference and sifting some significance from it; and that effort echoes our own in watching the *film noir*, since such films confront us with a sense of difference too, that between the way we usually see our world and the darker possibilities the films suggest. In that echoing we gain a heightened, if also disturbing awareness of our own situation, especially of our desires to control and explain a world that constantly asserts a control and a sense all its own.

By linking its narrative mechanism to these central motifs of possession and tangled communications, *Sorry, Wrong Number* enhances the atmosphere of difference and even suggests a possible cause. The almost biological drive for possession it describes seems to model an epistemological drive in the narrative, a desire to know or understand. In fact, possession becomes a kind of material compensation for our failure to know, hinting at how we often substitute acquisitions for understanding, trying to satisfy with things the sort of longing that things could never fill. As the acquisitive impulse—for knowledge, things, even others—gains strength, it becomes a binding force, imprisoning the individual within a "tangled network"—the very network by which we try to express or resolve those longings—and thus canceling out any gain it may have promised. For this reason, Leona's psychosomatic illness, despite its diagnosis, continues to cripple her and keeps her from escaping her murderer, while her murder, in turn, renders meaningless her new awareness of herself and of Henry's repressed needs. Through those linked motifs, *Sorry, Wrong Number* lets us see the full implications of its narrative mechanism, particularly how the effort it signals of appropriating, organizing, and mastering past events speaks ironically of the narrator's own bondage to a haunting past and the sense of otherness it holds.

The disturbing implications we note in *Sorry, Wrong Number*'s narrative technique can also help us see the conventional use of voice-over/ flashback in a new light. According to Foucault, there is a fundamental appeal to identifying the originating voice of discourse, to discerning the marks of "authorship." Our desire for ascription, he feels, masks our deeper "fear" of "the proliferation of meaning."[10] In effect, we block a potential proliferation of impulses and resonances by establishing an end point of discourse: a source, motivation, or supposed intention. The voice speaking about the past and directing all that we witness to some narrative closure in the present thus carries some measure of comfort or reassurance.

With *Sorry, Wrong Number*'s multiple voices, however, that measure assumes an uncomfortable burden of ambiguity and multiple meanings. They remind us that while the desire for authorship or ascription asserts control over and orders discourse, it also omits from consideration numerous generative and appropriative forces, a variety of authoring voices, such as those of culture, circumstance, or the unconscious. The desire to determine authorship, consequently, actually masks another sort of possessive impulse that both includes and excludes. In asserting the individual's place at the origin and design of discourse, we effectively bracket off a broad potential of multiplicity, ambiguity, or mystery, limiting meaning to a supposed intention or design. Appropriately, this is the very pattern Leona demonstrates when, confronted by numerous disturbing, alternate narratives describing her relationship with Henry, she dismisses them as the products of jealousy or ignorance, coming from "liars, liars."

This perspective, then, should cast a new light on the common *noir* use of voice-over/flashback. On the one hand, it can effectively evoke a disturbingly subjective realm, as we saw in *Lady from Shanghai*, or, as some critics contend, unmoor the narrative to drift in a sea of romantic revery.[11] On the other, it can also lend a kind of stability to the *noir* story, as we might argue is the case in *Double Indemnity* or the similar James M. Cain narrative, *The Postman Always Rings Twice*. In essence, it might help balance the narrative's disconcerting elements and ambiguous connections by establishing a perspective that, however ironically, implies a level of control, a focal point that limits "the proliferation of meaning" to which our world seems so prone.

Of course, in multiplying narrators and viewpoints a film like *Sorry, Wrong Number* upsets such a balance. Instead, it unleashes a nightmare of potential that always haunts the *noir* world—the potential of ambiguity, of multiple, indeterminate meanings, and of a self that is subject to unseen, unsensed forces. That this technique found only limited application might be due not just to its complexity, then, but also to the atmosphere it releases. For the multiple-narrator approach finally suggests more than a relativity of meaning or the subjective possession of significance. Simultaneously—and paradoxically—it evokes meaning's multiplicity and its elusiveness to produce the sort of paranoiac atmosphere that permeates only the darkest *noir* works. Within this realm of unbounded, proliferating meanings, the individual can seem, like Leona Stevenson, cut off from any hope of ordering or controlling her world, as she comes to resemble but another signifier in a disturbingly rich and confusing language system, one narrative line in a bewildering tangle of story.

Sorry, Wrong Number's introductory image, of the "tangled networks" that make up not only the telephone system but the very system of life in the modern world, evokes this predicament most eloquently. It illustrates the complex play of forces at work in modern society, linking individuals within a nexus of potential communication and possible meaning, even as it also binds them in the dark tangles of that human potential. It is a particularly disturbing vision, since it qualifies all hope and suggests a potentially fatal vulnerability in every effort to speak of this condition. This paradoxical predicament, though, is the very stuff of *noir,* and a reminder that one never really reaches any "wrong numbers" in the *noir* world. As Leona Stevenson's case shows, all lines seem disconcertingly to connect and every caller to bear a message of just how much the self is always bound within a realm of multiple, unforeseen, and inescapable connections. This connectedness, as a minimal hope and looming menace, is what the multiple voice-over *noir* perhaps too clearly charted for viewers.

NOTES

1. See Porfirio's "No Way Out: Existential Motifs in the Film Noir," p. 213, as well as Schrader's comments on the voice-over/flashback technique in his "Notes on *Film Noir,*" p. 284.
2. Kawin, *Mindscreen,* p. 6.
3. Gledhill, "*Klute* 1: A Contemporary Film Noir and Feminist Criticism," in Kaplan, *Women in Film Noir,* p. 17.
4. Quoted by Bazin in his *Orson Welles,* p. 58.
5. Foucault, *Language, Counter-Memory, Practice,* p. 124.
6. An additional and telling linkage between Henry and Evans might be seen in the former character's origins in Grassville, the hometown to which he longs to return, and the latter's desire to own some grassland on which to raise horses. In their common longings, both characters evoke a kind of pastoral or natural world from which they have been irrevocably separated. This pattern of broken links with a natural or pastoral world shows up in a number of other *films noir,* most notably in *The Asphalt Jungle* (1950).
7. Krutnik, "Desire, Transgression and James M. Cain," p. 34.
8. Ibid., p. 34.
9. Nichols, *Ideology and the Image,* p. 2.
10. Foucault, "What Is an Author?" p. 159.
11. For this emphasis on romantic subjectivity, see Schrader's "Notes on *Film Noir*" essay.

CHAPTER 5 ────────────────

Effacement and Subjectivity: *Murder, My Sweet*'s Troubled Vision

No doubt, it is not entirely my body that perceives; I know only
that it can prevent me from perceiving, that I cannot perceive
without its permission; the moment perception comes my body
effaces itself before it and never does the perception grasp
the body in the act of perceiving.
—Maurice Merleau-Ponty[1]

That's all I know on account of I don't see so well with my eyeballs
scorched.
—*Murder, My Sweet*

The *film noir*'s various developments of the voice-over also
point toward one of its most notable narrative experiments, with the
subjective camera. As we have noted, the voice-over usually works as a
kind of trope of consciousness, indicating that all we see and hear is, as
Bruce Kawin puts it, "mentally presentational."[2] That "mental" aspect
was developed primarily as a way of more forcefully involving viewers
in the narrative; but as a side effect it also suggested an alternative to
the way we usually see things, showing the relative as a possible route
to truth. Besides the stylistic emphasis on shadows, unbalanced compositions, and strange camera angles, this concern shows up thematically in a focus on the reliability of perception and a responsibility
we have to see our world and ourselves clearly, as films like *The Woman
in the Window* (1944), *The Dark Mirror* (1946), and *The Window* (1949)
illustrate. In light of these efforts, a *noir* attempt to turn seeing itself
into a sustained narrative device seems a natural development—one
whose first stirrings trace to an early *noir*, *Murder, My Sweet* (1944).

Despite its landmark status as a film in which, Carlos Clarens argues,
"the fully realized *noir* look first appears,"[3] and in which Raymond
Chandler's detective Philip Marlowe finds his first official screen incarnation,[4] *Murder, My Sweet* has received little attention. What makes this

omission significant is that the film also maps out the potential and the limitations of subjective narration that later *noirs* would follow. On the one hand, it crafts a privileged vision that at times calls attention to how we see in classical narrative; however, it also qualifies that vision with a sense of effacement that recalls Merleau-Ponty's description of our seeing. Initially, it promises to let us see like its detective protagonist, but it ends up in a "scorched" or blinded vision that hints of a threat in seeing too much and that gives reason to the film's efforts to pull back from the subjective. These poles already suggest the sort of ambivalence that would attach to *noir*'s efforts at subjective narrative. As it shifts between these poles, *Murder, My Sweet* explores a growing *noir* concern with how we see, and it begins to trace out how the subjective might be used to describe what Michael Wood, in his discussion of *noir*, refers to as "the ordinary places of modern life."[5]

Merleau-Ponty's comments imply that a paradox informs our seeing and haunts the very place of vision—our sense of self, our location in the world, and our placement in a cinematic narrative. While our physical presence lets us see, grants a vantage on and knowledge of our world, it also limits seeing, since our placement—our self—is the source of a frustrating effacement. Because of this nexus of what we see and what always escapes the gaze, he explains, we form "a deep-seated set of mute 'opinions'" about our lives.[6] And since we never really see *the self*, our efforts to articulate those "mute opinions" usually lead to "a labyrinth of difficulties" in terms of our involvement in what we see and, indeed, of our sense of self. Haunted by something that always escapes or effaces itself before our gaze, we constantly struggle to confront and understand our real selves and the world in which we seem to be meaningful figures.

Modernist narrative has explored various strategies for expressing this struggle and, in effect, overcoming it. The multiple narrators of Faulkner's *As I Lay Dying*, for example, win a kind of freedom over the limitations of individual perspective—and even over death—giving us a collective view, including the dead's vantage, on a single tragic event in a family's history. Jorge Luis Borges repeatedly fashions self-conscious narrators who describe their explorations of the "labyrinths" of narrative—labyrinths in which, as the narrator of his story "Funes the Memorious" illustrates, we can easily become quite lost. And in his many crime novels appearing roughly parallel to the *film noir*, Jim Thompson employs first-person and multiple narrators whose voices drone on, even when they are dying, to dramatize our human and narrational limitations as they seek some reprieve from them. What the self-awareness of such works accomplishes, as Kawin puts it, is to express their own "haunted" nature,[7] especially a sense of their very limits. In that struggle to express the ineffable, to acknowledge that it "is a limited system," the form confronts its own reality and triumphs over limitation. Kawin even suggests that such "systemic self-consciousness" is a key to the emergence of new genres, which spring from efforts at "dramatizing the limits of the old from *within* those . . . existing structures, so that the new genre appears to create itself out of the old."[8]

As an early *film noir, Murder, My Sweet* hints at this process, at a form in the process of emerging, and some of the terms of that emergence show up in its subjective techniques. By linking a subjective camera to its voice-over/flashback narration, the film fashions an intense awareness of point of view—one that verges on the kind of systemic self-consciousness Kawin describes. In foregrounding how we see in the movies and revealing the limitations of that vision, the film thus hints at a radical potential in *noir*. By bracketing and drawing attention to classical narrative's seemingly detached, objective, and stable perspective, rooted in a tradition of the ideal spectator and proper consumer of a dominant ideology, its subjective narration could well give us an insider's vantage on what usually seems outside and thus undermine the classical tradition. In this way, its subjective elements hold out a promise of much more than just greater audience involvement; it offers to take us beyond the normal borders of both classical narrative and the detective genre.

One way in which *Murder, My Sweet*'s subjective elements promise to move beyond these customary borders is by foregrounding how the cinema ideologically "places" us—that is, in our given political, sexual, and racial "opinions"—and thus opening up to our scrutiny the effects of cinematic "positioning." But while the subjective camera initially seems to make us more aware of our own place in the narrative, it also ultimately complicates the issue. For even as a subjective camera calls attention to our point of view, it also attaches a human burden to that vantage, the persona whose view we share and whose various characteristics and concerns that vantage illustrates. Consequently, the subjective view never simply or neatly exposes a narrative ideology, what has been called the fiction of the viewer, since it already portrays a fictional viewer, the figure through whom we see. And if the subjective camera suggests a dark labyrinth in which our seeing always seems to land us, we must remember that it is first of all that character's labyrinthine experience.

The character whose identity we temporarily assume, though, provides a comforting anchor for the subjective. In *Murder, My Sweet's* case, the detective Philip Marlowe offers an appealing identification, since he is by profession someone who can *see* especially well—a private eye—and who is skilled in maneuvering the dark world he inhabits. The various effects that here accompany our visual identification—looks of outward regard, partial glimpses of our "inhabited" body—thus reaffirm that identity and our involvement in the world of the narrative. However, that subjective vantage also "looks" false. As Kawin notes, most close shots produce an unnatural distortion and "leave out those portions of the face and body one's own eye normally sees," while subjective camera movements are usually "slower than eye movements (so the image can remain clear) and of a completely different nature: more akin to movements of the head, complicated by a neckbrace."9 Moreover, the visual absence of the character whose view we share adds a further effacement, akin to that which marks our seeing. With our vision inscribed in an enigmatic position, in a persona who is obviously not us, and thus in an otherness that remains a mystery of sorts, what we can see becomes defined by a correlative sense of what we cannot see, adequately understand, or even control. In effect, our point of view points to an effacement or focal slippage that undercuts any certainty about our place here or its implications. The result is a tension between absence and presence, between effacement and seeing, that stubbornly resists the resolution we desire and that a subjective camera seemingly promises.

The bracketed perception the subjective *noirs* offer thus never quite breaks free from the hold of classical narrative, especially its protagonist-oriented perspective, nor does it grant us full access to the position from which our "mute opinions" originate. Instead, it makes us aware of an effacement or frustration that attends even such a radical cinematic seeing. As Merleau-Ponty's remarks imply and as our subsequent readings of subjective camera films will show, the *noir* experiments with subjectivity produced no simple revelation of truth, and only a fleeting glimpse of what Bill Nichols terms "the image a society gives of itself in order to perpetuate itself."10 Rather, they fashioned a disconcerting sense of the labyrinth in which seeing and knowing are entangled, in effect, pushing toward, while never quite achieving the sort of systemic self-consciousness Kawin describes. While *noir's* subjective camera developments point to an awareness of cinematic seeing, then, it is the nature of the seeing self that these films most clearly explore, and appropriately in a mystery format.

In light of its potentially challenging nature, we should expect that *Murder, My Sweet* would follow the typical pattern of possibly disturbing Hollywood films. Far from fragile, the classical narrative is quite flexible, able to cope with a wide range of what we might term transgressive elements. It could recuperate them in various ways: by closing them within a dream, as in *The Woman in the Window;* attaching them to a rationalizing voice-over or frame, as in *The Postman Always Rings Twice* (1946); or even making them the subject of documentary-style exposés, as in *Boomerang* (1947). In fact, *Murder, My Sweet* employs several such recuperative strategies to balance its potentially disturbing effects. For example, like *Double Indemnity* it has an embedded flashback in which Philip Marlowe narrates his encounter with Moose Malloy and his girl Velma Valento, so the frame in which Marlowe talks to the police serves to motivate his flashback and to hold its disconcerting elements at a temporal remove. The film's humorous content—as Dick Powell plays him, Marlowe is constantly wisecrack-ing—also helps convert the disturbing into the stable, particularly when the menacing Moose Malloy appears. Its subjective elements similarly operate within a nexus of subversive and recuperative strate-gies, by turns embodying and denying effacement, evoking what can-not be seen but then turning it into the specular. These elements link the problem of the film subject—the detective and his dark view of events—to the general and potentially more disturbing problem of subject placement—the audience's vantage on the cinematic and real worlds—while at the same time deflecting the subjective's more unset-tling possibilities, particularly the sense that the self is a kind of haunting mystery with no solution. In sum, *Murder, My Sweet's* treat-ment of subjectivity illustrates much of the complexity and potential of a technique that later films, most notably *Lady in the Lake* (1947) and *Dark Passage* (1947), would use to make the everyday look strange, our own perspective seem unstable, and seeing and understanding appear to operate at some variance.

The first-person narration of *Farewell, My Lovely,* the Chandler novel on which *Murder, My Sweet* is based, clearly emphasizes the subjective. But as William Luhr notes, it is a "unique and idiosyncratic" sort of narration, since Philip Marlowe's point of view filters and comments on the characters, settings, and events.[11] Re-creating this effect, suggesting "that the way the film's events are perceived is as significant as what they are,"[12] posed a challenge for anyone trying to adapt Chandler's work, particularly since classical narrative's perspec-tive was essentially a given, implicitly a third-person, objective point of view. As a result, *Murder, My Sweet's* voice-over must do multiple duty, not only motivating the flashbacks and various subjective effects but also conveying the interpretive nature of the protagonist's consciousness through verbal descriptions that amplify or qualify what we see, subjectively reworking them, as if things were being presented in both an objective and subjective light. By pushing at the normal bounds of visual detachment in this way, this approach does hint at classical narrative's limits. It suggests that the entire narrative represents a mind at work, and is thus bound by the same limitations and potentially opens onto the same labyrinths as the mind.

Murder, My Sweet's subjective effects depicting Marlowe's driftings into and out of consciousness, as he is knocked senseless, choked, drugged, and shot, dramatically point up the film's challenge to normal perspective, as well as its efforts to disguise the gaps in our understanding that might thus be disclosed. A qualifying note may be needed, though, for there are actually few extended subjective shots of the sort that we find in several later *noirs*. While it freely uses the common visual formula of subjective shot-reaction shot, the film also manifests a kind of stylistic schizophrenia. Whenever the subjective begins to dominate a scene, its effect is pointedly qualified. Thus instead of simply showing events through Marlowe's eyes, identifying our point of view with the detective's, *Murder, My Sweet* uses two shot types that demonstrate the curious combination of subversive and recuperative impulses at work here.

The first of these types, and one for which the film is most noted, is usually described as a link to *noir*'s expressionist background. These are the shots that represent Marlowe's lapses from consciousness, such as when he is blackjacked while accompanying Lindsey Marriott. Marlowe's voice-over notes how "a black pool opened up at my feet. I dived in. It had no bottom," while at the same time an inklike stain gradually engulfs the image, effectively fading out the scene and disguising the ensuing narrative gap of several hours.[13] When, in a later sequence, he awakens from a drug-induced stupor in Dr. Sonderborg's "clinic," Marlowe comments on the smoke and the "gray web woven by a thousand spiders" that cloud his vision, while we see him through a smoked and etched glass that simulates his visual disorientation and distortion. While such scenes let us see as Marlowe supposedly does, though, we also, if illogically, see *him,* for he remains the central focus of the frame, even as we seem placed in his motivating point of view. Harking back to expressionism's efforts to objectify internal states, this peculiar combination of subjective and objective vantages in the same field of vision points to *Murder, My Sweet*'s peculiar strategy: its effort to evoke but control subjectivity, to deploy it but without the disturbing sense of effacement that might follow and point up the limitations on our cinematic seeing.

In a second shot type that resembles a purely subjective view, this strategy works more subtly. Reaction shots introduce several scenes and seem to motivate extended point-of-view shots. This vantage, in each instance, becomes an elaborate tracking shot, as if suggesting Marlowe's exploratory movements. When inspecting the Grayle beach house, for example, Marlowe first turns on his flashlight, and a cut shows the beam of light focused on a far wall, as if seen from his vantage. As the beam explores the room's dark recesses, the camera follows, suggesting the detective's slow, deliberate inspection of the place. However, without a cut to disturb its continuity, this long tracking shot eventually ends on a shot of Marlowe himself—the object of a shot that initially seemed to represent his point of view. As a result of several such scenes, a highly qualified kind of subjectivity emerges here. More than just an illusion or near approximation of subjective vision, these subtle shifts in perspective reveal the truly indeterminate point of view that characterizes the film, while they also point toward an abiding anxiety or distrust of that sense of effacement which would inform later, more extensive *noir* use of the subjective camera.

It is in trying to have it both ways, showing what Marlowe sees while also keeping him in focus, that this film evokes what Merleau-Ponty terms the "labyrinth of difficulties and contradictions" that impinges on our point of view. Of course, that effect is in many ways suitable for a *noir* detective film, since we expect a detective to be able to see and understand in ways that others cannot. But unlike more conventional film detectives, such as Sherlock Holmes, Nick Charles, or Charlie Chan, who mainly examine external events, the *noir* detective is typically involved in an investigation that brings his own concerns into focus. For instance, we might consider the cases involving *The Maltese Falcon*'s (1941) Sam Spade, *The Big Sleep*'s (1946) Philip Marlowe, *The Big Heat*'s (1953) Dave Bannion, and *Kiss Me Deadly*'s (1955) Mike Hammer. Each of these investigations turns into a case of self-exploration and discovery, as the detective gradually shifts focus from the outside world to the internal, to the self, as he discovers his need for love, his questionable morality, or perhaps his inclination to an almost antisocial violence. We could easily read *Murder, My Sweet*'s stylistic complexity in just this context, as aiming for such a dual focus on the world and on the self that would become a hallmark of the *noir* detective tale.

But perhaps more telling, especially since *noir* is often defined by its stylistic effects, is the way *Murder, My Sweet* thematically develops this concern with shifting perspectives. Since the film's intricate web of events originates in a search for a missing person, Malloy's girl Velma, effacement, or a haunting sense of an elusive figure, becomes a key concern here. The narrative's opening quickly sounds this chord, as Marlowe recalls how his involvement with Malloy started with an interrupted relationship, his own missed date with "soft shoulders," as he terms an anonymous girlfriend. This case of romantic caesura, observed as Marlowe gazes out at the dark, alienating city, strikes a subjective note—of a need for another—that, we surmise, often goes ignored because of the detective's professional commitment to an objective world that dominates his attention. By quickly repressing and replacing Marlowe's desire with Malloy's *case* of absent love, though, the narrative both sustains a subjective interest and objectifies that concern by transforming it into the case under investigation. Even as a kind of internal enigma appears, then, it is externalized, rendered as another's puzzle to be solved rather than a personal mystery that might too closely resemble our own deferred desires.

During Marlowe's subsequent narration, this fabric of objective and subjective concerns translates into an interplay between those who look and those who are objects of attention in a way that creates another challenge to recuperation here. As Marlowe's flashback begins, for instance, a ghostly image appears that suggests the potential blind spots in his vision, the limitations on a normal point of view. Alone in his office, Marlowe gazes out at the dark city skyline. The flashing neon lights, however, turn the window into a reflective surface that suddenly reveals the previously unnoticed and menacing Malloy. In subtending Marlowe's gaze, causing him to shift focus to the near surface, this reflection not only points up a blind space in the detective's perspective but also shows that the watcher is himself watched, the object of a gaze that seeks to appropriate—or in this case employ—him.

The sudden shift from seer to seen thereafter becomes a key motif, reminding us that no seeing is totally privileged or free from the impingements of the viewed world and casting a revealing light on the private eye as one whose gaze is never fully his own. It is a light that obviously plays on the film/viewer relationship as well, suggesting a reflexive impulse at work. Marlowe is hired by Malloy to see in a way that he cannot and thus locate the lost Velma. As Malloy's symbolic extension, then, he is constantly reminded that "private eye" means not *for the self* but *for another*. For this reason Marlowe always seems subject to another's possessive gaze. For example, when he encounters Ann Grayle at the Coconut Beach Club and learns that she has been watching him, he casually surveys the room and notices that Malloy is there too, observing him and Ann. When he excuses himself to see what Moose wants, Marlowe is treated like an acquired object, as Moose spirits him off, first to Jules Amthor's apartment, where he is beaten and questioned, and then to Dr. Sonderborg's clinic, where he is drugged and placed under observation. The effect of having the watcher persistently watched and reduced to an object for another is especially disconcerting, because it suggests the potential for a labyrinth of watchers and, ideologically, a level on which we are all possessed, our gaze subtended, appropriated, even permitted by a constantly effacing other—society, the movies, our psyches—that remains just beyond our view or understanding.

In developing this pattern, then, the narrative points to the impossibility of a single, stable point of view, and thus the limits to all seeing and knowing. Early in his tale Marlowe recalls how his role as watcher is reversed when he accompanies Lindsey Marriott to a rendezvous with some thieves. Initially, Marlowe had adopted a detached and amused perspective on his effeminate client, but on arriving at the meeting place he finds this vantage giving way to a feeling of complicity, a sense of his inclusion with Marriott in another's visual field: "We were watched. I didn't see anything; I felt it." When he is later knocked unconscious by some unseen figure, this unsettling shift from viewer to viewed recurs, as his subjectified reaction—a darkening screen and voice-over comment that "a black pool opened up at my feet"—fades into a shot in which Ann Grayle scrutinizes him. When Marlowe investigates Marriott's death by interviewing Helen Grayle, for whom the dead man had been acting, this pattern repeats. As a brief subjective shot-reaction shot series implies, Marlowe resumes his former perspective: we watch him reduce Helen to an object of visual pleasure, see his pleased look, and then view her tugging at her skirt to cover an exposed thigh. When Helen later comes to Marlowe's apartment, though, the play between seer and seen reverses. Finding him in his undershirt, she studies him and offers an objectifying appraisal, "You've got a nice build for a private detective." Her stance and remark bring both Marlowe and the viewers up short, for they repay the detective for his earlier view, while also subverting the privileged vantage from which he and the audience had previously appraised her.

At the same time, this reversal paints Helen's threatening nature in a new light for classical narrative. It defines her menace in terms of a reluctance to accept her status as an object of visual pleasure for an effacing audience, and thus in terms of a challenge she poses to the sort of privileged, voyeuristic vantage that film usually offers. A subsequent scene in which Marlowe and Ann search the Grayle beach house for Helen reinforces this effect. Finding no one, Marlowe turns his attentions to Ann, kissing her after the fashion which Hollywood tradition dictates for such dark and romantic settings. However, their embrace is interrupted—and our narrative expectations subverted—by laughter, as Helen emerges from a dark corner where she has been secretly observing the couple. Her entrance and observation point are from a position that, in the classical tradition, is treated as practically nonexistent, because it marks our own normally invisible vantage and could call attention to the voyeuristic implications of all cinematic seeing.

That Helen Grayle reveals this problem is appropriate, though, for it obliquely hints at her true identity. She is the missing Velma Valento, the former *show*girl whose very identity was defined by her status as a specular object. She has tried to cast off that identity, to become a spectator rather than a spectacle, thus moving into a normally effaced realm. In the fashion of so many *noir* threatening females or spider women, she represents what Janey Place terms a disruptive "desire for freedom, wealth, or independence."[14] Significantly, that "desire" takes the shape here of a longing for "freedom" from being *seen* in the conventional way and from being "placed" in society by that view. No longer a dancer and gangster's moll, Helen has become a respected member of society through her marriage to a rich recluse with "a morbid fear of any kind of publicity." In effect, she has become a new person by successfully reshaping the way she is seen. But if her success in effacing her previous role signals her threatening status, it is a threat that *Murder, My Sweet* eventually qualifies. For she finds herself trapped in a web of blackmailers—Mrs. Florian, Marriott, Amthor—who make it seem unlikely that she could ever finally escape from this world's constant interplay of seers and seen.

This is just one more way in which *Murder, My Sweet* pursues its stylistic and thematic compromise with effacement, a compromise that also shows up when Marlowe recognizes a similarity between himself and Helen. As we have noted, the subject's persistent disappearance marks most of the narrative and gives it a labyrinthine quality that points to the larger problem of seeing. While Helen has tried to vacate her identity as Velma, so too has Marlowe tried to omit the self from his investigation. This dance of effacement, however, only leads to murder after murder and plunges Marlowe into what his narration describes as a series of "black pits," each one "blacker than the others, and deeper." What Marlowe only belatedly recognizes is that *he* is a clue to the various mysteries under investigation, the only thread connecting these cases and leading through the labyrinth they form. Rather than a detached, external point of view, he *is* part of the field to be surveyed. And it is a mark of what he learns here that he finally adopts a new vantage, not just *from* the self but *of* the self; in effect, he learns to see himself anew. This new point of view admits his involvement in this world and, perhaps with the anti-isolationist attitude of the war still firmly in mind, cautions against a moral equivalent of effacement.

Preceding and clarifying the terms of this recognition is an unconventional use of the voice-over that accompanies Marlowe's drugged stupor at Dr. Sonderborg's clinic. Upon awakening to a vision of smoke and spider webs, Marlowe senses a kind of effacement, as if his body had become foreign, thinglike. Reaching for his sore throat, he notes that his "fingers didn't feel anything," in fact, that they seemed more like "a bunch of bananas that looked like fingers." More than a Sartrean "nausea," this feeling, along with the distorted, wide-angle view of his fingers we get, reinterprets the pattern of effacement that runs through the film. What halts this unsettling transformation and slipping away of the self is Marlowe's determination, an act of will he summons up in response to the smoke and spider webs that cloud his vision at this point. Marlowe recalls how he took command of his slipping consciousness, ordering it: "Okay, Marlowe . . . Okay, you cuckoo. Walk . . . and talk." It is an objectification of the self in the midst of this subjective sequence that matches the film's visual technique. It is also one that effectively saves his life by enabling him to escape from the clinic. At the same time, it shows the difficulty of achieving and maintaining an objective perspective, like that which the camera seems to adopt here. That view is, we recognize, a construct, but one that does not deny subjectivity or involvement; moreover, it is clearly useful for surviving in the world and coping with its mystery. By implication, that objective vantage seems a construct that the movies too adopt out of necessity, as a way of making their own mechanism more effective and unobtrusive, even of making narrative, in its root sense, as an *act of knowing,* possible.

This paradox, of an objectification of the self that captures a sense of the self's involvement, is also modeled in the narrative's frame. The opening and closing scenes of Marlowe sitting in a police station, his eyes covered by bandages as he explains what has happened, iconically present this paradox. The image of the blinded detective, his "eyeballs scorched," suggests a danger in subjectivity, in leading with the eyes or, in this instance, of getting too close to a gun's muzzle flash. Analogously, it also hints at a danger in looking too closely at the cinematic mechanism. However, even as he suggests an inevitable level of effacement, the blind detective, we should recall, represents a source of truth as well. If his experience with this labyrinthine world and its "black pits" has blinded him, it has also, in the best questing tradition, made him singularly able to "see" the truth, helped him to navigate the labyrinth. By enclosing sight within a frame of blindness in this way, *Murder, My Sweet* crafts a telling image of the sort of compromise that marks cinematic seeing and that subsequent *films noir* working in the subjective vein would explore in more ambitious ways.

The introduction of Marlowe's voice-over in the opening and closing frame scenes hints at this compromise. Each scene begins with the image of a bright light, metaphorically suggesting the possibility of revelations or enlightenment to follow, coming from Marlowe's voice. As the camera tracks back, though, we see that this image is but a reflection of an overhead light in the polished surface of the table where Marlowe sits. More than just an optical trick, a disorientation to mirror Marlowe's confusion, this deceptive image points to the limits that attend all seeing and insinuates how our desire for a certain *insight*—a privileged understanding of another or of the world itself— might well depend on what remains *out of sight*, offscreen, beyond our normal point of view.

Marlowe's subsequent discovery of Ann's presence at the police station, and with it of his love for her, thematically builds upon this simultaneous problematizing and recuperating of vision. In the tradition of classical narrative, Ann *is* the solution to Marlowe's most pressing "mystery." She is the girl he needs to be complete, a replacement for the "soft shoulders" mentioned at the start of his account. Throughout the narrative she has been presented, like "soft shoulders," as a kind of effacing figure. In the scene following Marriott's death, she shines a light on Marlowe and then runs into the dark as he awakes; later, in the Coconut Beach Club, she again disappears while Marlowe talks to Malloy. But in the film's final scene, Ann only seems absent; although she conceals her presence, Ann is with the police, listening as Marlowe talks about her. In effect, she objectifies and vanquishes the problem of effacement, recalls it but then recuperates the detachment and invisibility it seems to imply, just as Marlowe's blindness balances his subjectivity. Occupying a blind space that is not really blind, she appropriately sparks the narrative's return to the norms of classical cinema, which is marked as well by the film's romantic conclusion. In the final taxi scene, Marlowe smells the perfume on "Nulty," his supposed police escort, recognizes who is beside him, and asks for a kiss—from Ann. With their closing embrace and kiss, with an achieved love relationship that is the traditional measure of success, the film manages a satisfyingly romantic conclusion.

Murder, My Sweet does more than simply recuperate and stabilize what was a basically unstable perspective, though. In the development of *noir* narrative it is especially noteworthy both for the interaction it demonstrates between the seen and the unseen and for working out a thematic correlative to this interaction in its detective protagonist, who tries to efface his involvement in the world and assume a detached, objective vantage—paralleling the sort of effacement that traditionally marked the movies—only to discover the problems of such a stance. As we shall see, these developments surface more spectacularly in later *noir* subjective efforts, such as *Lady in the Lake* and *Dark Passage*. The former film, also adapted from a Chandler novel, uses a subjective camera to tie our perspective to Marlowe's for almost the entire film, so that, as the detective tells us, everything he sees we shall see. The result is a sense of immense but unsettling possibility, since every camera movement opens onto a blind space and doubles the labyrinthine sense by making our vision that of a constantly effacing figure. The film thus locates a disturbing instability and uncertainty in the character who must navigate the world and disclose its mysterious truths. The latter film uses subjectivity both as a tool of convenience, that is, to hide Humphrey Bogart's face until after his character undergoes plastic surgery, and to dramatize the plight of an individual forced into effacement, made to inhabit the unseen space that we and the movies typically ignore or deny existence to—the underworld, the offscreen, the subcultural. Because his actions are consistently misinterpreted, this character has to abandon his identity and his culture, totally efface the self, although it is a hard and unsatisfactory choice. But it is a choice that also implies how little choice we ultimately have, and in the best *noir* tradition emphasizes the unsatisfying conditions that the culture, the movies, and even our own natures impose on our seeing.

If it has received less attention than these later films, this is perhaps because *Murder, My Sweet* tries hard to be conventional. For example, Marlowe's easy humor clearly links him to earlier Hollywood detectives, like *The Thin Man*'s Nick Charles. And its frame device ultimately works to bind, qualify, and in some ways normalize the tale and its subjective elements. Like the police observing and interrogating the blind Marlowe, we adopt a vantage for seeing and questioning that never really loses its sense of authority, that never quite abandons the classical spectator position. While it successfully points to the difficult nature of all seeing by evoking the problems of effacement and blindness, then, *Murder, My Sweet* also maneuvers around these problems through its compositions, shifting perspectives, and frame-tale structure, and finally by erecting at the very source of all subjective vision here the image of the blinded detective. From our vantage we know that what he cannot see—Ann, for instance—is nonetheless there; and what he does not know for sure, he can easily surmise. Blindness is simply not a real issue, as Marlowe transforms the disturbing potential of the unseen into little more than an individual and temporary physiological problem, making the problem of effacement seem more apparent than real.

At the same time, though, the film traces a tension that signals its important place in the *noir* canon as a pioneer of later subjective narratives. Hardly just "an ambitiously arty misfire," as some claim,[15] *Murder, My Sweet* works at a compromise between the subjective and objective points of view that implicitly speaks to a concern with the problem of perception—a concern that became a *noir* hallmark. As we shall see, later works explored the problems and potentials of cinematic subjectivity in more extreme ways, in the process revealing, like the punches aimed at the camera in *Lady in the Lake*, the blind spots in our vision and film's tendency to efface the spectator, to place him or her at an unseen, privileged vantage that promises an objective truth. Within its limits, *Murder, My Sweet* questions this strategy by the very tensions it evokes and the problems of perspective it never fully recuperates. It is in those tensions, no less than in its models of recuperative activity, that this film contributed to the development of *noir* narrative and especially to its concern with how we perceive both the real and the cinematic worlds we commonly inhabit.

NOTES

1. Merleau-Ponty, *Visible and the Invisible,* p. 9.
2. Kawin, *Mindscreen,* p. 192.
3. Clarens, *Crime Movies,* p. 195.
4. For a history of film adaptations of Chandler's private eye, see Luhr's *Raymond Chandler and Film.*
5. Wood, *America in the Movies,* p. 100.
6. Merleau-Ponty, *Visible and the Invisible,* p. 3.
7. Kawin, *Mind of the Novel,* p. 14.
8. Ibid., pp. 16, 285.
9. Kawin, *Mindscreen,* p. 8.
10. Nichols, *Ideology and the Image,* p. 1.
11. Luhr, *Raymond Chandler and Film,* p. 10.

12. Ibid., p. 13.
13. Motivating such gaps is crucial to an effective subjective narrative, for the unrelenting subjective vision invariably limits the shaping power of the narrative and results in many purely functional scenes, there simply because they are the context of the protagonist's experience and field of vision. A loss of consciousness, whether through violence or sleep, can thus allow for narrative elisions that move the story along more efficiently, and it can permit more meaningful juxtapositions of events. Perhaps just as important, it allows us some breathing space, a momentary relaxation of that constant, forced identification of our eyes and our bodies with the film's narrator.
14. Place, "Women in Film Noir," in Kaplan, *Women in Film Noir*, p. 46.
15. Higham and Greenberg, *Hollywood in the Forties*, p. 38.

CHAPTER 6

"The Real Thing Is Something Else": Truth and Subjectivity in *The Lady in the Lake*

Most film histories describe Robert Montgomery's *The Lady in the Lake* (1947) as a curiosity piece, an interesting but ultimately wrong-headed attempt at creating a totally subjective narrative. As we saw in *Murder, My Sweet,* that effort partly traces to a desire to imitate the interpretive first-person narration of the Raymond Chandler novel on which the film is based. However, as the protagonist Philip Marlowe notes in the prologue, the subjective approach also has a more radical function here. Fastening us with a look of outward regard that already departs from normal film practice, he describes a disparity found in most popular narratives: "What you've read and what you've heard is one thing. The real thing is something else." Through the subjective, Marlowe promises to correct this disparity by letting us see things as he saw them, sharing the private eye's singular view of "the real thing." The result is indeed "something else," a film that challenges how we normally see in the movies, but without ever quite correcting that imbalance of which it spoke. In falling short in this way, the film probably assured its eventual status as a stylistic curiosity, but it also managed to suggest the full potential of a subjective camera narration.

Marlowe's opening claim implies that our normal *narrative* way of seeing—that is, how we see in most film narratives—leaves something to be desired. It is a shortcoming, I have already suggested, that the *film noir* tried to address in various ways. Its chiaroscuro lighting, dutch angles, and unbalanced compositions, for example, point to a stance like Marlowe's, and thus signal a level on which his comment speaks for the whole *noir* project; for these effects too challenge how we see our world—or at least how it appears through the window of classical Hollywood narrative. By disrupting our normal vantage, whether with an expressionist styling or, as *Murder, My Sweet* attempted, through various subjective effects, *noir* films could create a new visual experience and, implicitly, a more truthful view, even one that avoided cinema's normal ideological role as a collection of culturally sponsored and culture-fostering images.

This concern with a cinematic truth was essentially a by-product of various factors, but especially the technical developments of the war years. For instance, the appearance of lightweight, mobile cameras like the German Arriflex and the introduction of the highly maneuverable "crab" dolly that permitted longer takes[1] helped transform what previously was mainly a narrative punctuation, the subjective shot, into a viable narrative device, a sequence shot. Further aiding this trend was the interest in narrative experimentation we have already noted, an interest that traces back to Orson Welles's prewar plans to do a subjective version of *Heart of Darkness*.[2] With the critically and financially successful experiment with subjectivity in the prior Chandler adaptation, *Murder, My Sweet*, the stage was set, technically, conceptually, and financially, for further exploring this approach.

But in place of *Murder, My Sweet*'s modified subjectivity, *Lady in the Lake*'s makers planned a radical application of this technique. Fortunately, in the postwar context such stylistic experimentation seemed neither unworkable nor unmarketable. Robert Carringer theorizes that Orson Welles never realized his prewar subjective project because "the one thing as much feared in Hollywood as a runaway budget was radical innovation. *Heart of Darkness* had been dropped not only because it was too expensive but because Welles's plans to use first-person camera narration for most of the story were too experimental and commercially risky."[3] By 1946 when *Lady* started shooting, though, a calculable promise of commercial viability and a limited demonstration of its success combined to argue for using the subjective technique. The technique's compromised use in *Murder, My Sweet* had found a favorable response and Chandler's popularity was high, so it seemed an appropriate approach that might ultimately offer a more exciting rendering of his novel's first-person form. Finally, MGM would have the services of Robert Montgomery, one of its more popular prewar stars, who agreed to play Marlowe if he could also direct the film using the subjective technique. From the start, then, *Lady*'s radical style seemed to represent a compromise with a possible commercial payback, and at least a project with little real risk for a studio which, in 1946, was seeing its earnings soar to an all-time high,[4] as practically everything Hollywood produced in this flush time seemed to turn a profit.

While the film opened to generally favorable reviews, the critics did note a problem in its unconventional technique. Despite our sharing Marlowe's vantage, it was felt that this effect did not capture the private eye's experience, either radically or realistically. While only half serious, the reviewer for the *New York Times* hinted at the problem: "*You* do get into the story and see things pretty much the way its protagonist, Philip Marlowe, does, but *you* don't . . . get a chance to put your arms around Audrey Totter. . . . After all, the movie makers, for all their ingenuity, can go just so far in the quest for realism."[5] More to the point, another critic felt that the film suffered because "the unique powers of the subjective camera are left at the mercy of technicians schooled in conventional methods," with the result being a failure "properly to relate the individual onlooker to the image on the screen."[6] Indeed, the film does suffer from the viewers' ambiguous placement, for we seem to occupy a spot *near* the protagonist, but not really *his* position, and even that location is intermittent, interrupted as it is by several breaks in the narrative. Of course, the camera eye should never have been expected to stand in for the human eye; as the previous chapter noted, its perspective and sense of dimension, among other things, are quite different. Rather, as *Murder, My Sweet* also suggests, the subjective technique inadvertently pointed up something about those "conventional methods" that we normally overlook, namely, a troubling absence or effacement—what a contemporary reviewer termed a "visual ambiguity"[7]—that marks the normal cinematic experience. The problem, finally, is one of offscreen space, the area that *we* usually inhabit in film but that goes unacknowledged and unremarked (hence, the general proscription against the look of outward regard). The subjective camera calls attention to that normal absence, to our unquestioned, *given* point of view, and because it is so unrelenting here, this awareness frustrates the film's efforts at disguise or recuperation.

From the film's outset, we glimpse a disparity between the subjective's promise and its fulfillment. As Marlowe introduces the mechanism, he poses a telling challenge: "You'll see it just as I saw it. You'll meet the people; you'll find the clues—and maybe you'll solve it quick and maybe you won't." However, this promise, that our vantage will match the detective's experience, is one on which the film never makes good, for we never see all that Marlowe saw, meet the people he met, view every clue. The burden of such an unrelenting, all-encompassing vision proves too much for a narrative that, in the interests of effective storytelling, must leave gaps in our experience. It simply elides the unnecessary with invisible cuts, dissolves, and even straightforward breaks in the narration, such as when Marlowe sums up his case's progress. We could never really "solve it quick," as he proposes, therefore, because we never share his knowledge or his full *experience*—which might well, in the main, prove boring.

What we do share, and what various punches and kisses directed at the camera punctuate, is the larger sense of mystery evoked here. For in combination with these effects, the eye through which we see and experience Marlowe's mystery—precisely *because* it is not his, although *like* his—produces a sense of estrangement, a tense and truly tenuous identification with the narrator, while it also points up the gaps that invariably inform the stories we culturally tell and accept about ourselves. For these reasons, we find ourselves plunged into mystery, caught in a narrative trap of sorts that, for the film's duration, we cannot escape. In that trap of identification we wander a mazelike world, without any control over our movements; we confront unexpected threats and encounter inexplicable gaps of experience and understanding; and the goal at which we aim seems mainly one of escape. In reaching for a new cinematic style, a more interesting and involving way of telling the detective story, and a radical way of describing what, in this era, increasingly seemed a somber and confusing American experience, *Lady in the Lake* simply opened upon a darker, more disturbing, and ultimately more difficult perspective than Montgomery probably anticipated for his private eye experiment.

Certainly, the film's subjectivity produces a sense of mystery and of paradox that differs markedly from the usual atmosphere of detective narratives. As Pascal Bonitzer notes, that technique renders the detective an enigma, even though "he is the one responsible for solving the enigma."[8] Given our share in his point of view and the *double* mystery it thus unfolds, we almost invariably find it unsettling, its implicit commentary on our normally secure sense of self—not just our place in society but our very identities—not quite the sort of vision we expect from the movies or even relish. Of course, the buildup of details to ground our perspective—like reminding us that this figure works for "ten bucks a day and expenses"—implies some awareness of our possible estrangement. But Marlowe's frequent appearances as a mirror reflection, the two conventional scenes wherein he reports on his progress, and his concluding summary of the case do not add up to the sort of secure identity classical narrative usually offered. Nor do they dispel a sense of instability that Bonitzer views as symptomatic of the "blind space" that informs all film narrative:[9] the realm of the unseen, the offscreen, the place of our own perspective, and a spatial correlative for that mysterious sense of self the movies offer us.

One result of calling our attention to this blind spot or "partial vision" is that we thereby glimpse our place in a disturbing labyrinth: the labyrinth of narrative and of all such culturally produced structures, even the labyrinth of the self. Instead of some specific "real thing," consequently, we encounter a troubling sense of elusiveness; the viewer, as a stable, self-determining perspective, seems swallowed up in the act of looking, plunged into a structural labyrinth akin to what Marc Vernet describes as a "black hole"—the term he uses to describe the interruptions and disconnections that characterize *noir* narrative and by which "it raises more questions than it answers."[10] In effect, that encounter starts an awareness of a mystery that informs our every discourse about the real, as well as our whole sense of self.

A more promising fallout of the film's point of view is that it can make us acutely aware of our spectator position, here and in the broad cinematic experience. The constantly moving camera, the looks of outward regard that mark Marlowe's presence, and the punches and kisses thrown at the camera emphasize not only that our vantage is another's, but that it is always, even stiflingly, determined for us. Of course, the benefits of such a mindfulness are potentially great. As modernist writers like Borges, John Barth, and Thomas Pynchon have effectively shown through their narrative labyrinths structured like linguistic or semiotic problems, the path beyond narrative limitation might well be found *in* the very factors of limitation, for example, in language's own labyrinthine nature. Similarly, an awareness of the cinematic apparatus might well produce a kind of liberation from its manipulations. Julio Moreno saw in the film's technique just such a radical, reflexive promise, as the film attests to its one sure reality, "the place occupied by the spectator in the theater." Of course, while such a mindfulness gives us a new anchor in the real world, it also threatens the "imaginary world" whose "enchantment is broken, the narrative falls apart like a card castle."[11] But breaking that narrative "enchantment" could be productive too, if by blasting away film's illusion of objectivity, the subjective camera could also reveal how much cinematic seeing is always fashioned by camera and culture, rather than naturally given by reality itself.

The promise of *Lady*'s subjectivity was, therefore, both radical and implicitly paradoxical, since it suggested that our identification with the *private eye* might conceivably produce a new *public* eye, that is, a larger, more encompassing, and ultimately revealing vision of what

Marlowe terms "the real thing." In practice, though, we were being forced to accept the public eye of the camera as private, as "our" eyes, and the experience was distinctly discomfiting; it neither looked nor felt natural. The key problem with *Lady* may well be that it never could resolve this tension between promise and practice, thereby making amends for its broken "enchantment."

Recalling one of *Murder, My Sweet*'s subjective effects, *Lady*'s first subjective image is a tracking shot, indicating Marlowe's movement along a hall in search of the offices of Kingsby Publications. It is the kind of shot that recurs in the film, repeatedly creating a mazelike effect, as the starting, then halting, camera signals an eye and a human presence, randomly moving and constantly opening onto the new and the unseen. Adding to this effect is a series of images that establishes one of the film's recurrent patterns of disturbance. In this initial tracking shot, the camera pans right to inspect a door, then left to inspect a name stenciled on another door, before resuming its movement along the hall. A survey of the film shows that approximately forty-four additional shots focus on entrances, depict characters using a door for access or egress, or employ doorways or windows to frame characters and create multiple planes of focus. We soon come to expect that there is always another door to enter, something new, unsuspected, and possibly threatening yet to be encountered. For example, even after locating Kingsby Publications, Marlowe is directed to another door in the background, leading to the editor A. Fromsett's office, within which he finds still another, opening onto the office of publisher Derace Kingsby.

This emphasis on symmetrical structures and frames *is* helpful for composition; it repeatedly centers and stabilizes our point of view. In fact, this image pattern might well have been adopted as a kind of stylistic "ground" for the incessantly mobile camera. However, it also reminds us of a warning Marlowe posts in his introduction. As detectives, he notes, "You've got to watch 'em; you've got to watch 'em all the time, because things happen when you least expect them." Hence he tells us to stay on our guard, especially "when that door there behind you opens." Just who or what that "'em" stands for is never made clear. It may refer to characters the investigation will soon encounter, or perhaps the ambiguous "things" that are supposed to "happen." More likely, it is a generalization born of the larger sense of enigma or mystery that comes with being a detective, and that the very technique here fosters. The door imagery, then, hinting at something unstable in our own world, ever "behind" us or closed to our normal scrutiny, effectively codifies this effect.

In the initial tracking shot, Marlowe acts out this drama of instability and disorientation that recurs in the many later scenes wherein he seems to wander through a labyrinth, encountering doors that open onto other doors—and symbolically onto gaps in understanding that might never be closed. As this pattern develops, the simple act of opening a door takes on the flavor of the narrative style itself, becomes its image, with its constant sense of an unsettling opening. Marlowe's entry to A. Fromsett's office, for example, simply extends his mazelike movement by starting other revelations and mysteries that suggest how no truth will come "neat," be clearly perceived, or lack an enigmatic aspect. Thus while our expectations of this era lead us to expect the executive A. Fromsett to be male, we find behind her door a woman who has tried to disguise or deny her sexuality, as the name, masculine business suit, and icy manner attest. And this initial subterfuge looks forward to others, for while feigning interest in a manuscript Marlowe submitted, she tries to assess his ability as a private eye in hopes of employing him to locate Chrystal Kingsby, her boss's missing wife. Since her reasons for interfering in Derace Kingsby's affairs go unstated, another level of mystery and speculation quickly develops. Consequently, we quickly sense how simply opening a door can lead to various enigmas, extending the labyrinth from a stylistic level to a thematic one. On both levels the film hints at a disturbing continuity between this world's enigmatic nature and the mystery behind all human identity and motivation.

Eventually, this door imagery merges with another hallmark of subjective narration, the look of outward regard, to suggest the limits on our seeing that qualify all sense of "the real thing." Agreeing to find Chrystal Kingsby, Marlowe questions those who have been involved with her, starting with Chris Lavery, a playboy who previously jilted Adrienne Fromsett. Meeting Marlowe at the door, Lavery looks directly into the camera and at first refuses him entry. After admitting Marlowe, he throws a punch toward the camera that, a subsequent fade implies, knocks the detective out. Clearly, maneuvering the labyrinth is a difficult and at times dangerous affair, as Marlowe admits when he describes his occupational "sickness"—"reoccurring black eyes." When he returns to Adrienne's office, she too looks into the camera and asks angrily, "How did you get in here without being announced?" It is the same sort of challenge that later greets the detective's intrusion on Kingsby's Christmas party. When his investigation subsequently reopens the case of a supposed suicide, Florence Almore, Marlowe is again refused entrance, her parents staring into the camera as they bar the door to their home. While these looks of outward regard are essential to establishing Marlowe's narrative "presence" and imply that the filmmakers felt viewers needed to be reminded of their subjective vantage, they also serve to fix our point of view and thus bar it from the sort of free vantage it seems to enjoy in classical narrative. If the profusion of doors here seems a visualization of the narrative style, then, so do the many instances of barred, difficult, or challenged entry appear an outgrowth of the mobile camera eye and its exploratory impulse. For this pattern of resistance reminds us of both the subjective's limitations and the everyday world's reluctance to see or be seen in a new or revealing way.

Characterizing *The Lady in the Lake,* then, is this fundamental link between its point of view and the images it reveals, as the one consistently finds its reflection in the other. We can begin to gauge the importance of that link in Michel Serres' account of our common desire for an objective or "real" knowledge: "There is only one type of knowledge and it is always linked to an observer, an observer submerged in a system or in its proximity. And this observer is structured exactly like what he observes. His position changes only the relationship between noise and information, but he never effaces these two stable presences."[12] Even the subjects of Marlowe's gaze reflect this play between mystery and boundary, as if mirroring the very tension that molds his subjective view. For instance, while she employs him to find Chrystal, Adrienne also tries to limit or direct Marlowe's probings, telling him to avoid Lavery and concentrate on the cottage at Little Fawn Lake where Chrystal was last seen; "Go back to the lake," she tells him, "you did fine there." When his investigation reveals Adrienne's relations with Kingsby and Lavery, she coldly notes, "It's none of your affair," and tries to fire him. In similar fashion, both the crooked cop DeGarmot and his superior Captain Kane try to limit Marlowe's efforts, warning him not to bother the citizens of their jurisdiction and to stay out of San Pedro. When the detective suggests there may be a link between a body found in Little Fawn Lake and the later murder of Chris Lavery, Kane dismisses the idea of a larger mystery, telling Marlowe, "What do I care about a drowned dame in a lake? I got a body in here and that's plenty enough for me. . . . Let's confine ourselves to what went on here. . . . That's all that's in my jurisdiction."

This sense of jurisdiction, though, already points toward another, deeper level of truth these characters do not want probed. Adrienne's angry reaction to Marlowe's stare—"Why are you looking at me that way?"—emphasizes the sense of boundary here, of depths or reasons beyond which one should not go. Her comment brings the detective's gaze—and our own—up short, forestalling any effort to render the private as public, by implying that there are things the subjective eye should not look on without permission. And at the same time, it adds a sense of mystery to this nexus of looks: a mystery in her character, as her wariness at being seen implies,[13] and even an enigma about our looking, which depends on a "why" beyond any explanation, only given in Marlowe's subjective gaze. What that elusive reason hints of is a level of unknowing and curiosity that underlies and impels not just our point of view but, after a fashion, all cinematic seeing.

It is appropriate that Adrienne sounds this note of limitation, for she most clearly embodies the problem of perceiving truth here. As we have noted, her dark business suit and upswept hairdo project an almost masculine appearance, one supported by her success in a man's world; as Kingsby notes, Adrienne has "worked herself up to a position of importance." At the same time, she seems sexually experienced in a way that distinguishes her from most female characters in this era's films. Her relationships with Lavery—Marlowe discovers her handkerchief in his bedroom—and with Kingsby—her Christmas gift to him is a bathrobe—were implicitly intimate. And in trying to manipulate Marlowe, she turns to a sexual allure, much as, we might imagine, she has done with her boss. While Adrienne thus functions in a variety of roles—the sexless executive, the femme fatale—that protean capacity also makes her a disturbing and potentially threatening figure, another locus of mystery facing Marlowe. Kingsby only emphasizes this view, noting that he knows little about her: "her past life and background [are] blank." While Marlowe eventually takes her into his confidence, some doubt remains. So, when she asks him to "quit being a detective," he confesses that he "can't until this thing is over," for otherwise he could never "be sure" about her or her feelings for him.

But Adrienne simply codifies the ambiguity that marks all the characters Marlowe encounters. Lavery, for instance, notes that "Miss Adrienne likes to romanticize," yet he too seems almost a fictional creation. The lover of both Adrienne and Chrystal, he is described by the former as a Swede but greets Marlowe in a heavy Southern accent. And while Derace Kingsby apparently encouraged Adrienne's romantic aspirations, he shows a very different side on learning that she has hired Marlowe. Reacting in a way that speaks of his own duplicity, he tells her, "If I've ever said anything endearing to you, it was because I was lonely."

Such disguised motivations combine with a pattern of masked identity to sketch a depth of duplicity or elusiveness in all of the characters here. In searching Little Fawn Lake, for example, Marlowe discovers the body of a drowned woman, initially thought to be Muriel Chess, the caretaker's wife, later presumed to be Mildred Haveland, but finally identified as Chrystal Kingsby. Mildred, who we learn murdered Chrystal, also easily shifts identity, at one time posing as Lavery's landlady while ransacking his house, and later as Chrystal in an effort to extort money from Derace. Such instability, also seen in DeGarmot, who is both a police detective and Mildred's accomplice, eventually evokes a similar potential in Marlowe, who plants his identification on a drunk at one point to avoid being picked up by the police, and later poses as Kingsby in order to trap Mildred. It is as if the play of elusive or indeterminate identities comes full circle, back to the original enigmatic narrating figure, who is effectively the source of these other unstable identities. And that circularity reminds us, much as the visual style itself implies, that there is no level free of the enigmatic, no figure—including the viewing self—without a depth that defies scrutiny.

The implications of this interweaving of subjectivity and problematic identity become clearer in the context of Stuart Marshall's suggestion that Marlowe's vantage serves as "the agent of the viewer's desire."[14] Through Marlowe, after all, we gain a voyeuristic pleasure of the sort that propels later films like *Rear Window* (1954) and *Peeping Tom* (1960), although that pleasure is less sexual in nature than empirical, as the film's opening disarmingly avows. The desire to which this film and its subjective view finally caters is that of seeing clearly, looking into the depths of our culture and ourselves, threading the labyrinth that is our personal and cultural condition. At the same time, it is a desire that recognizes a danger in its satisfying gaze; that is, our looking could encounter a mirror, our seeing open onto a reflexive dimension, so that in examining these enigmatic characters and their mysterious world we might also glimpse our human mystery—our problematic, elusive, and ultimately enigmatic identity. Thus we find a curious double pull sourced in the subjective camera here. On the one hand, it seems to hold us aloof, relieved of complicity in this world or its disturbing shape by the very difference of our perspective—and our difference as well from the other characters in the film. But on the other, it projects an image of instability and binds us to this world through those looks that signal the camera-as-Marlowe's presence. The subjective, of course, quickly loses its impact, especially the sense that it is *somebody's* view, without the repeated cues that also pull us into the seen world, trap us in a sequence of looks, and mark the pattern of complicitous gazes that ultimately compose the world. If what comes into focus, then, is not quite the "real thing" initially promised, it is a most unexpected *in*sight, a glimpse of our own mysterious aspect.

It may be for this reason that *Lady in the Lake*, like *Murder, My Sweet*, finally exchanges its radical promise for a position of stability, identity, and qualified truth, in the classical narrative tradition. Of course, on one level the detective genre always involves a compromise. As John Cawelti explains, its dual impulses of "ratiocination and mystification" work "in a tense and difficult relationship to each other," but their balance is what makes the tale effective.[15] Significantly, Marc Vernet has observed a variant of this pattern in the *film noir*. In what he terms a "filmic transaction," the *noir* narrative alternately threatens and reinforces the structures and patterns of our lives by letting us relish darkness, while also maintaining "a pleasant and comforting belief against the contradictions of reality."[16] This paradox usually depends on a framework of rationality and traditional beliefs that can be threatened without being overturned. With *Lady*'s unsettling style and the dark vision it projects, though, such a compromise might seem impossible, for its emphasis on instability from the start leaves little stable ground to return to at narrative's end. And thanks to the film's subjective technique, its element of "ratiocination"—a drive to make "the real thing" visible—risks uncovering its own deep-rooted pattern of "mystification," reason's own enigmatic aspect, and thus revealing how much it shares in its opposite's nature.

While *Lady* begins in a subversive and revealing posture, though, it eventually retreats from that stance at every level. In fact, its efforts at recuperating a conventional reality strain at the film's avowed concern with the real. The extended tracking shot, like that which opens the first subjective sequence, illustrates the pattern of stylistic recuperation at work here. While it never disappears from the narrative, that mobile subjective shot is eventually grounded in a way that almost neutralizes its disturbing, labyrinthine effect. When Marlowe is pursued by DeGarmot, for instance, the tracking shot of him walking and then riding down the dark city streets first focuses on a mysterious black car from which the detective is being watched. Given this emphasis, the camera then locates the car's image in Marlowe's rearview mirror, so we can watch its pursuit from that vantage. This shift largely cancels our sense of Marlowe's rapid driving through the twisting streets by shifting attention from a view of his *motion* to the *fixed* mirror image of a car. A variation of this transfer occurs when Marlowe meets Mildred Haveland, posing as Chrystal. As he approaches, she looks away into a store window, hiding her face from the detective and from us; and when she moves off, he follows closely, so that his vantage becomes a conventional camera's, his own enigmatic identity and movement temporarily displaced into Mildred's faceless figure. Correspondingly, the shot of Marlowe's hand dropping grains of rice to mark his trail hints of a different impulse at work here—as does the unmotivated break in the narrative at this point, which is covered by a dissolve. No longer an agent of mystification, Marlowe is dedicated to mapping the labyrinth and dispelling enigma. In fact, even the key images of mystification, the doors and windows, take a recuperative shape. Trapped in Mildred's apartment, Marlowe is about to be shot by DeGarmot. Through a large background window, though, we glimpse a fire escape on which, after much delay, Captain Kane appears, gun poised to rescue Marlowe. Thus what suspense Marlowe's precarious position initially generates dissipates into an image of justice's operation, when that rear window becomes a portal of wish fulfillment and marks a return to normalcy.

But the greatest weight of recuperation is borne by Marlowe and Adrienne, whose difficult early relationship dissolves in a promise of love and marriage. In keeping with the film's initial stance, the detective and the editor seem in pointed contrast: he is committed to the truth of experience, she to a world of manipulative fictions. Interestingly, Chandler had sketched a rather different situation in his script—a conventional love relationship. As William Luhr notes, his adaptation followed a typical Hollywood romantic formula, with "Marlowe and Fromsett going over the evidence together; she approaches murder from a literary standpoint, perceiving the evidence as a fictional detective might, while Marlowe gives the 'real life' approach."[17] However, Chandler's script was not used, and the subjective narration, with its sense of an isolated, estranged perspective, emphasizes the distance between Marlowe and Fromsett, just as it does that between the audience and the viewed world. His disdain for what she publishes thus finds its opposite in her scorn for his writing, seen when she promises to "slash the emotion right out of it." And his reluctance for, as he puts it, "getting mixed up with tricky females who want to knock off the boss's wife and marry him for themselves" prompts her cynical rejoinder that "every man has his price." As Montgomery redefined their relationship, then, there seems little reason for a shared investigation, much less for romance, since Marlowe and Adrienne show little trust in each other and represent very different attitudes toward the truth.

However, this gap abruptly disappears when the narrative takes a more conservative turn. Following the period's conventions, Adrienne, who initially seems the typical *noir* "black widow," would have to be recuperated or destroyed. But the transformation that occurs is an extreme of recuperation that suggests just how disconcerting the image of an aggressive, almost masculine woman was in an era when many men found themselves supplanted by a mobilized female work force and the traditional family structure radically upset. From her initial concern with catching a millionaire—"There's more than one Kingsby on the Christmas tree and I'll shake one loose yet," she tells Marlowe in a hard-boiled tone to match his own—and manipulating the males around her, Adrienne becomes Marlowe's loving girlfriend, caring for him after his car is wrecked and cooing, "I just want to be your girl." In a remark that reworks her earlier comment about every man having his "price," she looks into the camera and tells Marlowe, "All I really want is to own you." This appropriation, though, betokens loving support rather than a threat to the detective's integrity, and thus marks her conversion to a socially acceptable role. If, as Michael Renov suggests, we view the typical *noir* female "as the figuration of 'style' itself, in the sense of a signifying surface,"[18] then this change's significance becomes clear. Since she has been emblematic of the subversive, Adrienne also symbolically becomes a focus for much of the narrative style's disturbing effect. As a result, her redemption serves an extra function, vicariously swerving the narrative back into a conventional line as well.

Appropriately, a change in Marlowe parallels this shift and reflects on the radical claims he initially made for the narrative. Openly scornful of the sensationalistic pulp fiction Adrienne edits—magazines like *Lurid Detective* and *True Horror Tales*—he proudly notes that his writing differs because it is "based on a true case." As his introduction emphasizes, Marlowe stands for the truth of experience, which he sees as our access to "the real thing." So when Adrienne tells him how to investigate Chrystal's disappearance—"I read a story once about a killer who left clues," she offers—he cuts her off with a disdainful remark that measures the difference between his experiential world and her read one: "*That* was a story." However, this pattern later reverses when Marlowe anticipates that Mildred may be setting a trap for him. "I read a story once," he remarks, as he plots to leave a trail of rice for Adrienne and the police to follow. That his remark is more than just a comment on Adrienne's attitude can be seen in the narra-

tive's resolution. When Kane demands an explanation of the whole
Kingsby case, Marlowe brushes him aside with an announcement of
his new occupation: "I'll write it and see that you get the first copy out
of the typewriter."

While this version might differ from the truth of experience, as
Marlowe has said the "read" usually does, it marks his new perspective, as the film's nonsubjective epilogue certifies. Marlowe, we learn,
will move to New York and become a writer, doing stories based on his
experiences, which Adrienne will then edit into publishable form.
Perhaps this pairing represents a new and desirable synthesis, a literature of truth born from the marriage between a man of experience
and vision and a woman of print and pulp literature, between one who
knows "the real thing" and another who understands how to shape
and sell it. At least this seems the recuperation the film wants to
suggest: a subversive stance certified through its embrace by a status
quo that is itself radically altered for the better.

This compromise, however, masks a retreat from the film's initial
vantage, for it hints that the detective's plain view of truth *needs* such
shaping and translating. In Marlowe's early comment, "I'd decided I'd
write about murder; it's safer. Besides, they tell me the profits are
good," we might see an awareness of this situation and a readiness to
compromise his truth-teller's role for a "safer," more profitable occupation. At any rate, the conclusion, with Marlowe and Adrienne
leaving the sordid world of Los Angeles for New York, also implies an
abandoning of the detective's role, along with its realistic point of view
that promised to make his writing different and valuable. While a
social self may have been fashioned and a social structure reaffirmed
here, these achievements thus come at some cost. If the detective is
indeed important to society, his ability to act and his access to truth
affirming what Cawelti terms "the myth of individualistic justice" able
to overcome "the power of evil and chance in the world,"[19] Marlowe's
prying private eye and solitary action remain at odds with his new
cultural role. As a result, those traits must either be discarded or
adapted to a social—or economically profitable—end. Marlowe's marriage and choice of a stable literary life suggest such a taming of the
detective's potentially threatening, asocial aspect. And that result mirrors the film's compromised nature, for with detection itself aban-
doned, we sense how much of the truth of human experience must
remain "something else," beyond the private eye's prying, revealing
gaze.

The film's conclusion in a conventional "objective" view of Marlowe
and Adrienne underscores this compromise. Releasing us from the

subjective and its promise of "the real thing," this shift returns us to the film's starting point, a place apparently sanctioned for Marlowe's supposedly subversive narration. This shift not only suggests that the narrative is all a sort of performance of Marlowe's "writing," but it also appropriates the subjective vantage's unconventional, supposedly radical thrust as a kind of "special effect," a contained and calculated sensation of a type appropriate to the very pulp literature and popular style Marlowe has scorned. Given the disconcerting effect of its subjectivity, the film in this way frames and defuses a technique that has proven both useful and challenging. That technique has spotlighted the manner and manipulations of popular narrative, and even used Kingsby Publications' lurid magazines to suggest popular film's own patterns. But even as we metaphorically glimpse film's preoccupation with marketing, audience appeal, and, above all, profits, the subjective technique also argues for this particular film's *difference* through its concern with "the real thing." Meanwhile, the labyrinth that leads within, the enigma of the self and the world it inhabits, briefly surfaces, only to be effaced by narrative's end. It is thus fitting that Marlowe's final address strikes a chord of reassurance rather than subversion, for in the tradition of cinematic contradiction, it can both certify a return of normalcy in the film and also assure us that "the real thing" has indeed been served.

In the wake of *Lady in the Lake*, as we shall see, other *films noir* pursued this subjective path with varying effectiveness. However, no subsequent film attempted the degree of subjectivity *Lady* did. *Possessed* (1947), for example, contains only one long subjective sequence, and it allots that perspective to the film's deranged heroine, as she is wheeled into a hospital and confronted with a coldly detached, rational world. In *Dark Passage* (1947) the sporadic point-of-view scenes belong to an outcast, escaped criminal who cannot prove his innocence, so his vantage signals his position outside normal society. *The Dark Past* (1948) combines these circumstances; its short subjective scenes represent the dream visions of a killer who, the film's psychologist narrator notes, is criminally insane and unable to function properly within society. The very partialness of these perspectives, their use in otherwise largely conventional narratives, not only distinguishes these films from *Lady in the Lake* but also contributes to their effectiveness and audience acceptability. For those partial vantages become emblematic of possible but *aberrant* variations in how we see our world. In general, they never quite displace the normal or directly assault our sense of reality and self.

Equally telling are the associations the subjective takes on in these films. It signals an outsider's view, one far different from that of a private eye who, if alienated from his world, also represents its most deeply held values. The later films in this mode link the point-of-view shot to a derangement, criminality, or alienation that is mysterious, complete, and open to no real recuperation. It thereby hints of a self that has become inexplicably trapped in a labyrinth, tormented by gaps in understanding, and prey to "something else" that we can never quite identify, save that we sense—and indeed *hope*—it could not possibly be "the real thing" our experiences outside of the movies have acquainted us with. These films do present a mystery, but with the exception of *Dark Passage* it is not *our* mystery; rather, it is an experience of enigma we can relish with little sense of responsibility, in a return to the sort of voyeuristic vantage that the subjective's radical thrust at truth might have challenged.

In *Lady in the Lake* what Vernet terms the "defensive structures"—of the movies, the moviegoing audience, and the culture that produced these images—are all overturned to some extent, but that assault, at least initially, works too well, strikes too close to home, that is, to our sense of normalcy in all these realms. If the detective's chief task, as Cawelti argues, is to carry out a "quest for justice" and to reassert an order in his world,[20] he cannot easily do so if both he and the everyday world, the spectator's world, are linked to the enigmatic and the labyrinthine, or if he is himself seen as a figure of violation. Such associations jeopardize the very structures he must ultimately save or reinforce, and in the process jeopardize the popular function of the detective narrative as well. For these reasons, *Lady* reaches for a rather unconvincing reinforcement, although one that points up just how tenuous our cinematic and cultural hold on "the real thing" actually is. What this film's subjectivity does successfully show, despite the recuperative structures that qualify and control its effect, then, is a vision of the depths that tug at both our sense of self and the narratives we fashion to disguise that powerful pull.

NOTES

1. For a discussion of the technical developments that influenced the *noir* stylistic, see Salt's chapter on "Film Style and Technology in the Forties," in his *Film Style and Technology*, pp. 287–308, and Kerr's "Out of What Past?"

2. Accounts of Welles's subjective camera project can be found in Higham's *Films of Orson Welles;* Rosenbaum's "Voice and the Eye: A Commentary on the *Heart of Darkness* Script"; Leaming's *Orson Welles,*

pp. 174–80; and especially Carringer's *Making of "Citizen Kane,"* pp. 1–15.

3. Carringer, "Orson Welles and Gregg Toland," p. 658.

4. For a discussion of MGM's financial situation, see Gomery's *Hollywood Studio System.* In 1946, Gomery reports, the net profits for Loews, Inc., MGM's parent company, were 17.9 million dollars, an increase of 5 million dollars over the previous year.

5. Review of *The Lady in the Lake, New York Times,* 24 Jan. 1947: 18.

6. Brinton, "Subjective Camera or Subjective Audience?" p. 360.

7. Ibid., p. 360.

8. Bonitzer, "Partial Vision: Film and the Labyrinth," p. 58.

9. Ibid.

10. Vernet, "Filmic Transaction," pp. 6–7.

11. Moreno, "Subjective Camera and the Problem of Film in the First Person," pp. 357–58.

12. Serres, *Hermes: Literature, Science, and Philosophy,* p. 83.

13. As an indicator of how Adrienne embodies and objectifies the larger tensions operating here in both the characters and the subjective mechanism, we might consider a scene in which she stands before the mirror in her apartment, her back to it as she glares at Marlowe, who is reflected in the mirror and thus physically present for us as he is in few other scenes. Her arms behind her in a gesture that suggests simultaneously her vulnerability and her defiance, she seems to challenge Marlowe to unravel her mystery. The ambiguity surrounding her is thrust home by the suggestive images that flank her robe-clad, alluring figure. On one side, her hand reaches toward a flat, sculpted shell that suggests Venus and female sexuality; and on the other, her arm directs our gaze to a series of phallic glass wedges that recall the threatening masculinity she has already evidenced. With Marlowe objectified here, she thus becomes the repository of the enigmatic, as if made to bear the weight of mystery that has previously attended the point of view itself.

14. Marshall, "*Lady in the Lake:* Identification and the Drives," p. 40.

15. Cawelti, *Adventure, Mystery, and Romance,* p. 107.

16. Vernet, "Filmic Transaction," p. 8.

17. Luhr, "Raymond Chandler and *The Lady in the Lake,*" p. 30.

18. See Renov's "*Raw Deal,*" p. 19. His point about the female character as "a metaphor for style itself" derives from Derrida's *Spurs: Nietzsche's Styles.*

19. Cawelti, "*Chinatown* and Generic Transformation," in Mast and Cohen, *Film Theory and Criticism,* p. 509.

20. Ibid., p. 504.

7

Seeing in a *Dark Passage*

Ever see any botched plastic jobs?
—*Dark Passage*

As its title hints, *Dark Passage* (1947) offers one of the blacker, more disturbing visions in the *noir* canon. It is a film that not only speaks threats, as the remark above suggests, but links those threats to its subjective technique. Embodying that subjectivity is escaped convict Vincent Parry, whose face is on every newspaper's front page; for him every look, each random glance seems menacing, freighted with a promise of recognition and recapture. Against that menace, plastic surgery seems his only hope to eliminate the face everyone is looking for. But qualifying that hope is his fear of the surgery's outcome. That fear surfaces in a dream, wherein Parry's point of view becomes a nightmare montage of pregnant glances, menacing looks, and large, disembodied eyes—all tied to his fear of, as the surgeon ominously puts it, a "botched plastic job" that could distort his identity, making him "look like a bulldog . . . or a monkey." What makes this fear more significant is that Parry has already undergone one botched job, in the trial that unjustly turned him into a kind of freak, a convicted murderer for whom every look is threatening. In fact, his fugitive status is the primary motivation of his subjective gaze, which in turn symbolizes this prior misidentification and mutilation of the self. His dream, then, both reflects Parry's own anxiety and points toward a larger concern we have observed in other subjective narratives with how we see and are seen, and with how these varying perspectives affect our sense of self.

As the previous chapters have noted, the *film noir* adopted various strategies for questioning our normal perspective. Typically, the form paints the familiar urban environment in disturbingly dark colors, making the everyday seem suddenly menacing. The subjective point of view that dominates *Dark Passage*'s first half, though, goes a step further by linking how we see the *world* with how *we* are perceived.

It thereby raises a potentially threatening question about the self: whether our sense of identity is a culturally given or self-determined thing. In fact, its investigation into the nature of identity most clearly distinguishes this film from its subjective-technique precursors and illustrates what was probably the most complex line of development this narrative style took.

Although released just eight months after *Lady in the Lake* and the last *noir* to make extensive *narrative* use of subjectivity, *Dark Passage* is seldom seen in the same stylistic light as the earlier film. When it is discussed at all, usually because of its pragmatic application of the subjective,[1] it is treated as another instance of Hollywood turning the avant-garde to a conservative end. Most historians see its subjective technique as just a clever way around a narrative dilemma posed by the film industry's star system. Since Humphrey Bogart, who plays the fugitive Parry, was one of the period's preeminent stars, the film's makers faced an especially difficult task in suggesting a pre- and post-plastic surgery leading man. Certainly, no disguise would look quite natural on Bogart's face or prove acceptable to his many fans. But with the subjective camera, director Delmer Daves could circumvent the problems that arise when a nearly iconic figure must appear—and work convincingly—in the role of a man with two faces.

While this practical strategy works effectively and results in a style that adds significantly to the film's themes, contemporary reaction suggests that it was little appreciated, partly because, unlike in *Lady in the Lake,* the subjective was used sporadically. Bosley Crowther, for instance, felt that Daves merely "confused things by using a subjective camera at the start, so that it sees things as through the eyes of a fugitive," before settling down "to the conventional use later on."[2] Drawing on our observations about the earlier subjective-camera films, we might speculate that the real source of confusion lies less in the shift from a subjective to a conventionally "objective" vantage after Parry's surgical bandages are removed than in the kind of spectator placement and identification that results. After all, the film situates our point of view not in a detective or conventionally heroic persona, as in *Lady in the Lake,* but in the alienated figure of a convicted murderer and fugitive who can never shed his outcast status. As a result, there is a level on which the misidentification Parry feels as an unjustly convicted murderer models our own unease at the forced union of our perspective with his. So our attitude toward the world we see is darkly colored from the start, and in light of the failure of Parry's surgery to alter his predicament along with his face, to grant him real freedom from proscription and pursuit, abandoning the subjective does little to alleviate the anxiety created by our initial identification.

The film's opening sequence establishes a pattern of boundaries and their violation that characterizes this relationship between seeing and identity as the rest of the narrative develops it. As *Dark Passage* opens, a slow pan from left to right introduces San Quentin prison and surveys its impregnable nature: the surrounding water, the prison's broad walls, a guard tower, and finally a guard with rifle held ready. However, another pan in the same direction then undercuts this initial note of limitation. It shows a road leading away from the prison, and moving along it a truck loaded with steel drums, in one of which someone is crouched. These parallel camera movements evoke an imposing cultural boundary, but then question it by showing a possibility for escape or transgression, almost as if preparing us for the stylistic transgression that follows, as the film shifts—or escapes—from the objective vantage of classical narrative to the subjective point of view that dominates the succeeding scenes.

When the film shifts to the subjective, though, it also establishes the problem of identity involved here. As its occupant rocks the drum in which he is hiding off the truck and down a hill, we take his point of view, seeing from inside the drum as it rolls and sharing the disorienting vantage that results. But when the drum comes to rest, the sense of disorientation lingers, for the camera stays inside it while its occupant, whom we only see from the back, staggers out. The shot suggests a distance that attaches even to visual identification—a level on which the character whose point of view we share remains estranged from us.

Once the perspective of this stranger, Parry, takes over, that tension again translates into an interplay between limitation and escape. Reprising the initial series of pan shots, Parry scans the countryside looking for an escape route, but all he sees is a blocked road, as several motorcycle patrolmen race by. While a subsequent pan in the opposite direction suggests a possible escape route by revealing another road onto which Parry frantically scrambles, this effort at boundary crossing is pointedly qualified, conditioned by subjective glimpses of a bordering fence, of Parry's hand tentatively grasping the fence rail, and his anxious voice-over comment, "I've got to start taking chances." Of course, we might expect the anxiety level to increase here, since the initially detached, objective point of view has given way to an involved, subjective one, that of a fugitive and social outcast. But the ease with which a road can seem by turns an escape route, a barrier to freedom, and an unknown realm in which one must take "chances" suggests the tension that marks this world and colors all seeing here—our own and Parry's. So even as Parry searches for a way out, his perspective emphasizes how he remains bound within this world, how the blank space that he inhabits via his subjective gaze—and that we inhabit through him—is not a space of total freedom, despite its location outside the film frame, but another prison of sorts linked to his identity. It stylistically embodies the San Quentin—as well as the misidentification that put him in prison—from which he continually flees.

Dark Passage's introductory sequence thus sets up a complex relationship between seeing and identity endemic to its subjective "gimmick." As the narrative centers around Parry's searching gaze, ever alert for pursuit or a look of recognition, it also increasingly underlines a disturbing instability, lodged stylistically in the absence of that point of view from the screen, and thematically in Parry's fugitive status. Through his subjective vantage Parry essentially disappears, his narrative presence shifting into what Pascal Bonitzer refers to as "blind space"—the area outside of the camera's field of view.[3] And this stylistic escape parallels Parry's desire to evade the imprisonment society has dictated. However, the fallout from the retreat into blind space is a pervasive sense of "enigma or suspense"[4] that carries over to our own placement here, and thus to our sense of identity. Despite our status as culture-bound beings, then, we find it hard to embrace that absent identity, particularly given the classical tradition, in which identity and viewer identification are so fundamentally intertwined.

Besides, there is another stylistic marker here that stands in the way of any self-effacement and hints at the inescapability of identity. To function as a point of view, after all, a subjective camera must repeatedly remind us of its fictional embodiment; for without the appropriate cues, our *sense* of the subjective wears off, dissolves into a traditional third-person view. Thus marginal views of Parry's hand and arm, noted in the previous pan shots, frequently cue us to his presence. As we noted in *Lady in the Lake*, though, the exchanged glance, the look of outward regard by another character, bears the main burden in this regard, linking the narrative's outside or blind space to the inside, on-screen space the protagonist occupies in classical narrative. It is especially through the pattern of exchanged looks that *Dark Passage* develops a crucial relationship between seeing and identity, suggesting both the longing for freedom or escape that drives Parry and the persistent power of placement—of recognition, capture, and imprisonment—that characterizes the world in which he moves, much as it does the circumstances in which we usually view films.

Logically, this pattern of exchanged glances initially centers on

Parry, for whom every look is a potentially identifying, accusatory one, and every subjective gaze informed by a level of visual paranoia. The early scenes in which someone confronts and questions him particularly emphasize how his point of view opens onto a question of identity. Parry's subjective view introduces three characters who by turns offer help for and threaten his escape: Baker, who gives him a ride after his jailbreak; Irene Jansen, who picks him up and conceals him after his fight with Baker; and Sam the cab driver, who directs him to a plastic surgeon. While each one offers a needed ride that takes him further away from San Quentin, each also quickly recognizes Parry and gazes at him in a seemingly threatening way. Their repeated looks into the camera suggest how every gaze is potentially cognitive, binding Parry into this world and the imprisonment it has prescribed for him. More than just indicators of his point of view, then, these reciprocal looks contribute to a pervasive paranoia around the look; they fashion a fear of recognition and placement within the false identity of a murderer that society has forced on him. In effect, each of these stylistic cues reveals a drama of identity being played out here, for each carries a threat to misidentify, by seeing in a culturally determined way, and through that misidentification to recast in Parry's psyche the prison he has just fled. These paired or exchanged glances thus point up a fundamental limit to identity—its dependence on how we see ourselves *and* how others see us—here embodied in Parry's fear of being seen for who he is and what he is not.

In a ripple effect, this pattern of glances, as well as its freight of estrangement and anxiety, extends from Parry to various other, similarly alienated characters. In fact, it is this nexus of threatening looks and misidentifications that ultimately makes *Dark Passage* one of the most disturbing *films noir*. After Irene picks Vincent up, for instance, his fear of the exchanged look transfers to her, for in helping him she gains a measure of guilt, becoming misidentified with a murderer. Appropriately, at this point Parry's subjective view temporarily stops, as Irene hides him under some canvases she has been painting—hides him under her "perspective," as it were. But in driving Vincent to her apartment, Irene experiences the same menacing looks he has. First, at a roadblock she exchanges glances with a policeman, who questions her and perfunctorily searches the car; next, with a motorcycle patrolman, who follows her car, pulls alongside, and stares at her; and then with that patrolman and a tollbooth attendant, who also questions her. As a stand-in for her hidden passenger, Irene thus runs a gamut of accusing glances that emphasizes the boundaries she has crossed—a roadblock, a tollbooth, society's proscriptions against helping a convict; and those boundaries underscore how she has compromised her own identity in concealing Parry's. Her assumption of his place in this chain of visual exchanges hints that they occupy a similar place in society. But it is a fitting connection since, as we later learn, she too is haunted by a misidentification and bound by the past—by the memory of her father's conviction for a murder he did not commit. Her efforts on Parry's behalf are motivated by her desire to dispel this haunting past and overcome the boundaries that proscribe her life too.

This pattern applies to Sam the cab driver as well, who also recognizes Parry and sees something of himself in the fugitive. After Vincent's initial subjective view of Sam, we watch the two in medium shot through the cab's windshield, Sam looking ahead but glancing at his rider from time to time via the rearview mirror, and Parry watching his interrogator while trying to stay hidden in the shadows of the back seat. A single subjective shot, showing Sam's head in the lower left of the frame and his eyes in the mirror in the upper right, objectifies the sense of menace that has previously attached to such exchanged glances, but in a way that also suggests an ambiguity about Sam: he seems simultaneously the watched and the watcher, both vulnerable and threatening, much like Parry himself. And to reinforce that dual identity, a passing police cruiser makes Sam, like Irene, into a specular object and ironically calms Parry's fears. While Vincent hides in the backseat, Sam exchanges glances with the police, as Irene did, presenting himself in place of his fare as the object of their suspicious scrutiny. Explaining this sympathetic action, Sam remarks that "From faces I can tell a lot." It is a reply that, in the context of his later "I study people's faces," strengthens the link to Parry by emphasizing how he too constantly watches and sizes up people. But perhaps more important, it suggests at least a possibility for proper identification and a level on which the gaze need not be defined by a nexus of fear and menace.

This brief displacement of Parry's vantage into conventional shots of others who share his experience accomplishes two tasks. First, it immediately links Parry and his fugitive status to many of the people he meets, so that he becomes emblematic of others who have been similarly misidentified or denied an identity by their culture or by circumstance. Irene, for example, responds to Vincent's remarks about his isolation by noting how she feels as if she "was born lonely," and recalling how impotent she felt in the face of that powerful cultural mechanism, the judicial system, when first her father and then Parry were tried: "I wanted to help . . . but all I could do was write crazy letters." Sam strikes an identical note when he confesses how "a guy gets lonely driving a cab." Skeptical, Vincent responds in a way that describes his own problem: "What's lonely about it? You *see* people." Of course, seeing people—and possibly being seen—is Parry's curse, as he subtly echoes Sartre's comment in *No Exit* that "Hell is—other people."[5]

What Sam drives home, though, is something that Parry implicitly understands, namely, how seeing and a sense of self can seem quite at odds. Thus he explains, "I pick people up and drive them places, but they never talk to me." Although Sam indeed *sees* people, they act as if he does not exist, denying him an identity even as his look apparently begs for acknowledgment and identification. Parry too longs to be seen, but without the misjudgment and condemnation that is his lot; that is, he longs to be recognized for what he really is, an innocent and ordinary individual. The problem, as we have already noted, is that seeing implies certain limitations. For instance, the world Parry inhabits judges, identifies, and condemns largely on the basis of appearances, and it values little such supplements as Irene's "crazy letters" or Vincent's pleas of innocence. It is a situation that resonates for the cinematic world we inhabit as well, as it points to a disparity between what we are and what we see on the screen, between the identity we bring to the movies and the cultural image we view, that in which the films strive to place—or misidentify—us.

Dana Polan has hinted at a second effect of this shifting perspective when he describes it as a "mutation" of classical film narrative. Because of this shift, he offers, "the narrative and the image come apart, refusing to provide any but the most meager of certainties and centerings"[6] about the people we see or the world depicted. While aptly indicating *Dark Passage's* divergence from a classical model, this notion of unraveling needs qualification. In light of the developed relationship between Parry's point of view and the film's pervasive sense of misidentification, loneliness, and alienation, we might see the narrative as struggling for a different kind of centering that speaks directly of this longing for identity. In fact, what center there is here resides in the gaze, in the anxious, often suspicious, and questioning look that recurs, and in so doing signals this world's anxiety. In this way, Parry's subjective gaze merges into a thematic development of limitation and longing.

Even as it works against a conventionally "centered" narrative, then, the shifting subjective vantage here seems to project its image into the world around and to find its reflection in the people with whom Parry mingles and increasingly finds something in common—particularly that they feel as misperceived and consigned to society's periphery as he does. The anxiety-laden looks with which *Dark Passage* abounds, therefore, not only create a sense of fragmentation and alienation but they also underscore how its subjective effects and narrative decentering contribute to the notion of a shared, if unwelcome, social identity. For the world this film describes, finally, is one populated by various sorts of isolates, prisoners, and fugitives from imprisonment, a human panorama of what Robert Porfirio terms the "existential identity" of *film noir*.[7]

What finally saves Parry from recapture and imprisonment, though, is not a special talent for seeing nor, analogously, the ability of the subjective viewer to stay out of frame. It is, in fact, that network of similarly lonely and isolated types he discovers. Besides Irene and Sam, this group includes Dr. Walter Coley, the unlicensed plastic surgeon who lives and works in a walk-up apartment on a dark side street, and George Fellsinger, who prefaces his offer of a place to hide with the comment that Parry is "the only person who ever liked me." Yet another such isolate, a night watchman, accidentally helps Parry escape from a detective who recognizes him in a diner. The film's penultimate scene shows the importance of these characters. As Parry waits for a bus to the Mexican border and freedom, he anxiously eyes a policeman checking the depot and overhears a conversation which a middle-aged man, alone and apparently down on his luck, strikes up with a similarly dispirited woman seated nearby. The woman nods approvingly as the man laments the general isolation of people in modern society; "There was a time when folks used to give each other a helping hand," he offers. In their shared recognition of this problem and of their mutual plight, though, this man and woman find a measure of reassurance and a common ground of understanding that prompts the man's final, affirmative remark, "We've got something in common; we're both alone." This qualified affirmation, despite circumstance, not only prepares for a later scene with the man and woman seated together on the bus, smiling as they apparently head off to share a new future, but it also suggests how *Dark Passage* tries to recuperate its most disturbing elements by locating a sense of society and of new identity, even amid its images of a pervasive isolation and alienation.

The widespread misidentification and denied identity that we see, though, helps explain why the subjective camera's exit after Parry's plastic surgery has such little effect on the narrative. Parry's physical transformation, which motivates this stylistic shift, only marks the point at which he becomes irretrievably bound to the cultural identity unjustly imposed on him. After tracing him to Irene's apartment, Baker identifies the new Parry and tries to blackmail him by threatening to expose Irene as his accomplice. But in struggling with his tormentor, Parry *becomes* a killer by accidentally throwing Baker over a cliff. Still hoping to square himself with the law, Vincent then confronts his late wife's best friend Madge, who, he realizes, is responsible for framing him and sending him to prison. When she refuses to sign a confession, he offers a comment that points up another transformation underway: "In every paper in the country I'm a killer. I never thought it possible to kill anybody until this minute." More than a threat to prompt Madge's cooperation, his statement amounts to a recognition of the predetermined, "fated" role he seems bound to—a role immediately corroborated when Madge backs up and accidentally falls to her death from the apartment window.

In one way, this death neatly resolves the narrative, since it almost providentially achieves a measure of justice and revenge, without imposing an avenger's action and guilt on Parry and further troubling our identification with him. At the same time, though, her fatal plunge plunges Vincent into a hopeless position. For her disappearance— literally into thin air—mocks his desire to reappear in society, his name cleared. It also renders his own disappearance essential, since he will predictably be charged with Madge's death too, and without her, as she had taunted him, "you can't prove anything, because I'm the proof." Ironically, then, this guiltless revenge only solidifies his guilt in society's eyes and leaves Vincent feeling even more trapped by circumstances. His identity as a "killer," trumpeted by every newspaper headline, is only strengthened, given all the more appearance and authority of fact in the absence of his person and of a voice to counter this dominant discourse.

It is a situation Madge predicted when Vincent first revealed himself to her; prophetically, she told him, "You'll never be able to prove anything because I won't be there." His curiously parallel rejoinder, "You'll never get away from me because I won't let you out of my sight," not only suggests the narrative's heavily ironic character[8] but also those limitations on "sight" *Dark Passage* repeatedly scores. Earlier, we noted a distinctive feature of Parry's point of view, how it seems to open by turns on the possibility of escape and entrapment, and thus constantly to point up an anxiety that surrounds seeing and being seen. This tension afflicts those around Parry as well, who similarly display an apprehensive, even suspicious, gaze that is the badge of their own alienation, the very look of isolation. With it, the individual holds others at a distance, ever suspicious of their motives. And through this look the individual tries to avoid or control the contingencies of his world, even to escape its most disturbing boundary, an ambiguity or indeterminacy that besets the sense of self.

Certainly Parry's effort to find his wife's real murderer fits this pattern, for what he is looking for is some reason in the improbability that he senses, a cause for the destructive misidentification he suffers from. Thus he tells Irene, "I've got the Indian sign on me. It seems I can't win. I've got to start out and prove who killed her." What he wants is a *visible* sign in place of the invisible one he senses, some evidence of the frame that has bound him to an identity, imprisoned him in San Quentin, and trapped him in a paranoid existence.[9] However, the ease with which such signs, especially the evidence he sorely wants, can simply slip away, even as he vows not to let it "out of my sight," shows the elusive nature of all certainty, even about the self, here. Starting from Parry's subjective, and thus different, view, *Dark Passage* draws out the real pain of difference, delineating the various levels of frustration that circumstance and cultural conditioning impose on seeing and on the self.

David Lavery has argued that such a connection between seeing and frustration is symptomatic of the anxiety we commonly experience in the modern world. Today, he says, "we feel the pain of an alienation unique in history. But alienation is simply another name for longing in an advanced, perhaps terminal stage."[10] He further suggests that longing in our culture, especially for some certainty about the self, is typically "eyeborn": "we long the way we do because we have given such prominence to our vision";[11] thus we surround ourselves with the very images of our desires. Through our seeing, in the movies no less than in our daily lives, we gauge our separation from the world and from those around us who, in contrast, seem to possess a secure and easy sense of identity or to inhabit a comfortable place of their own. Seen in this context, *Dark Passage*'s emphasis on Parry's anxious gaze and almost paranoid fear of every reciprocal look becomes a fitting way of evoking an alienation common to modern culture, as well as of modeling the interplay of desire and its frustration at work in the *film noir.*

But using the subjective in this way also brings several risks that suggest why this narrative method would find little further application. Given a forced identification with Parry's point of view, audiences naturally share his feelings of anxiety and displacement in a way that classical narrative never encouraged. As noted earlier, the resulting "confusion" critics like Crowther sensed probably derives as much from these imposed feelings as from the simple shift of subjective placement here. For the combined weight of a character's displacement from the screen and society can be an uncomfortable burden, one that makes viewers feel how tenuous their own situation is, especially how much it depends on a culturally permitted perspective, on how we too might be seen or even be rendered invisible by an attitude that works to maintain the status quo.

In the strained resolution *Dark Passage* achieves, we can detect an effort to counter this effect, much like the recuperative strategies found in *Murder, My Sweet* and *Lady in the Lake*. With a justice of sorts attained by Madge's and Baker's accidental deaths, Parry escapes across the Mexican border and then to Peru, where he hopes Irene will someday join him. Her appearance there at the film's end suggests a love triumphant over all circumstance. But it also seems like an affirmation in spite of events, certainly in spite of Parry's inability to prove his innocence and of the exile from both his country and his true identity that the couple must then endure. While Parry has escaped from a nexus of accusing and imprisoning glances, it is at such a great cost that his achievement rings hollow. For ultimately we sense just how binding that sense of placement and its attendant misidentification are, since he overcomes them only by a normally unacceptable, even impossible option: by abdicating from his culture and his identity, opting instead for a world in which he will always be a foreigner, the very embodiment of *alien*ation.

We have earlier discussed another risk to this narrative technique, one closely linked to our spectator placement. The subjective camera not only ties our view to a character's, it also emphasizes that film is always a directed—and hence manipulated—way of seeing. But as we also noted, part of the basic ideological task of classical narrative is to disguise "the process of representation itself, the investment of meanings as a material social process."[12] In calling attention to its directed vantage with a subjective camera, a film like *Dark Passage* threatens to reveal the mechanism of production; and that effect easily opens onto the sort of visually based paranoia Parry feels, potentially hinting at the manipulation of the film audience as well.

The final scene suggests an awareness of this narrative problem and an effort to recuperate it. At this point the film not only reverts to a conventionally objective vantage but also structures its resolution around its most disturbing feature, Parry's gaze. In a shot sequence that recalls Bogart's introduction in a more conventional narrative, *Casablanca* (1942), we see a drink brought to a table, a hand take it up, and then the formally dressed Parry, seated alone in a cafe, apparently at ease in his anonymity here. This "quoting" of the earlier film suggests one option available to the fugitive, as the film evokes a romantic soldier-of-fortune mythos of a sort associated with Bogart. At the same time, the sense of isolation and anonymity Parry projects resonates peculiarly in *Dark Passage*'s context. While singled out by the camera, he seems to be just another patron, quietly enjoying himself. Although it is the sort of anonymity that he had previously desired, Parry now seems in search of some identification, some look of outward regard, as the close-up of his gaze implies. Far different from his earlier anxious and fearful look, his gaze now appears purposeful, directed hopefully toward the cafe's entrance. In effect, his prior fear of eye contact has been replaced by a *desire* to see someone—Irene Jansen—who will see and identify him. The mutually happy exchange of glances that heralds her arrival, and which we view in a conventional shot-reaction-shot sequence, completes a transformation of the look here and reclaims a level of normalcy for the film. That transformation effectively pronounces the gaze—both Parry's and our own—innocent again, freed of the limits to seeing and being seen that *Dark Passage,* during its subjective portion, so disconcertingly revealed.

If the *film noir*'s experiment with subjective narrative was relatively short-lived, this may be mainly due to the disturbing implications that a film like *Dark Passage,* even with its pragmatic use of the technique, points up. For while the extended point-of-view shot effectively translated the human gaze as a measure of isolation and alienation, it seems, like the threatening figure of Madge here, to have operated too near the edge, too close to the bounds that limit our vision and condition our very sense of identity. As Bill Nichols suggests, though, every work of art holds two equally significant possibilities: "its potential to liberate/its threat to habituate."[13] In terms of their ability to reveal how we normally see our world, both within and outside of the film experience, the subjective *films noir* achieved some level of cinematic liberation; at least our perception of how certain types of film narrative work was potentially altered. But since its prosperity partly depended on fostering the normal conditions of production and representation, the American film industry also tended toward a standard of habituation, which translated into a reluctance for formal experimentation and an impulse to qualify or rein in its effects. While *Dark Passage* seems to want it both ways, it never convincingly reaches the expected level of habituation. But then that may be the surest sign of the film's achievement and of its important place in the *noir* canon. For in comparison to subjective camera predecessors like *Murder, My Sweet* and *Lady in the Lake*, it at times lets us see too much, and as a result speaks too clearly of how our seeing is conditioned and channeled by our nature and our culture. In this way, its subversive eye opened wide on the darkness that inspired the *noir* form, while also ensuring that this eye would seldom open in quite the same way again.

NOTES

1. See, for example, Bernard F. Dick's discussion of *Dark Passage*'s subjective technique in his *Anatomy of Film*, pp. 67–68.
2. Crowther, review of *Dark Passage*, p. 11.
3. Bonitzer, "Partial Vision: Film and the Labyrinth," p. 58.
4. Ibid., p. 59.
5. Sartre, *"No Exit" and Three Other Plays*, p. 47.
6. Polan, "Blind Insights and Dark Passages," p. 30. As Polan uses it, the notion of a "centering subject" represents a point of focus and identification that facilitates our access to and placement within the film narrative. I would argue that we are fundamentally "placed" here, in fact that *Dark Passage* is largely *about* our inevitable placement within society and a socially determined identity. In order to talk about placement in this way, though, the film necessarily had to take a new stylistic approach.
7. Porfirio, "No Way Out: Existential Motifs in the Film Noir," p. 216.
8. Overlooking the ironic value of such lines and occurrences, Polan simply attributes them to a breakdown in classical unity; as he offers, "the narrative of *Dark Passage* is one in which dramatic coincidences occur so often as to break any question of plausibility, of narrative as a logical unity." Of course, "plausibility" and narrative unity are hardly the same thing, and while *Dark Passage* may often seem to strain the former, there seems a most disconcerting logic to its narrative, one which Polan offers a glimpse of when he relates Sam's story of a man with a goldfish bowl to life as "a kind of bowl—where you can never escape bumping into someone who knows you." These elements fit most logically into the pattern of concerns noted here with seeing and being seen and with the threat to identity that accompanies the exchange of glances. See Polan's "Blind Insights and Dark Passages," p. 31.
9. In the introduction I cited a passage from a film made in the same year as *Dark Passage, Out of the Past.* Just before confronting a group of criminals who have set him up, the film's protagonist, Jeff Bailey, tells a cabdriver friend, "I think I'm in a frame [but] all I can see is the frame. I'm going in there now to look at the picture." It is a

comment worth repeating here, since it clearly echoes Parry's plight. The sense of a "frame" is pervasive in *noir* and is crucial to both of these films. Of equal significance, though, is the characters' similar longing to *know*, to discern whether they are simply victims of bad luck—"the Indian sign"—or if their stories are being told for them, related by some narrating, binding, framing force. What these and various other *films noir* similarly describe is a consuming, at times self-destructive, drive to see or tell (*Out of the Past* is a voice-over/flashback narrative) about these forces that seem to narrate us, and by so doing to effectively turn the tables on narration.

10. Lavery, "Eye of Longing," p. 25.
11. Ibid.
12. Nichols, *Ideology and the Image*, p. 2.
13. Ibid., p. 290.

8

The Transparent Reality of the Documentary *Noir*

The cinematic image grasps only a small part of the visible; and it is a grasp which—provisional, contracted, fragmentary—bears in it its impossibility.
—Jean-Louis Comolli[1]

If the subjective-camera *films noir* never quite gave us the sort of radical shift in cinematic style that some of the technique's proponents envisioned, it is partly because we tend to overestimate film's ability to make the real world visible. As Jean-Louis Comolli reminds us, even the seemingly most realistic films afford only a "fragmentary" grasp of our world, and that partial vision depends on a kind of narrative paradox. For while they appear to make the world newly visible, render its reality transparent, they only manage this feat by straddling film's limits, disguising "the very blindness which is at the heart of this visible."[2] We have already glimpsed traces of this strategy in several types of *noir* narrative, but it is crucial to the semidocumentaries that emerged in the immediate postwar era.

Films like *Boomerang* (1947), *T-Men* (1947), *The Naked City* (1948), and Henry Hathaway's many forays in the form, notably *The House on 92nd Street* (1945), *Kiss of Death* (1947), and *Call Northside 777* (1948), at first glance seem to do away with many of the period's usual narrative conventions—and constraints. In fact, like the subjective-camera *noirs,* they appear to take no pains to hide the cinematic mechanism. Rather, in a reflexive tendency unusual for the era, they often acknowledge and even appropriate that mechanism as part of their realistic strategy. This forthrightness combines with a pattern of voice-over/flashback, location shooting, archival footage, and factual story lines to produce what seems like a radically realistic technique for examining the modern scene. But as a closer examination shows, that combination lets these films play the cinematic game of transparency and disguise, of belief and disbelief, in a more complex way. For despite their elaborate armature of realism, they never quite avoid the limitations Comolli observes, and they leave us today with a sharp sense of how tenuously "real" even such "documentary" films can be.

Classical film narrative, of course, has its own arsenal for creating an impression of transparency or seamless realism. Through conventions of continuity editing, shot-reverse-shot sequences, and third-person point of view, for example, it implicitly argues that what we see is a dependable, truthful view of our world.[3] These practices allow traditional narratives to invoke what Colin MacCabe terms a "dominant discourse" of reality, wherein "the relationship between the reading [or viewing] subject and the real is placed as one of pure specularity. The real is not articulated—it is."[4] In short, we take the reality of what we see for granted. Our status as *viewing* subjects of a "pure specularity" lets us assume that a film's point of view is objective and primes us to accept unquestioningly what we see.

By the postwar period, though, this strategy had become strained. Audiences accustomed to the newsreel and documentary as a way of obtaining war information, impressed by the actuality of Italian neorealist films, and intrigued by the emerging *film noir's* realistic themes were ready for a new level of film realism, one successfully demonstrated by films like *The House on 92nd Street* and *Boomerang* and developed by directors like Hathaway and Elia Kazan, and the producer Louis de Rochemont. In fact, the appearance of these and a spate of similar films inspired *New York Times* critic Bosley Crowther, usually a conservative voice in film criticism, to call for an "extension of [their] documentary style" to "our average American films."[5] And indeed, a more realistic style, modeled on these films and indebted to the influences noted above, was clearly emerging.

The formula for the semidocumentary *noirs* seems most indebted to a pattern popularized by the newsreels, especially de Rochemont's *The March of Time*. Often credited with opening up a "creative" vein for the documentary film, de Rochemont had developed a formula that, as one critic describes it, involved "taking a story based on fact, photographing it in its actual locations, and producing a newsreel-like effect in a feature-length film."[6] More precisely, he fashioned a narrative of history and current events by combining normal newsreel material with stock footage, a narrating voice-over, and "the reenactment of an event so effectively that it simulates reality itself."[7] When he turned to feature films at Twentieth Century-Fox with productions like *The House on 92nd Street* and *13 Rue Madeleine* (1946), de Rochemont made this formula into a popular narrative model that in time would be copied by various *noir* filmmakers.

The earliest of these films, *The House on 92nd Street,* well illustrates the narrative pattern that emerged. With its true story line of the smashing of a German spy ring in wartime America, it might well have been a lengthened *March of Time* episode. As an introductory title tells us, it was "photographed in the localities of the incidents depicted, . . . wherever possible, in the actual places the original incidents occurred," and apart from the principal players, all of the FBI personnel seen in the film were actually employees of that agency. As a complement to this realistic texture, the film also incorporated footage of the real spies, originally taken by the FBI with hidden cameras, and that footage, thanks to the bridging effect of a voice-over narrator, blends smoothly into the narrative. Of course the story, "adapted from" government files, is hardly a mundane one. Even beyond the impact of wartime anxieties, the narrative offered a transvestite German spy and a leading man, Lloyd Nolan, who had already established a persona of sorts in various "B" detective films. De Rochemont and Hathaway wanted to link the documentary's reputation for truth and objectivity to the best standards of Hollywood narrative, especially to studio-quality cinematography and a classical narrative style. In the process, they developed a pattern already implicit in the *March of Time* series, wherein the concern with conveying fact is wed to Hollywood's prior and even primary commitment to an entertainment that would satisfy the public's tastes and desires.

As we might expect, that pattern did result in a somewhat problematic style. As John Tuska notes, "the *noir* visual style" of these films, which argues for their inclusion in the form, at times works in almost "direct contradiction to the narrative structure."[8] In fact, what signals their *semi*documentary status is a consistent and calculated slippage from a documentary "look." Repeatedly, films like *The House on 92nd Street, Boomerang,* and *Call Northside 777* shift from the conventions of narrative, *noir* lighting, and unusual camera angles to a realistic documentary style, as they set about making truth both dramatically effective and comfortably acceptable. One result of this shifting is a tension between scenes that by turns evoke the dark, expressionistic world of more conventional *films noir,* and the naturally lit location images we associate with documentary. In other instances, this tension centers on the film's subjects, as the narratives announce a broad social focus, such as juvenile delinquency or corruption, only to pursue it through a traditional strategy of character identification that makes the cultural concerns those of an individual with whom we identify and sympathize.

What these results suggest is a kind of compromise built into these films by their twin pull to both reveal and dominate truth, to appear transparent while filtering reality through a traditional narrative mechanism. So while these works, like other *films noir,* might expose the criminality and destructive desires at work in our culture, they usually do so in a nonthreatening way that distinguishes them from the darker *noir* mainstream. Yet they are not quite traditional narratives either, for they do make visible and talk in a straightforward, factual way about things that often went unseen or unsaid in conventional films. Moreover, they identify their subjects as neither purely fictional nor metaphoric, but as *representative* of real-life people, situations, and events, while they establish a distanced, omniscient voice *of history,* as it were—their voice-of-god narration—to introduce, comment upon, and link their various sequences that appear as if in flashback. In this way they draw on our tendency to valorize the real and on the authority of the seemingly objective, detached vantage we normally associate with the scientific method to qualify their treatment of a sordid subject matter and make its narratization seem like transparent documentation.

Of course, our popular narratives usually try to disguise contradiction and to represent, as Louis Althusser explains, "not the system of real relations which govern the existence of individuals, but the imaginary relation of those individuals to the real relations in which they live."[9] Despite their narrative compromises, though, the semidocumentaries threaten this task in a way that suggests their importance in American film history. For in the best *noir* tradition, they implicitly challenge how we see both the cinematic and the real world, and in the process promise to reveal the very shape of the imaginary. While counterbalancing the documentary impulse—and its subversive potential—with narrative might blunt this effect, it also forces on us a problematic, shifting perspective that threatens to point up film's controlled point of view and thus spoil the game of conventional film realism. Thus the blending of documentary mechanisms with narrative never quite produced the transparency or warrant of truth that these films initially seemed to promise.

Their curious solution to this tension becomes clear when we examine the pattern of contradiction in these films. For instance, while the initial titles explain that *The House on 92nd Street* contains such sensitive factual information that "it could not be made public until the first atom bomb was dropped," that *Boomerang* is "based on fact," and that *Call Northside 777* "is a true story," the films also point up their status as *cinematic constructs*. Thus the latter two films begin with tight close-ups not of the "case files" that supposedly inspired them but of the film scripts themselves. While *The Naked City* opens with an aerial shot of New York, offering a revealing vantage on the city, the accompanying voice-over is identified as that of Mark Hellinger, the film's producer, who tells how the actors "played out their roles on the streets, in the apartment houses, and in the skyscrapers of New York itself" and describes the locale that contributed this "true story" from among its store of eight million.

T-Men offers a more elaborate example. It moves from opening travelogue shots of Washington, D.C., to a medium shot of Mr. Elmer Lincoln Iren, former head of the Treasury Department's enforcement division, who looks directly into the camera and reads a prepared statement about his bureau's work. From this report, which he holds so we can see it (thus underscoring the *document*ary nature of his remarks), he cites statistics, outlines the present structure and duties of his arm of the Treasury Department, and recalls its past achievements, especially its part in smashing the Capone gang. But he then produces another file, which he describes as a "composite case"; it is, in effect, a narrative drawn from and relying for credence upon the sense of authority that has been so laboriously established. A dissolve bridges the shift from this real figure to an invisible voice-of-god narrator, who proceeds to recount this "composite." But what results is a composite not simply of various factual events or case histories but of fact and fiction, of naturalistic camera work and conventional narrative, as the film simultaneously attests to its discourse's truth *and* admits the filmmaker's shaping, intrusive hand. While we might interpret this strategy of gradually moving from fact to fictional construct, or of introducing the filmscript drawn from a case history, as the triumphant possession of narrative by what Michel Foucault terms discourse's "will to truth,"[10] it also suggests another facet of that will to truth, namely, a tendency to disguise its impelling forces and desires.[11] It is a strategy that points to the basic pattern of these films, as they establish a basis of truth that opens onto fiction but then mask the jointure by producing another level of apparent truth, one paradoxically sourced in their cinematic nature.

In effect, the documentary *noir*'s realism depends on a kind of reflexive posture, as it acknowledges its filmic mechanism or mirrors it in the element that is normally its primary disguise—the narrative. Thus films like *The House on 92nd Street, Boomerang, T-Men, The Naked*

City, and *Call Northside 777* invoke what seems like a narrative para-dox: although fictions, they attack the fictive in order to assert their own truth; and while asserting the unbiased, even uncinematic nature of their documentary eye, they evoke the filmic apparatus by describ-ing how a technology of observation and communication lets them accurately record and assess reality. By so doing, they *certify* their point of view, mark off a space of truth that seems transparent and beyond question simply because it has already been admitted and implicitly questioned.

The House on 92nd Street, for example, not only recounts a true spy story, it shows the hidden movie cameras used in the government's surveillance of the spies and even incorporates some of the footage those cameras produced. Similarly, *T-Men* surveys the various observa-tion techniques employed by the Treasury Department to fight crime and protect the citizenry, while also showing how its own prying eyes— the T-men—are usually monitored to ensure their protection. Of course *The Naked City,* with its reflexive commentary about "the motion picture you are about to see" delivered by the producer as he describes his film's level of realism, represents this strategy's most straightfor-ward development. These films and others like them typically let us glimpse the cinematic apparatus at work, either metaphorically or directly, by way of verifying their ability to record reality and access its truth. By making us aware of film's usually obscured relationship to the real, they can then reassure us on some fundamental, if unex-amined, level that their own view is reliable and revealing.

Boomerang, described by James Agee as the best of these "locale" films,[12] clearly illustrates this strategy. From its initial establishing shot, it announces a desire to offer a revealing, transparent vantage. As an anonymous narrator notes that "the basic facts of our story happened in a Connecticut community much like this one," we view a dizzying 360-degree pan of a bustling downtown area. This unusual circular shot immediately asserts a kind of transparency; it suggests that we can see everything, as if nothing could be withheld from our sweep-ing, high-angle view of the town's life. Of course, the camera's own privileged position, which is also the narrator's, remains concealed, not outside but unperceived, there at the very center of the panorama we view. This curious shot thereby hints of an inside that will remain outside here, a part of the cityscape in this case that cannot be seen because it is our own point of view, although rendered invisible by the very camera movement that seems designed to suggest how compre-hensive our perspective is. In this initial effect we glimpse the double nature of the vantage of these films, as they ideologically turn the inside out, implying how our view from within the culture might easily open onto an objective and factual vision of our world.

Reinforcing the sense of a comprehensive and transparent view is the focus on two sorts of activity that follow the murder of a clergyman in this Connecticut town. First, documentary-style footage details the police work that Reverend George Lambert's death sets in motion: rounding up witnesses, searching for clues, questioning suspects. It is the sort of surface perspective newsreel audiences were used to, one complemented here by a series of montage effects common to both documentary and narrative film that traces the investigation's lack of progress: inserts of newspaper headlines and editorial cartoons criticizing the police's ineffectiveness, juxtaposed with shots of various townsfolk—firemen, customers in a barbershop, people by their radios, reporters discussing the case, women hanging their wash—all eager for a solution to the crime that has upset the entire community.

With the comments of these townsfolk, the film slips into the realm of traditional narrative; but even as it does, it also implies, as if in compensation, its access to another level of truth usually unseen by the documentary eye. Thus in the style of classical narrative, we glimpse the political turmoil that has developed around the case and become fundamentally linked to it. From a close-up of a headline reporting the state legislature's call for action, the film cuts to a reaction shot of Police Chief Robinson, remarking that his murder investigation is "turning into a political three-ring circus." Besides linking the documentarylike scenes of investigation to the narrative proper, this shift gives us privileged knowledge of a political struggle between the Reform party in power, which finds the police failure embarrassing in an election year, and the opposition party, headed by newspaper owner T. M. Wade, who sees the floundering investigation as a great opportunity for propaganda and an opening for his return to power. Even as the narrator describes the "overzealousness of the public," then, we see *through* this commotion, in a way the public cannot, to the larger issues at stake here, while we also recognize how much of the truth of this situation remains blocked from the public's eye, because they lack the encompassing perspective the narrative purports to offer.

Even as it looks beneath the investigation's surface to sketch this world's complexity, though, the film also insinuates how elusive truth remains. On the level of the investigation, for instance, a montage of suspects being rounded up is accompanied by a voice-over comment on "the nebulous figure conceived in the minds of the seven witnesses," a figure so vague that "the mere fact of wearing a dark coat with a light hat" became sufficient cause for arrest. For this reason, even after several witnesses pick John Waldron, a vagrant, from a lineup, Chief Robinson hesitates to claim a breakthrough in the case; as he cautiously puts it, "All I've got is a guy." And despite political pressure, State's Attorney Henry Harvey is equally cautious in prosecuting the case. The police psychiatrist's inability to identify Waldron as a "homicidal type" troubles him, and his eagerness to see a ballistics report on Waldron's gun, the product of what he terms "a more exact science," emphasizes his desire to find a reliable truth. As a result, Harvey's subsequent and repeated comment that "it seemed like a well nigh perfect case" does not so much reassure as hint of an uneasiness he feels and a depth of truth that continues to evade the documentary eye.

Underscoring this sense of uncertainty is the film's political focus, that shows how guilt and innocence have become almost irrelevant to those in power. Seen relaxing at his country club, T. M. Wade seems detached from events and little concerned with truth; as golfers play in the far background, he sits in shade and comfort, telling his employees how to aid Waldron's defense: "I don't care if he's guilty or not. I've got an election to win, and the only way I can do that is to make Harvey look bad." The Reform party, though, reveals a disturbingly similar attitude. Public Works Commissioner Paul Harris, for instance, reminds Harvey that "we have to win an election, and to do it we need a conviction." When Harvey is noncommittal and outlines the troubling ambiguities of his case, the narrative opens onto still another level of truth connected to these political machinations, as Harris pulls a gun and threatens Harvey because he fears a threatened government investigation might expose his illegal practices—reveal the reform that is not reform but corruption itself. What *Boomerang* attempts to do at every level, in fact, is to *admit* the possibility of uncertainty, ambiguity, limited perspective, but ultimately only to counter that potential by showing how its broad and penetrating view affords another, deeper level of truth in compensation.

On a larger, structural level as well, *Boomerang* demonstrates this strategy of testifying to its own integrity while admitting the sense of doubt and anxiety to which such *films noir* usually spoke. The grand jury hearing that makes up the film's last third points up this effect, by forming a second level of voice-over/flashback narration, coming from Harvey's address to the jury. The resulting series of flashbacks essentially mirrors and affirms the film's original narrative voice. While it admits that Father Lambert's murder remains unsolved, it dramatically illustrates the unpopular truth of Waldron's innocence—which is, we are led to believe, a far more difficult truth to reveal than even the real murderer's identity. Just as the film purports to offer "basic facts," so Harvey's address to the grand jury begins from a primary concern he announces at the start of the hearing, "that all the facts be scrutinized with the utmost care and in an impartial manner." In fact, a subjective shot from Harvey's point of view of *The Lawyer's Code of Ethics* underscores our feeling that his testimony comes from "a completely honest man," as even his political opponent Wade styles him.

But what follows is not just a testimony of and to truth by a speaker whose veracity has repeatedly been certified; it is a testimony given in the very *manner* of the film's narrative and its asserted truth, that is, as a series of flashback re-creations of events on which Harvey comments. In a way that recalls the film's introductory titles, Harvey describes how he and his staff have, faithful to the facts, reenacted the murder events in order to certify the eyewitness testimony they have received and to determine beyond all doubt Waldron's guilt or innocence. Thus, these reenactments reflect the film's own status as reenactment, while the truth they conclusively show—that Waldron was not the murderer—becomes a kind of validation of the film's similar documentary strategy.

It is as if the film itself were on trial, its method for revealing truth called into question. With this trial as the narrative's dramatic climax, the film can assure us that even in a re-creation of reality, the truth will out. The unpopularity of that truth, as Harvey feels compelled to defend the person he is supposed to prosecute and prove innocent an individual whom both his political party and the general public want as a scapegoat, sheds further light on the film's strategy, which admits local doubts and ambiguities, even the *movie*ness of its documentation, but only to more strongly affirm the larger truthful impulse that drives the narrative. Harvey's actions especially reassure us by implying that his narrating voice, like the film's own, operates without any personal bias in the service of truth. But, lest we miss the point, it is also made more conventionally when Harvey's political cohorts propose to run him for governor if he convicts Waldron and he repudiates the offer, telling his wife that he could be as happy "in a one-room flat" as in the governor's mansion.

While the initial suggestion that Harvey could be a voice of either truth or duplicity implies a hard choice that he must make, Harvey has been so set apart from the politicians of his party, subject to the narrative's penetrating eye as no other character has been, that there hardly seems any room for doubt or a conflict of motivations in his character. After the pattern of classical narrative, we see into his intimate family life and past history, learning much about his character, while no other figure is similarly examined. As a result, his own commitment to truth, like the narrative's, seems clear and absolute. In effect, the narrative testifies to his character and concern with truth, just as he reminds those in the courtroom of the hearing's purpose to document truth. These multiple levels of attestation in turn reassure us about the film's commitment. However, this interdependence of testimony, like the ultimate truth Harvey reveals, namely, that the murderer cannot be located, that the truth the public is eager for cannot be made known, also admits the limits to any commitment—or to the most searching documentary eye. Even the most truthful perspective, we are told, can see only so far.

In attempting to resolve its murder-mystery plot satisfactorily and thereby fulfill our generic expectations, though, the narrative tries to close up this ambiguity with a strategy that reasserts its special capacity for an outside or revealing vantage. A flashback to Father Lambert's life, motivated by the voice-over narrator, and several scenes during the inquest insinuate the real killer's identity. This information, of course, makes it easier for us to adopt the narrator's point of view as he remarks on the "overzealousness of the public," while it also lets us see the officials' eagerness to satisfy public emotions as a kind of scapegoating. More important, we follow Waldron's prosecution and listen to his protests of innocence with a better sense of how difficult it is to distinguish truth from falsehood, and how easily one can be mistaken for the other when we are immersed in a situation and unable to view it objectively, from outside. It is a point Alfred Hitchcock would pursue far more disconcertingly in probably his darkest foray into the *noir* form, *The Wrong Man* (1956). From our vantage here, though, the trial seems mainly a clash of confused motivations— the political aspirations of Harvey's party and those of T. M. Wade, Police Chief Robinson's concern with solving the murder and removing public pressure from his department, the public's desire for some revenge or sign of justice, and Harvey's concern with the case's ethics—and that tangle of motivations clearly jeopardizes the quest for truth.

While these tangential dramas are being played out, though, we repeatedly observe the reactions of the real killer, one of Lambert's parishioners who he recommended be institutionalized because of a dangerous psychosis. In the first courtroom scene, the camera singles him out as a curious spectator, in medium shot registering his pleased reaction as Harvey notes that three witnesses have placed Waldron at the murder scene. The shot is repeated to show this mysterious figure's shock when Harvey then announces that, despite the testimony, he believes Waldron is innocent. And to indicate that this man does not just symbolize the crowd and its general reactions, a shot shows him seated while all around stand in shocked protest at this unexpected announcement. A subsequent long shot of him alone in the courtroom after the other spectators exit—a high angle shot from the front of the room, as if from the judge's bench—completes a visual pattern of singling out and then indicting the real killer. It is a pattern that has provided a privileged view shared by none of the film's characters, suggested a level of knowledge available only to us, and thereby ensured our attitude toward the demonstration of Waldron's innocence.

The factual demonstration of innocence that follows should be quite satisfactory to a removed, uninvolved spectator, to a documentary eye concerned simply with discerning fact and attesting to truth. However, as the narrator comments at the film's opening, "the death of a man like Father Lambert leaves a gap in any community"—perhaps not unlike the sort of gaps that period audiences had begun to sense in their own world. As we have noted, *Boomerang* sets about closing such gaps, rendering blank spots in its point of view unnoticed and its reality transparent, thus disguising the contradictions in its structure. To balance Father Lambert's death and lend a sense of meaning to these events, then, two other deaths occur. First, Paul Harris shoots himself in the courtroom, his gun firing immediately after Harvey shows that Waldron's gun could not have been the murder weapon. This sequence metaphorically links Harris to Lambert's murder and hints that at least his death has served a purpose. Although accidentally, it has helped expose and root out corruption in this community and visited justice upon one individual responsible for that corruption. Second, the figure singled out as the real killer dies in a car wreck. A close-up of the newspaper headline announcing Waldron's innocence also shows a picture of the real murderer who, in his disordered mental state, assumed a police car was after him and crashed his car into a tree. While the narrator notes that the murder of Father Lambert "was never solved," this image, as if emanating from a distance beyond that of the narrative consciousness, hints otherwise. Like "Rosebud" in *Citizen Kane,* seen from a privileged vantage as if in proof that there is some "answer" to Kane's enigmatic life, the newspaper close-up here supplies a solution—and a comforting *resolution* to the narrative. It suggests a providential justice watching over and at work in this world, giving meaning to even the most senseless acts and guaranteeing justice despite our fears of its absence.

Of course, to be both narratively effective and acceptably realistic, this sort of resolution has to come from a view outside the world described here. Faced with what seems like a breakdown of the moral order—the senseless killing of a priest—and the failure of the police to assert justice, we need an almost godlike perspective to affirm that an order persists, despite our limited view of its workings. The resulting affirmation, though, comes not from the film's documentary vantage—the facts it observes or the history its voice recounts. Rather, the cultural system itself seems to voice our anxieties about the availability of truth and meaning, and, in the absence of other assurances, to draw from the culture's store an old and powerful ideology, really a theology, that might yet afford an answer. The comforting message that concludes the film, that Henry Harvey was in reality Homer S. Cummings, who eventually became Attorney General of the United States, corroborates this marriage of outside and inside perspectives. For even as it reaffirms the narrative's documentary character, its precise correspondence to recorded human history, it also testifies to a benevolent *providence* in which, despite our anxieties, we might still trust. As the narrative pulls back to reassert its documentary vantage, then, it also falls back for certification upon the very system it purports to examine.

Although not produced by de Rochemont, *Call Northside 777* shows the influence of his narrative approach and demonstrates a more overt use of this self-corroborating and self-referential tactic. Clearly mindful of how much our belief in filmic reality depends on a narrative's stable point of view, this film in various ways calls attention to its own perspective, but only to better establish that its perspective, like *Boomerang*'s, is extrasystemic and thus to suggest that the reality it perceives is indeed transparent and true.

Although praised for its "actuality settings and authenticity in photography,"[13] *Call Northside 777* begins not on a documentary note but with a shot of what is clearly marked as the film's "shooting script." However, this filmic reference hints less at a distance from truth than an alliance here between the cinematic and the real. For a title tells us that what follows is "a true story" of Chicago, shot in "the actual locales associated with this story." Inserted archival footage of Chicago emphasizes this sense of actuality and, like *Boomerang*'s panoramic introduction, suggests an all-seeing eye. Along with a stentorian voice-over describing the city's resurrection after the great fire of 1871 and its reconstruction as a "new Chicago," this opening firmly establishes the film's historical context, while it also appropriates the sort of authority we normally attach to the historic.

The film's true focus, however, is not so much history as the shape man gives to it. As the voice-over notes in a curious but telling transition, "That history is on record and the record is kept by the newspapermen who have made Chicago's papers great." What makes this sudden shift to the newspapermen meaningful is its centrality to the film's efforts to marry the real to the imaginary, history's vantage to that of traditional film narrative. For one of classical narrative's devices for establishing a position of authority is to link our point of view to a central character's, anchoring our vantage in a developed, conceivably real persona. Such identification gives the narrative a direction or goal and orients our perspective to its achievement. As long as what we see and hear relates to that goal, we feel we are seeing all that can or need be seen. Since the historical is from the first identified with the film's stated point of view, the civic vantage—and responsibility—of Chicago's newspapermen, character and history thus seem fundamentally linked in a "normal," cinematic way.

In this way character helps to structure what we term the cinematic imaginary.[14] Drawing on Lacanian principles, various critics have suggested that film places viewers in a special relationship to the world it depicts. They see that world as seamless, whole, already constituted for them—and naturally meaningful. Of course, it is actually an *imaginary* relationship, a technological version of Lacan's "mirror stage."[15] That relationship is based in the film's images, fostered by our own imaginations, and usually intent on disguising its carefully crafted, partial, and even symbolic status. And the key to preserving that relationship in classical narrative is character; through our identification with a central figure who serves as a kind of reflection of our own identity, we are made to seem a part of that world and to see its reality not as a symbolic creation, but as an extension of our own.

In keeping with this pattern, *Call Northside 777* uses one reporter to focus our point of view, voice the sort of skepticism we often feel in the face of an institutionally "given" reality—which we might associate with the Hollywood film—and inject a reflexive element that seems free from any institutional resonances. The reporter McNeal reopens the case of two men convicted of murdering a policeman many years earlier. His character, like those of the imprisoned killers Frank Wiecek and Tomek Zaleska, is based on a real-life figure, James P. McGuire, whose *Chicago Times* articles helped a wrongly convicted murderer win freedom. The star status and filmic associations Jimmy

Stewart brings to the role, though, inevitably focus attention on his personality, shifting our concern from the murder case and wrongful imprisonment to the investigator and thereby redirecting our gaze from a long-standing, unresolved mystery to a familiar, seemingly transparent character.

Like the typical protagonist of classical narrative, McNeal is a goal-oriented, psychologically motivated character, whose point of view we can embrace not only because of the associations Stewart allows but also because he reacts much as we might in similar circumstances. Assigned to investigate a scrubwoman's efforts to prove her son innocent of murder, McNeal approaches his task reluctantly, even cynically. At best, he feels, it could be a "human interest" story, a "yarn" good for a quick, sensational headline. Aware of how seductive such appeals are and of the self-serving stance such popular stories often take, though, he warns his wife—and implicitly us too—"don't you start believing it." And even when his articles attract public attention, McNeal remains detached and skeptical, viewing the story as little more than a technical challenge, as he looks for "sock, mass appeal," an "angle," "something to hit the public with." What he comes to personify in the process is the very self-serving, sensationalistic attitude we often associate with Hollywood narrative, which prompted calls such as Crowther's for a new approach to film realism.

However, his cynical attitude gradually disappears, as McNeal becomes involved in his investigation and committed to Wiecek and Zaleska, even accepting their story of innocence with no real proof. Thus he decides to pursue it, despite his editor's business-based decision to kill the story after its initial impact passes. In fact, the developing narrative really concerns McNeal's shift from cynicism to belief more than the convicted men's exoneration, and rightfully so, since this is also the thrust of the reflexive story unfolding here. It is as if he speaks for the film industry about its newfound commitment to truth, when McNeal explains how he "went into this thing believing *nothing*" but found himself compelled by the truth, unable to put the story aside until he had seen it through. In Wiecek's initial response to McNeal's stories—he terms them "writing without heart"—we can glimpse the significance of this newfound zeal. What he locates in this story, and what his own writing increasingly reflects, is a human commitment and feeling previously absent in his work, despite all of his technical skill, and even in his life. It is a new commitment that, the film implies, models the film industry's own.

Supporting this shift, as well as the subtle appropriation of the real by the imaginary here, is a recurring image of reality as a puzzle awaiting assembly. Starting with the initial high angle shots of Chicago, especially its railroads and stockyards, the film attributes a mazelike quality to the city. This characteristic resurfaces when McNeal, in a montage of street scenes, searches for Wanda Skutnik, the only witness to implicate Wiecek and Zaleska in the original killing. This sense of a labyrinth both emphasizes the reporter's impressionistic view of the city and reinforces our notion that he is a searcher for truth. At the same time, this motif takes a symbolic form that anchors the documentary and location footage within a fictional context and clarifies its meaning. Agonizing over the case and his inability to sort out the guilt or innocence of his subjects, their lack of transparency, McNeal finds he cannot sleep and turns to a jigsaw puzzle we have previously seen him and his wife working on. In a pointedly ironic comment, his wife asks, "What's the matter; won't the pieces fit together?" and then reminds him that "Pieces never make the wrong picture. Sometimes you're just looking at them from the wrong angle." In linking the puzzle motif to the case study, the enigmatic to the question of point of view, this scene deploys a metaphor, a common device of classical narrative, within the documentary context to shape its realistic presentation and assert a dominance over it. But equally important is how it models the need for and availability of a proper "angle" for understanding reality, here patterned on the puzzle's imaginary example. With this model the film can at the same time reaffirm its documentary thrust and link that vantage to classical narrative's own normal position of dominance.

The film's climax amplifies this effect by using the reflexive to reinforce our sense of the real and, as it does in *Boomerang,* to close any further gaps between the fictional and documentary. To discredit Wanda Skutnik, McNeal seizes upon a photograph showing her and Wiecek together, apparently prior to her identifying the man she claims never to have met before. To prove the suspected date, he subjects it to a new enhancement process that can enlarge a photograph's smallest portion to reveal previously invisible details. Then, to reach a parole board meeting in time, he uses another technological development, a device for reproducing and transmitting pictures over long distances. What McNeal produces in Wiecek's support is an image of reality: blown up, transmitted, and scrutinized from a new angle in order to reveal truth. In effect, it is a trope for the film itself, evoking not only the cinema's ability to capture, transmit, and reproduce reality's images but also—and most important—its ostensible purpose of rendering transparent otherwise veiled truths. In privileging the film apparatus and its techniques in this analogous way, *Call*

Northside 777 testifies to film's ability to transmit reality and to the documentary *noir*'s special power to provide a normally unavailable and telling vantage on our world. Through such technical prowess, we are assured, films can provide the images we *need* to see, those that might hold a key to our own truth or that might, after a fashion, free us, as they do Wiecek, from imprisonment by and within a fictional world.

This technologically propelled truth is not simply revealed, though; it is set in opposition to an entrapping world of fiction. For Wiecek and Zaleska are not just victims of mistaken identity but of a pointed fictionalizing coming from Wanda Skutnik and supported by police and judicial negligence or corruption at various levels. Since McNeal's efforts to reopen the case promise to reveal flaws in the whole justice system, he finds that the case records have been moved to a restricted site, and that, as one policeman offers, "the word's gone out to keep away from you." What makes these efforts to maintain the story of Wiecek and Zaleska's guilt more significant is the larger narrative pattern they reinforce. In the world *Call Northside 777* sketches, fictionalizing itself becomes the true antagonist, the impulse to veil or disguise reality the culprit against which the film's documentary strategy is mobilized. Fittingly, in this instance too technology helps confirm the truth, as McNeal uses a hidden camera to photograph the secret case records and a polygraph machine to test Wiecek's innocence. These elements, as well as the polygraph expert's belief that Wiecek is innocent, support our own feeling that events have been distorted, fictionalized, and then wrongfully treated as the truth through their passage into public record.

What makes this technological victory over the fictional even more important, though, is that it is the only victory that can be won here. McNeal does gain Frank Wiecek's freedom, but not because the real killer has been caught, only because the various mechanisms the reporter deploys render Wanda Skutnik's testimony transparent. Wiecek's friend, Tomek Zaleska, however, remains imprisoned, as the ultimate truth, the identity of the real murderers, continues to elude McNeal. Of course, that elusiveness goes unstressed if not unnoticed, since it ill accords with the film's emphasis on a documentary "truth," as well as with its effort to affirm film's vantage on the real. But in its partial and slippery truth, in the film's discomfitingly open rather than comfortingly closed resolution, we glimpse the limits of the semidocumentary's transparence. In effect, the partial "grasp" of these films becomes clear.

In this context, Bosley Crowther's description of *Call Northside 777* as "a slick piece of modern melodrama"[16] becomes a telling comment on its narrative strategy. The melodrama is, after all, a highly shaped and fundamentally affirmative fictional mode. As John Cawelti explains, it takes as its guide "the moral fantasy of showing forth the essential 'rightness' of the world order."[17] For all of its efforts to examine and offer "special insight" into the criminal justice system, *Call Northside 777* is ultimately dedicated to this sort of affirmation. It supports the social institution it examines, accepts the problems it lays bare, and in the process adopts a paradoxical posture that marks the very bounds of the visible.

Emphasizing this melodramatic thrust is the film's coda, spoken by the formerly cynical reporter and metaphoric voice of the semidocumentary. When Wiecek is released from prison, McNeal is there to congratulate him, noting that "It's a big thing when a sovereign state admits an error. And remember this: there aren't many governments in the world that would do it." After the fashion of *Boomerang*'s providential ending, we here learn that, in time, the American system will work and that justice will eventually prevail. In this comforting context, it seems fitting for Wiecek, despite his eleven years in prison, his wife's remarriage, his child's adoption, and all that the narrative has documented—perjured testimony, police cover-ups, official disinterest in justice—to agree that "It's a good world outside." It is as if his nightmarish experience extended no further than the prison walls, and the continuing plight of his friend Tomek Zaleska could simply be forgotten in light of this other victory of truth over an imprisoning fiction.

Thanks to the brightly lit location shots of Wiecek's release and the narrator's repetition of that coda, Wiecek's initially halting assertion gains in conviction and supports the film's final emphasis. By stressing the importance of a proper perspective for seeing truth, this ending effectively salvages the *intent* of the film's documentary thrust from any unsettling implications we have glimpsed. As compensation for a small, individually localized failure in the social system, McNeal, Wiecek, and the film audience have gained a significant and valuable vantage. They have learned to see things with the sort of encompassing view that, it is implied, the semidocumentary typically enjoys. *How* we see—that is, our "angle"—thus comes to seem more important than *what* we see; and indeed, that is a considerable point, one that affirms an essential thrust of the *film noir*, as a form that questions our normal point of view and, in its stead, provides us with a more revealing one. At the same time, though, it allows a local, unsettling truth to be submerged, albeit with some difficulty, within a global, reassuring truism. In this context, we might see Wiecek's final remark as reflecting both the desire and the achievement of these films. For they all eventually lay claim to a special perspective, one that seems located outside of the world to be viewed and that promises us a specially revealing vantage on our world. If that outside, almost divine vantage often blurs the immediate human predicament, it is nevertheless a valuable position. From it, the world can indeed seem like a "good" place, at least a realm where justice, truth, and meaning ultimately hold sway, despite occasional appearances to the contrary.

As both *Boomerang* and *Call Northside 777* demonstrate, the semi-documentary's point of view is never quite as distanced and objective, as fundamentally focused on the real, as its title cards, newsreel-type footage, or voice-of-god narrators might imply. Rather, it is mainly concerned with asserting a *need* to see in a certain way and affirming its ability to satisfy that need. But as Comolli indicates, a truly detached, penetrating cinematic vantage is almost impossible, so all that these films might ever hope to offer is a semblance of transparency, or the system's own view of how it might look from outside.[18] Because of this bind, some critics would exclude the semidocumentary from the *noir* canon. For while it, like most *films noir*, focuses on dark passions and criminal actions, set in the modern American cityscape, it finally implies that these elements are less typical manifestations of our culture than temporary disruptions in a largely orderly and properly functioning social system. As this study suggests, however, the narrative paradox that these films demonstrate, their straddling of narrative limits, clearly points to their kinship to the *noir* family.

In commenting on the great number of crime films in this period, Siegfried Kracauer posed a question that speaks to the affirmation the semidocumentaries achieve, and thus to their difficult task of marking off a position for a limited critique of American society. He asks why "a creed that had a real hold on its adherents would . . . need to be so explicitly and superficially proclaimed."[19] Of course, our normal desire for freedom from anxiety always prompts us, individually and culturally, to try to close any "gaps" we see in our system—in the self, society, even the movies. But in aligning our voices and point of view, in effect our public consciousness, with a voice and imagery that spoke a certain cultural or ideological truth in the guise of a detached, objective narration, these films never quite provided the answers or indictments they promised. Rather, they typically bracketed their disturbing subjects within an unconventionally realistic but reassuring, even melodramatic, format, which has the effect of muting their potentially disquieting voice. As a result, what these works, like many other *films noir,* most clearly reveal is less the reality of postwar America than their audiences' *desire* and even deep-felt *need* for a reality that might match their assumptions about their world. Unable and perhaps unwilling to be released from this system, from a habit of thought, viewers could at least seek some confirmation that, as Frank Wiecek says upon his release from prison, it is indeed "a good world" when viewed from "outside." The documentary-style *noir* sought to confirm that hope.

NOTES

A portion of this chapter appeared earlier in the *New Orleans Review* (copyright 1987 by Loyola University, New Orleans) and is reprinted by permission of the *New Orleans Review.*

1. Comolli, "Machines of the Visible," p. 760.
2. Ibid.
3. For an elaborate discussion of these techniques of transparency, see Bordwell, Staiger, and Thompson, *Classical Hollywood Cinema.* Bordwell summarizes this practice as evidence of "Hollywood's pride in concealed artistry" (p. 24).
4. MacCabe, "Realism and the Cinema: Notes on Some Brechtian Theses," in MacCabe, *Tracking the Signifier,* p. 39.
5. Crowther, "Imitations Unwanted," p. B1.
6. See Archer's "Elia Kazan—The Genesis of a Style," p. 6.
7. Elson, "De Rochemont's *The March of Time,*" in Jacobs, *Documentary Tradition,* p. 107.
8. Tuska, *Dark Cinema: American Film Noir in Cultural Perspective,* p. 192.
9. Althusser, *Lenin and Philosophy and Other Essays,* p. 155.
10. See Foucault's "Discourse on Language," p. 219.
11. For a detailed discussion of this pattern in Foucault's thought, see White's essay, "Michel Foucault" in Sturrock, *Structuralism and Since.* In his gloss of Foucault, White explains that while "discourse wishes to 'speak the truth,' . . . in order to do this it must mask from itself its service to desire and power, must indeed mask from itself the fact that it is itself a manifestation of the operations of these two forces" (p. 89).
12. Agee, *Agee on Film,* I.275.
13. Crowther, "Imitations Unwanted," 2.1.
14. For a discussion of the concept of the cinematic imaginary and its relation to our notions of film realism, see MacCabe's "Theory and Film: Principles of Realism and Pleasure," in *Tracking the Signifier,* pp. 64–67.
15. For the most elaborate discussion of this relation between the film apparatus and Lacanian concepts, see Metz, *Imaginary Signifier.*

16. Crowther, review of *Call Northside 777*, p. 29.

17. Cawelti, *Adventure, Mystery, and Romance*, p. 45.

18. Comolli describes this paradoxical working of the cinematic apparatus as follows: "what makes it falter makes it go" (p. 760). See his "Machines of the Visible" essay.

19. Kracauer, "Hollywood's Terror Films," p. 134.

CHAPTER 9 ───────────────────────────

The Evolving Truth of the Documentary *Noir*

The trend is obviously toward greater realism, toward a more
frequent selection of factual American themes, toward the theory
that motion pictures should not only entertain and make money,
but should also give expression to the American and democratic
ideals; to "the truth" as we, the citizens of democracy, accept it.
—Philip Dunne[1]

In the documentary *film noir*'s various strategies for demonstrating its realism, we can see more than just the American cinema
pushing at its inevitable limitations. They also suggest a kind of evolutionary development that the *noir* form was linked into. Writing in the
heady aftermath of World War II, Philip Dunne foresaw a promising
shift in American film. Our wartime experience with the documentary, he felt, would prove a narrative watershed, leading to a new
realistic style with which our films could speak truths we commonly
understood but which usually went unspoken. A few years later André Bazin, the dean of realist film critics, reiterated this hope, but in
the context of a larger cinematic evolution he saw underway. For
Bazin, film was, at root, enacting a kind of myth of realism—the "myth
of total cinema," as he put it—that was edging us ever closer to a
perfect imitation of human reality.[2] And in the postwar film scene,
particularly the Italian neorealist movement, he saw clear evidence of
this development, numerous examples of "the general trend of cinema . . . toward realism."[3] But just as the neorealist style gradually
changed, producing what must have seemed to some the almost opposite developments of Visconti's operatics and Fellini's surrealism, so
did the documentary *noir* gradually veer from the direction Dunne
foresaw.

Dunne's optimistic assessment of the semidocumentary's potential
rested on several obvious and ultimately quite problematic assumptions: first, that there was a consensus about our "American . . . ideals"

or "truth"; and second, that "the words *truthful* and *documentary* are nearly synonymous."[4] If the former notion was a holdover of wartime idealism, soon dispelled by national and international realities, the latter signaled a more entrenched belief that also underlay neorealism, a belief in what we might term the representational relation, in a dependable connection between what the camera, properly directed, might record and truth itself. Both of these assumptions would eventually be laid bare and undermined by the semidocumentary *noir* in the course of its development, first by its very focus on fissures in our consensus—a focus that brought mixed reactions to the "truth" of the films; and second by a gradual evolution *away from* a truly documentary style. In fact, this evolutionary pattern most clearly shows the tenuous ties to the real that always marked these films.

Following Dunne's lead, James Agee in 1947 praised the large number of documentary-type crime films then appearing as evidence of "a new and vigorous trend in U.S. moviemaking."[5] But in just over a year that "vigorous trend" seemed almost played out, with few examples appearing in 1949 and 1950, the most noteworthy being *City across the River* and *The Sleeping City*. This short life span might be due to the radical potential we have ascribed to the semidocumentary. In their focus on cultural failings, problems of corruption, flaws in the legal system, and juvenile delinquency, films like *Boomerang, Call Northside 777,* and *City across the River* mount an ideological assault that we see in few other *noirs*. Films like *Double Indemnity, The Lady from Shanghai,* and *Sorry, Wrong Number* center more on a kind of internal darkness—what Foster Hirsch describes as the individual's "struggle with powerful inner forces"[6]—than on broad social issues. At the same time, the *noir* documentary uses a different and potentially disconcerting voice to address these problems. As we have noted, its conventional elements—true stories, location shooting, use of non-actors and high-grain film, voice-of-god narration—by their very difference make us aware of classical narrative's contrived realism, which depends on such things as continuity editing, shot-reverse-shot sequences, and third-person point of view. In the process, they threaten that style's effectiveness by implicitly showing it to be a fashioned, contrived mode, its reality not so much an extension of *our* world as of a conventional *cinematic* world which might or might not speak to our situation.

By grounding their social commentary in a factual context, by aligning narrative with the newsreels of the day, these films also challenged the way audiences saw their world. Although these films may reflect a desire for some new means of expression or a longing for truths neglected by classical narrative, then, we might expect an uneasiness at the "sound" of their voice, which uttered things the "citizens of democracy" would probably find unsettling. Thus we might be surprised by the response of a generally conservative critic like Bosley Crowther, who praised the use of real settings and the naturalistic photography of the semidocumentaries, as he argued for extending this style to the broad range of American film.[7]

Crowther, though, was already behind the times, for by 1949 (when he was writing) that potentially radical style was proving open to a far from radical application. Parker Tyler hints as much when in the same year he ascribed the strength of these films to their "positing a theoretical *actualité* behind every effect of action, lighting, and makeup in creative film, no matter how melodramatic, formal, or artistic such effects may be."[8] What Tyler observes is a telling narrative tension within these films, which are finally marked not so much by a difference in "effects" between them and conventional narratives, but a change in the *conviction* those effects lent to narratives that were largely traditional, even melodramatic in shape. Admittedly, none of the early documentary *noirs* achieves the sort of harmonious resolution that characterizes most film melodrama. In fact, what clearly signals their *noir* status is a slippage that usually accompanies, and even undermines, their efforts at resolution. As examples we need only recall the unsolved murder in *Boomerang, Call Northside 777*'s Tomek Zaleska, who at film's end remains wrongfully imprisoned, or *Naked City*'s implicit question of how people with our culture's every benefit could go so wrong. But these films and their successors do evoke a broadly melodramatic paradigm, as they posit a local upset in a generally moral social order and, usually through a heroic figure's courageous action, eradicate the disturbing element and restore a semblance of right.[9] Given unsettling subjects, these films minimized their disturbing impact by encoding those subjects in a narrative tradition of problem resolution, even though that paradigm was ill-suited to postwar circumstances.

As a result, the documentary techniques themselves gradually began to function less as tools for revealing and attesting to truth than as part of a formal rhetoric of belief that might be applied in reassuring ways. Thus, later documentary *noirs* could simply corroborate a preexisting truth, that is, the viewers' consensus of what the real world—or the reel one, depicted in the movies—was actually like. As an illustration, we might consider a film like *City across the River*. Its opening spurred a public outcry against its depiction of juvenile delinquency, and the studio responded by addressing not the film's subject but its technique. In a variation on voice-of-god narration, newspaper columnist Drew Pearson opens the film, testifying to its facticity and urging viewers to see its naturalistic narrative, shot on the streets of Brooklyn, as a vivid warning of what "could just as well have happened in any large city where slum conditions undermine personal security and take their toll in juvenile delinquency." Protests by several Brooklyn citizens' groups against the portrayal of this American "truth," of a culturally determined delinquency and crime, prompted the distributor, "as a friendly gesture, to drop all mention of Brooklyn from its advertisements," while the producers offered a stylistic alteration: "after much consultation," the *New York Times* reported, they "decided to tone down the offending foreword."[10]

In the following year *The Sleeping City* brought a replay of this pattern of public outcry and industry reaction with its depiction of New York's Bellevue Hospital. Its exposé-style story of murder and drug thefts among the hospital's interns and attendants sparked a reaction that the studio tried to quell with a prologue apologizing for the film's disturbing themes. Richard Conti, who plays an undercover detective posing as an intern, introduces the narrative with a tribute to Bellevue and the "public servants" who staff it.[11] Of course, by affirming the film's fictional nature in this way, the prologue effectively reverses the original intent: to raise consciousness about the contradictions in our culture by revealing the ills plaguing even our institutions of healing. And by assuring viewers not just that Bellevue and its employees are *different* from what the film depicts but that, *despite* all realistic appearances, the film is basically grounded in fiction, the appended opening reconstitutes the sort of gap between film and reality that the semidocumentary style was supposed to bridge. In this case, the semidocumentary's mechanism has simply become a manipulable set of signs to be arranged not to evoke truth but to serve a popular belief, namely, whatever the movie industry and moviegoers might find most acceptable or least threatening. In effect, truth and belief have become quite distinct concerns.

As we can see, the semidocumentary came to signal two contrary attitudes, both a desire and a fundamental fear—a longing for a voice and the sort of radical truths it might speak, linked to an uneasiness at any speech that might upset the way viewers perceived and believed in their world and, indeed, themselves. What this paradoxical stance already hints at is an ongoing shift in the form, although hardly of the sort suggested by Dunne. This evolutionary pattern basically takes two forms.[12] One shift is stylistic, as the cachet of facticity gradually drops away from the documentary style's components. For example, the voice-of-god technique becomes increasingly personalized, brought down to earth, until it is hardly distinguishable from the sort of voice-over found in films like *The Lady from Shanghai* and *The Postman Always Rings Twice*. At the same time, these films also refocus their subjects, turning more to the universal patterns of human desire and weakness than the social questions explicitly posed by works like *Boomerang* and *Call Northside 777*.

In effect, both style and theme pull back toward the identifiable and less-threatening orbit of classical narrative, thereby reprieving audiences from the challenge of that "radical" style. Within a recognizably fictional context, cultural problems could not only be safely noted but also easily—if impractically—resolved. At the same time, we find a number of films that clearly draw on this documentary form, deploying its realistic bias in a way that speaks of a continuing desire for some means of addressing the modern American situation. But even as these works suggest a discomfort with our options for talking about such things, they also point up classical narrative's syntactical power to adopt such a lexicon into its own signifying system.

A film like *The Naked City* suggests the broad directions of this evolution. For while it appears at the height of the form's popularity, it looks toward a shift in both narrative style and subject matter. Unlike the anonymous, authoritative narrators of films like *Boomerang* and *Call Northside 777*, *Naked City*'s voice-of-god emanates from its producer, the former New York newspaper columnist Mark Hellinger, whose roots are discernible in the tenor and inflections of his remarks. As he addresses the viewers—"Ladies and Gentlemen, the motion picture you are about to see is called *The Naked City*"—he emphasizes that we are watching a film, a fiction that draws on his familiarity with New York and its denizens. As our prior discussion of the semidocumentary's strategy notes, this comment, along with his remarks on the picture's casting and location settings, hints at a modernist, reflexive narrative, and at least a different level of realism here. The hope is that by exposing the film apparatus, the narrative might also expose the convention-bound realism of classical narrative and the ideological mechanism that attaches to it, thereby winning some freedom from both, staking out a position beyond their normal influence.

A shift in tone, however, blunts that reflexive thrust. Reacting to Hellinger's familiarity, which Sarah Kozloff terms his "lyrical, Whitmanesque tenor,"[13] Bosley Crowther described the film as "Hellinger's personal romance with the city of New York,"[14] while James Agee commented on its "mawkish" handling of standard police fare.[15] Such assessments suggest the sort of narrative shift that has occurred. It is as if the voice-of-god has descended to our level, taken human form—

as a film producer—to grant us a privileged view of this world. And the narration's general character underscores this "earthly" attitude, for it is consistently conversational, using first-person pronouns, present-tense verbs, reading the thoughts of various characters, and even acting as our surrogate, talking back to a character like the fugitive Garza—"Take it easy, Garza. Don't run!" he remarks. The result is a tension between the narrator's familiar, subjective sensibility and the sense of authority and realism at which the film seems to aim. Of course, the narrator remains all-knowing, judgmental, guided by a purpose of his own, even as the conditions of that omniscience become more problematic. As Kozloff suggests, the subjective elements linking his otherworldly position to our culture-bound one might simply be intended to "make it more palatable and forestall criticism for open didacticism."[16] However, those narrative elements also strain our sense of reality all the more and point to an increasing uncertainty about the sort of perspective these films offer.

Hellinger's democratizing voice, moreover, has a significant corollary in the story he tells. For *The Naked City* does not examine a social dilemma or exemplary issue of any sort. It simply begins by introducing various representative types—cleaning woman, radio announcer, newspaper typesetter—and the commonplace activities in which they are engaged. When we see a murder in progress, then, we accept that, as the narrator notes, "this too is routine." Throughout its length, the narrative emphasizes the everyday, as if the normality of these events sufficiently certified their truth. And the film's conclusion reiterates this theme: "There are eight million stories in the naked city. This has been one of them." This change in emphasis from the remarkable to the routine has important implications for the documentary *noir* project, since it shifts attention from cultural problems to issues that are at once both more universal and more personal—problems of violence and desire shown in a naturalistic context. In fact, it seems that in this concern with the everyday the documentary current clearly merges with the *noir* mainstream to focus on the "powerful inner forces" that move us. For these films are struggling to document equally the self and society, and especially the darker forces that drive both.

The ideological fallout of such "routinizing" is also noteworthy, for the various events and motivations dealt with become less disturbing or threatening, if at the same time less susceptible to remediation. In the case of *The Naked City*, this strategy was deliberate, as screenwriter Malvin Wald relates: "I explained [to Hellinger] that in combining the artistic documentary technique of Flaherty with the commercial product of Hollywood, a safe subject matter should be used—murder, a police story."[17] Of course, a "safe subject" makes fewer demands on viewers. Murders based on greed or desire never really challenge our sense of how we live or what social responsibilities we bear. Moviegoers are simply invited to see themselves a bit more clearly and thus to understand better the intricate workings of human nature.

To illustrate these shifts in the semidocumentary, I want to examine two films that suggest the different narrative patterns that developed. *The City That Never Sleeps* (1953) is one of the last *films noir* to use most of the documentary style's trappings, but it is also a work in which those characteristics become more personal, less assertive, clearly turned to a different end. *Panic in the Streets* (1950), in contrast, discards many of the form's characteristics—in fact, some might question its inclusion here since it lacks many of the defining documentary traits—even as it redirects much of its social thrust. It exemplifies a strain of more influential, apparently realistic, routine-life films that eventually appeared. If the former film signals the swan song of the semidocumentary in its more didactic form, the latter suggests the power which a simpler conception of realistic cinema would increasingly exercise, and which would prove one of *noir*'s more important influences on American film narrative.

Although a late entry in the semidocumentary form, *The City That Never Sleeps* clearly echoes earlier films of this type. Recalling the opening shots of films like *Naked City, Kiss of Death,* and *City across the River,* it starts with a pan of the Chicago skyline that quickly establishes the urban setting and the fact that it was shot on location. Meanwhile, an anonymous narrator offers an introduction that echoes Hellinger's *Naked City* prologue in both tone and posture: "I am the city, hub and heart of America, melting pot of every race, creed, color, and religion in humanity, from my famous stockyards to my towering factories, from my tenement district to swank Lake Shore Drive. I am the voice, the heartbeat of this giant, sprawling, sordid and beautiful, poor and magnificent citadel of civilization. And this is the story of just one night in this great city. Now meet my citizens."

If a bit corny, this opening is also more truly Whitmanesque than Hellinger's, going his romantic posture one better. It effectively anthropomorphizes Chicago by making the narrating voice the city's own. If other documentary-style narrators seem like intermediaries between audience and subject, journalistically reporting on specific problems in particular locales, this voice subjectifies reality; we listen as a spirit of place and people talks about a typical if dark side of its own life. In character, it is at once proud but unpretentious, civilized yet folksy, thanks partly to the incongruous southern accent that Chill Wills lends to Chicago's persona. This involved, subjective consciousness, moreover, sets up a tension with the visual code of the opening images. The extreme long shots of the city that usually open such films normally signal a detached, objective perspective, and thus a level of facticity that the narrative supposedly has; but these images represent a kind of self-display, the city intimately opening itself to our gaze in the narrative about to unfold.

This initial coding is further disrupted when the voice-over takes a moralistic turn that echoes a tradition of film fantasy more than the *film noir*. Introducing several characters, the narrator tells how this night will prove crucial for each one. Policeman Johnny Kelly in particular is described as "a man who tonight has reached a crisis in his life." Dispirited by the seemingly dead-end nature of his job and a strained marriage, he plans to resign from the force and run off with a striptease dancer, Sally Connors. It is to help him through this dark night of the soul that the film's narrating "spirit" manifests itself, appearing as a sergeant with the appropriately universal name of Joe. Taking the place of Johnny's usual partner on night patrol, Sergeant Joe provides a sounding board for Johnny's gripes, lectures him on his duty, and helps him overcome various temptations, including the lure of a $5,000 bribe by a crooked lawyer, before finally disappearing when Johnny decides to accept his lot.

The recurrence of Joe's voice at the film's conclusion, announcing that in the course of this night some people, "like Johnny Kelly, are being born again, and the city never sleeps," clearly echoes *The Naked City*'s conclusion. But it does more, by also emphasizing how this narrative serves as a kind of moral exemplum and hinting at a level of moral guidance implicit in classical narrative. In fact, in light of the film's premise, its incarnated narrating voice probably resembles that of a film like Frank Capra's *It's a Wonderful Life* (1946) more than other documentary-style *noirs*. The Capra film's "head angel" narrator almost literally embodies the voice-of-god and its incarnation of Clarence the guardian angel prefigures *The City That Never Sleeps*'s Sergeant Joe. Of course, while the earlier film lengthily establishes its fantasy context, the later one tries to disguise or deny that kinship with its dark and sordid imagery. As a result, its moral stance can seem rooted in reality itself and the lessons experience can teach us.

A further disruption of the semidocumentary style shows up in the film's reflexive elements. In the prior chapter we described how, in various ways, films like *The House on 92nd Street, Boomerang,* and *Call Northside 777* refer to the filmic nature of their documentary eye, or at least to the usefulness of a technology of observation and communication for recording and assessing reality's truth. By admitting the workings of the cinematic apparatus, either directly or metaphorically, these films reaffirm their ability to record reality and access its truth, thereby reassuring us on a fundamental if unexamined level that the point of view they afford—and that film in general offers—is both reliable and revealing, fit for our belief.

While *City That Never Sleeps* displays what may be the most elaborate pattern of reflexive elements among the semidocumentaries, it does so in a jarring and almost paradoxical manner that suggests the sort of contrary impulses—toward realism and toward the norms of classical narrative—which increasingly tugged at such films. On the one hand, it uses such documentary techniques as the prologue and voice-over to evoke almost a fantasy realm of guardian angels and tutelary spirits and to announce from the narrative's very start its fabulistic impulse. On the other hand, it develops a pattern of reflexive references, but not so much as the other semidocumentaries do, to disarm skepticism and stake out a separate realm of belief by distinguishing itself from classical narrative; that strategy here serves, if clumsily, to indict illusion, to question all image production—by implication, even its own.

Drawing on the work of Jacques Lacan, Bill Nichols explains how film's "representations" typically "fix us in an imaginary relationship to the material conditions of existence,"[18] while also trying to disguise the imaginary—or image-constructed—nature of that relation. In effect, the film experience reconstitutes Lacan's "mirror phase"[19] by fashioning with its images a sense of self or an identity that we can comfortably embrace. Ideologically speaking, we might think of that identity as a pattern of belief to which we are to conform. It feels reassuring, just as we feel good about our sense of self, so long as it seems natural, unconstructed, nonimaginary. And indeed such a naturalness, sourced mainly in the film's narrative voice, is part of the discourse of *The City That Never Sleeps*.

But this film also traumatizes the imaginary, cracks the mirror as it were (and we might begin to see a rationale for the number of *films noir* in which cracked mirrors are central to the plot, from *Lady from Shanghai* [1948] to *Nightmare* [1953]). For *City That Never Sleeps* launches an assault on a world of illusion that almost seems like a strike at the cinematic imaginary. To this end, it establishes a theatrical context, much of its action occurring outside of, within, or backstage at the Silver Frolics nightclub. Two focal points dominate the exterior scenes and reveal the sort of divergence between image and reality that the reflexive usually suggests: first, we see a marquee advertising the "Follies International" from Paris; and second, a window display shows a mechanical man inviting passersby into the club. Despite the marquee and the girls' exotic names, though, the dancers here are just tired locals, as their accents and gum-chewing habits show, while the mechanical man, we learn, is a failed actor, his face painted silver as part of his act, as well as a psychic defense against his life's many disappointments.

The world these people inhabit is also marked by artifice and deception. Emphasizing this point, extreme long shots from the audience's vantage repeatedly show the stage through netting or other props that obscure our view, while also suggesting a trap of fate or circumstance into which the characters, for all their show of glamour, have fallen. The backstage scenes then build on these themes by underscoring the disparity between the real world and the burlesque show. At the same time, Johnny Kelly's view of Sally's striptease act from backstage, her disparaging remarks about the audience, and the attitudes of the other employees toward the club's patrons reveal a cynicism in those who purvey these illusions and a disenchantment with both their own sordid world and the seedily glamorous one they project. Sally, we learn, wanted to be a ballerina, and Greg Warren, the mechanical man, a legitimate actor, but through circumstances both have been, as she bitterly notes, "ground down to this." Their disdain for the world of spectacle and titillation they help fashion suggests how the individual can be ruled, against his will, by the very discourse in which he participates.

This accumulation of details about images, actors, performance, and audiences could well be directed at our traditional view of the filmic apparatus. For it might remind us of how film can play upon and cater to our sense of the imaginary, working not in the service of truth but as a purveyor of illusions for the profit of others. It also threatens to reveal how much we are ourselves constructed by that play of images, our sense of self dependent on illusion. Of course, in pointing out this disparity between illusion and truth, the film dares us to glimpse its own contradictions. With a kind of schizophrenic bravado, it implies that it is, essentially, something other than a film—or at least different from other films. Its narration's ingenuous claim, after all, is that it is reality's own "mindscreen,"[20] manifesting itself and showing its metaphoric contempt for all that is not truth, not reality.

In keeping with this attitude toward the imaginary, the voice-over introduces a cast of characters who seem almost nightmarish metaphors of the filmmaker and filmgoer. Ruled by the imaginary, the characters here singlemindedly traffic in and pursue illusion. Thus

Johnny Kelly, as an antidote to his alienation, pursues Sally and plans to run away with her. To finance this escape, he agrees to some illicit work for the lawyer Penrod Biddel, whose promise of easy money is tellingly linked to a promise to help fashion a new self, to "make a big man" of Johnny: "I've helped a lot of people. It's a hobby of mine to take a human being and give them [sic] glamour, confidence, polish." The same lures—wealth and a new image—also attract Sally. Her ambition to be a ballerina now forgotten, she longs to leave her job as the Silver Frolics's star and go to Hollywood, land of illusions, where with Johnny she might start anew. To do so, though, she must leave Greg Warren, whose mechanical man act is just an excuse to stay close to her and disguise his unrequited love.

In this reflexive context, his role looms most significantly. As fascinated pedestrians watch his "act," the nightclub barker poses a question about him—"Is he mechanical or is he real? Watch him walk, watch him move, then guess whether he's made of wax, metal, and putty, or if he is flesh and blood"; the same question might well be posed of everyone here. For in varying degrees they all play roles, denying their true nature, even their humanity, by adopting a tough, illusory exterior in order to hide a vulnerable or damaged psyche. Sally's remark, that "Chicago is the big melting pot and I got melted but good," typifies the attitude behind their efforts to project another, tougher, less vulnerable self-image. However, this tendency also suggests a level on which they all resemble actors in a film, people trying to be something they are not. This pervasive role-playing is central to the film's general indictment of the imaginary.

With the presentation of the film's dual antagonists, the lawyer Penrod Biddel and his former henchman Hayes Stewart, the emphasis on illusion finds its clearest focus. Their introductions emphasize that both are basically showmen, dedicated to projecting a false image and profiting from it. For instance, our first glimpse of Biddel fittingly is through a camera's viewfinder, as his picture is taken to illustrate a story on his status as the city's most powerful criminal attorney. That this image represents a carefully cultivated role intended for public consumption and at odds with the truth quickly becomes apparent when Biddel interrupts the session to take a call from Johnny about an offered bribe. In fact, Biddel's reputation emphasizes how much his life depends on illusion, since he helps criminals only to gain power over them and so turn their illicit talents to his own use.

His most successful project has been Stewart, whose introduction also contains a telling image, that of a rabbit in a cage. The rabbit recalls Stewart's earlier career as a magician and signals the talent for illusion that he has since turned in another, criminal direction; as the narrator explains, under Biddel's tutelage "his greed [became] so much greater than his conscience that he began picking people's pockets, and his career as a hoodlum went on from there." At the same time, though, the image hints at Stewart's own imprisonment, his subservience to Biddel. In this introduction, consequently, we glimpse the sort of paradox that characterizes both Stewart and his supposed master Biddel. While intent on making himself, like the rabbit, disappear from Biddel's grasp, Stewart remains fascinated by illusion, both the sort of which his own magic is composed and the images of "glamour" and "polish" that Biddel has provided and uses to control him.

It is primarily through these characters who influence Johnny Kelly's life that the film sketches both the great lure and the dangers of the imaginary. While the others alter the trajectory of their fates by relinquishing illusion, Biddel and Stewart finally fall because of their commitment to the illusory and its power. Thus, even as his power and influence give the lawyer mastery over the criminal, we see how he too is bound by certain illusions. An old man, he believes that his young and beautiful wife Lydia, a typical *noir* "black widow," loves him. But she has fallen for the younger Stewart and what she ironically describes as his "magic touch," and conspires with him to murder Biddel. Once freed from Biddel's hold, though, Stewart faces a new image problem, for Lydia witnesses the killing and, consequently, inherits a portion of her husband's power over Stewart. Killing her only turns the screw tighter, since he must then also silence Greg Warren, who, from his window post, sees her death. It is as if each step in maintaining an image of innocence, in deploying the power of illusion to escape from a dark reality—in this instance, the master illusionist Biddel—only draws Stewart's secret self further into the open, leading him closer to the same fate as Biddel and making it clearer that his true nemesis is the lure of illusion itself, of the manipulable image.

The film's conclusion dramatically completes this indictment of the illusory by contrasting an individual who is bound by illusion to one who resists its lure and thereby locates his true self. Stewart, as we have seen, suggests what can happen to someone who gives himself over to a world of illusion. Presented as the magician's potential double, Johnny too seems drawn to Biddel's orbit by promises of money, power, and "glamour," but is finally able to resist those lures. In shooting Johnny's father, Stewart makes the threat explicit, as the corrupt role model literally displaces, kills off, the proper one. That killing, however, jolts Johnny back to a sense of his true self, as he decides to act like the policeman his father was and he really is, bringing Stewart to justice. Their climactic confrontation atop the elevated's tracks evokes both their doubling and this ultimate difference. Too far away for anyone to distinguish pursuer from pursued, cop from criminal—in effect, their difference blurred—Johnny tosses his badge to those watching and in that move renews his claim to his real-world identity as a policeman.

It is an awakening that heralds several others at this point. For Greg has served as a decoy to draw Stewart out, and his heroic act prompts Sally to see him in a different light, as if his metallic paint had suddenly become transparent. She promises to abandon her job and her plans to run away in order to, as she puts it, "straighten out and have a good life" by doing "the husband and wife routine" with him. Showing how the last vestige of illusion disappears with that genuine commitment, Greg begins crying while still performing his mechanical man act. He thereby breaks the illusion he has been paid to create, as a close-up and audience reaction shots emphasize. In this way *City That Never Sleeps* completes its indictment of and retreat from a theatrical, illusory world. Those who traffic in illusion, specifically Biddel and Stewart, have been killed because of their commitment to that realm, while Johnny, Sally, and Greg have found the needed strength to abandon the illusory, accept their true selves, and even locate the possibility of "a good life" in the process.

The film's final scene, wherein Johnny meets his wife Kathy in the street, suggests a return to normalcy after a nightmarish period. Shot with a filter that lends a soft, almost romantic aura to the early morning setting, the scene conventionally promises future happiness; and that promise is affirmed by the narrator, who notes that now "Johnny Kelly is home, home to stay." But this conclusion reaches for more than just normality. By working the film's vision of corruption and alienation into a moral shape, it implies that society's ills are largely due to our inability to cope with limitations, an inability that leads us to embrace illusions and false images instead of the values of love, home, and family that have traditionally been a source of both individual and cultural strength. More than just a conservative ending, this melodramatic resolution suggests how much the semidocumentary by this time had become a shaped form, determined more by the dictates of the imaginary, including its innate capacity for disguise, than by the thrust of truth.

Further blunting any radical potential and countering the film's almost anticinematic stance is a strategy of displacement that underlies its indictment of the imaginary. As we have noted, because it can disclose the imaginary's mechanism of illusion, the reflexive can threaten a film's ability to construct the imaginary relationship of individuals to their world. The film's voice-of-god narrator and its focus on a world of entertainment and spectacle suggest such a reflexive impulse at work, but that impulse ultimately takes a conservative turn through the displacement of its critique. First, of course, the narrative incarnates its voice-over, literally making the imaginary real through Sergeant Joe, whose constant message is to accept the status quo. By displacing what is normally an objective, certifying voice from outside to within the narrative—in the process suggesting that the outside view *is* the inside one—the film blunts the reflexive, implying that the imaginary here *is* the real and that this melodramatic pattern wherein good and evil are so starkly arrayed is the very image of reality. On a second level, some patterns of the imaginary are displaced into patterns of corruption and wrongful desire that can then be indicted while the larger patterns of life remain untouched. With the imaginary limited to the aberrant, the corrupt, the selfish impulse, our normal sense of the real can finally go unchallenged.

Equally curious in effect is the film's focus on illusion, false images, the lure of spectacle—the very basis of film narrative. These elements, *City That Never Sleeps* implies, alienate the individual and can undermine both the self and the social contract. Given this motif's cinematic resonance, we have to wonder if the film is working against itself by raising doubts about its own images and their function. As our discussion of *Call Northside 777* showed, a film might call attention to its nature simply to affirm its singular access to truth. And in light of its peculiar strategy of displacement, this focus in *City That Never Sleeps* does make some sense. For if the film aligns the imaginary with what we tend to see as realistic in such narratives—the dark, normally denied images of corruption, for instance—then it also makes sense for it to challenge what we usually perceive as real—the film's "documentary" images, for example—and to realign our conceptions with the melodramatic patterns of conventional narrative. Such a paradoxical strategy suggests an increasing difficulty with the documentary technique, especially with successfully blending an impulse to truth with one for entertainment and cultural reassurance. Of course, it also points to a pattern of contradictory assumptions that show up in many films of this period. Thus we find works as different as *High Noon* (1952) and *Invasion of the Body Snatchers* (1956) being read alternately as conservative or liberal tracts, as warnings about the need to confront the threats from outside our society, and as illustrations of our own destructive paranoia. In such films, just as in works like *City That Never*

Sleeps, we see demonstrated how much influence the imaginary continued to exert on evolving film efforts at showing the truth.

In the course of what I have termed the semidocumentary "evolution," many of the form's conventions simply fall away or, as the strange voice-over of *City That Never Sleeps* demonstrates, blend into more conventional narrative structures. But even so, the attitude toward the real that spurred these films lingers in *noir* narrative. As Colin MacCabe reminds us, our impression of film realism depends on "obscuring . . . the relation between text and reader [or viewer] in favour of a dominance accorded to a supposedly given reality."[21] This sense of a "given reality," its truth manifest, operates powerfully in a number of *films noir* that spring from the semidocumentaries. While conventions like the voice-of-god narrator, prologue, and factual subject matter tend to disappear, the use of location settings, documentary-style photography, and non-actors seems to take root in mainstream narrative. Typifying this development are films like *Panic in the Streets, The Asphalt Jungle,* and *Union Station* (all 1950), all of which suggest a retreat from the semidocumentary's radical posture. In fact, they clearly recall classical narrative in one major respect; for they efface our position as subjects of a narrator's direct address, thereby transforming us from participants in an imaginary discussion about reality to invisible consumers of film imagery. Still, they advance the semidocumentary's thrust by developing a more forceful image of the everyday, which results in an at least equally involving sense of the real.

As with any historical development, we can trace the lineage of these other *noirs* to various forces that might each claim an element of parentage. We have already noted the considerable impact of Italian neorealism on postwar American cinema. Its "direct, documentary-style rendering of life," location shooting, use of non-actors, and implicitly social message clearly mirror the developments we see going on in the *noir* semidocumentary.[22] Films like *Open City* (1945), *Paisan* (1946), and *Bicycle Thieves* (1948) confirmed the appeal of the small human drama, of the commonplace. In effect, they demonstrated authenticity's dramatic power, especially its ability to exert a conviction and appeal beyond the documentary context; or as Cesare Zavattini, one of the movement's pioneers, put it, "to make things as they are almost by themselves, create their own special significance."[23] Advancing that goal, though, is a particular strategy that resembles one we have already observed in the *film noir.* As André Bazin offers, neorealist films strove for "a particular way of looking at things," a perspective that did not simply disguise itself, as in traditional Hollywood cinema, but that tried to avoid interfering with reality, "never making reality the servant of some *a priori* point of view."[24] The resulting vantage seems to open onto the real world in a way that conventional Hollywood narratives seldom managed.

While the semidocumentaries were also concerned with point of view, Bazin is careful to distinguish Italian neorealist films from their American counterparts. "Neorealism," he explains, "is more an ontological position than an aesthetic one," more the attitude behind that perspective than just a set of conventions that mark it. Thus in 1952 he could look back on the disappearing semidocumentaries and, drawing a comparison to neorealism, explain that "the employment of its technical attributes like a recipe do [*sic*] not necessarily produce it, as the rapid decline of American neorealism proves."[25]

A film like *Panic in the Streets* clearly tries to go beyond the "recipe" approach Bazin notes, even while it uses many of neorealism's basic techniques. Filmed on location, primarily on the New Orleans waterfront and in the French Quarter, it employs a number of nonprofessional actors, closely follows the rhythms of everyday life, makes the camera as much as possible into an uninvolved observer, and takes a decidedly social perspective. But we should not forget that *Panic in the Streets* is shaped at least as much by the same industrial forces that helped form the semidocumentaries as by any aesthetic considerations. Its location shooting, for instance, was probably encouraged by rising labor and production costs in Hollywood, the emergence of small production companies whose studios were essentially the city streets, and new developments in camera, lens, and sound technologies. Then too, the film ultimately shies away from the proletariat-as-protagonist situation of so many neorealist films in favor of a more conventional Hollywood approach, using recognized stars—in this instance, Richard Widmark and Paul Douglas—in the leading roles and building the story around the personalities of the characters they play. Perhaps most important, the situation that these figures face is not a simple problem "in the order of things," as Bazin describes the situation of *Bicycle Thieves*,[26] but rather a potentially calamitous visitation of plague that, the film notes as it looks toward the emergence of a "disaster" genre in American cinema, threatens to devastate the nation.

Panic in the Streets, in effect, combines the neorealist influence with compatible industrial circumstances, the inevitable patterns of Hollywood narrative, and the dark vision of *film noir*. That very combination of ingredients perhaps explains both the power of such films and a weakness that accompanied later developments of the documentary *noir*. This film was, we should also note, directed by Elia Kazan, who established his credentials with the successful semidocumentary *Boomerang*. As a result, we might reasonably expect some continuity with the earlier film's style, as well as evidence of the director's maturation. However, Kazan's personal history, as a "friendly" witness for the House Un-American Activities Committee investigating supposed communist influence in the film industry, already suggests a certain shift from the vaguely populist stance of *Boomerang*, and thus a potential dissonance that we might find in his later films.[27]

While the overt mechanisms of documentary disappear, *Panic in the Streets* does emphasize the commonplace, using life's daily events to help shape its narrative. But to the commonplace it adds something unusual, even singular—an outbreak of plague that motivates a search for several killers who were in contact with the disease's carrier. The film's title, as well as its thematic thrust, ultimately proves more metaphoric than descriptive, suggesting a larger significance to the everyday activity of fighting disease and healing the sick that the narrative details. To further this effect, the film links medical routine to a detective formula, while also allying its protagonist, Dr. Clint Reed of the Public Health Service, with police detective Tom Warren to track down the possible plague carriers during a forty-eight-hour "incubation period." Through the sense of urgency and the traditional pattern of detective narrative that result, then, *Panic in the Streets* effectively marries the eventful and the ordinary. In the process, it also points up how much significance, how much "truth," hides in the everyday world and the commonplace experience.

Drawing attention away from the improbable combination of doctor and detective is a metaphoric pattern the film develops to link its disparate elements and to reach for a larger significance. Nearly every scene of the film centers around a highly realistic element, a concern with eating or food, and this focus gradually evolves during the narrative into a meditation on a common *noir* theme, the various forms that human appetite takes. Through this emphasis, in fact, the film grounds its implicitly social concern—with crime as a kind of disease of the social order—in the sort of fundamental human problems that the semidocumentary, following neorealism's lead, had increasingly taken as its focus.

In the broadest sense, as a variant of desire, appetite frequently provided a central motif for the *film noir*, as *The Lady from Shanghai* well illustrates. At the same time, it was also often used simply to suggest the everyday, the normal world wherein the play of desire can so readily and quickly surface to wreak havoc. We might think, for instance, of *Mildred Pierce* (1945) and how Mildred's struggle for survival, as a single mother with a family to raise, is measured in the chain of restaurants she establishes. *The Postman Always Rings Twice* similarly uses its diner setting to establish a context of appetite and its repression, which in turn impel the adultery and murder that occur. In such films, this motif both helps to build up a realistic backdrop for the actions that will occur and carries a metaphoric weight, pointing to the inner forces that drive us, seemingly beyond all conscious control.

Working both ways in *Panic in the Streets*, the appetite motif forges a subtle yet crucial link for the film's two main story lines—the murder of a plague-carrying immigrant and Dr. Reed's family life. Following the opening sequence, in which the illegal immigrant infected with pneumonic plague is robbed and killed, we watch his autopsy. Shot on location in the city morgue using non-actors, the scene seems highly naturalistic, and the running conversation between the coroner and a colleague adds to this atmosphere; their minds are obviously elsewhere than on what seems to be a routine task, as they discuss where to go and what to eat for lunch. But more than just an isolated instance to paint a realistic context or even to signal official indifference to such events, this conversation starts a pattern of connection here, as the film begins to sketch a world that revolves around consumption and outlines the cultural consequences of such an attitude. Thus, we first see Dr. Reed, who must locate the murderers and possible plague carriers, at his home as his wife complains that she cannot pay the grocery bill, while their son eats his dinner. Reed's low-paying government job—and by extension his devotion to public service—is quickly established as the cause of his family's financial troubles, their "hunger," if you will. However, the ranking of public duty over individual appetite soon proves to be the key to stopping the plague, capturing the killers—symbolic of the plague—and ultimately ensuring the best life for his family.

The detective-style drama that follows emphasizes this contrast, largely in the pattern of classical film narrative. Practically every step in the detection process occurs against a backdrop of personal appetite that we come to see as the chief obstacle to Reed's efforts. Assigned to work with detective Warren, Reed and the detective begin planning their strategy at a diner, where each voices his reluctance to work with the other. After agreeing to set aside their personal differences, they start their quest at a seamen's hiring hall, where Reed barters for information by offering not only a cash reward but a free dinner. Predictably that appeal pays off, for in a "greasy spoon" diner across the street he learns that a shrimp boat captain ferried the alien ashore. Although skeptical of Reed's contention that his passenger was contaminated, the boatman eventually names the ship from which his passenger disembarked and even lets Reed inoculate him, but without disrupting his meal of an oversized "po' boy" sandwich. When Reed and Warren locate this ship, they again find a captain unwilling to help or to disturb his routine to listen to them; "I'm going to finish my breakfast" is his only comment. But in keeping with the central motif here, a frightened cook then comes forward. He recalls the stowaway because he had been bribed to prepare special meals, particularly shish kebob, that suggest the passenger was an Armenian.

Having traced the plague's source through this food chain of sorts, Reed and Warren adopt a similar strategy to track down the alien's killers in New Orleans. Thus they resume their search with a list of the city's Armenian restaurants. While one restaurant's owners, John Nefaris and his wife, recognize the dead man's photograph, they refuse to say anything for fear that the Board of Health will close their place. At this point, a deep-focus composition of the sort that typifies this film and the realistic style of the postwar cinema reveals an important piece of information, one that suggests the complex nature of this world. For even as Reed and Warren leave, we glimpse the killers—now plague carriers—they are seeking, at a booth in the rear of the restaurant. There two men, Blackie and Fitch, question a third, Poldi, about the man they killed and whether he had brought anything valuable ashore. Of special interest is the "business" accompanying their interrogation, since it casually comments on their relationship. As they question Poldi, Blackie and Fitch take the food from his plate and eat it, suggesting in the process the play of appetite that has already begun to turn the gang members against each other, as they suspect their partner of holding out on them. This disintegration of the group, in essence its self-consumption, is what finally leads Reed and Warren to them and results in the film's climactic chase across several food warehouses on the docks. After escaping from a coffee warehouse, Blackie is trapped when he tries to board a banana boat; appropriately, it is the rat guard on the ship's cable that thwarts him and binds him within another food-related metaphor, as a kind of vermin preying on the normal human food chain.

This pervasive emphasis on food and eating, as I have outlined it, does more than simply establish a realistic context for the action. For it is within this routine concern that *Panic* locates its major thrust, particularly the social focus that suggests the neorealist influence. Examining the plague's various manifestations in myth and literature,

René Girard found it to function as "a generic label for a variety of ills that affect the community as a whole and threaten or seem to threaten the very existence of social life. It may be inferred from various signs that interhuman tensions and disturbances often play the crucial role."[28] If we look for such a basic correlation between the plague and social disorder in *Panic,* we shall find it precisely in the film's almost scene-by-scene evocation of appetite. It is appetite, after all, that surfaces every step of the way in the search for the killers/plague carriers, and it is this motif that links the various corrosive or destructive forces at work in this world. In effect, it metaphorically points up a common but dangerous focus on the self and the satisfaction of individual appetite to the total disregard of the larger social implications of such self-centeredness.

In fact, the natural corollary to the film's motif of consumption is its exploration of the relationship between the individual and his society. The dark, shadowy, often unbalanced compositions that dominate the film and stylistically link it to the *noir* mainstream not only hint at a precarious and threatened world but also point toward the rapacious characters who inhabit it. Blackie, Fitch, and Poldi, for example, clearly prey upon the weak and unwary, and, as we see, eventually upon each other as well, as they try to appease their own appetites. The various sailors, dockworkers, and ordinary citizens depicted here, though, seem little different. They appear generally unconcerned and willing to accept such criminality and self-interest as the natural order of things, since they too are intent on satisfying their own desires. In this instance, the awkward rhythms of some of the non-actors reinforce this sense by suggesting that the characters may be so preoccupied with their personal concerns that they cannot give full attention to—or even believe in—the cultural crisis at hand.

In melodrama, it is the isolated individual, in this case Dr. Reed, who usually must speak for society and its interests, embodying an alternative to such concern with self-satisfaction. Despite police skepticism about his warnings of a plague and their pleas of impotence—"We can't find an unknown killer in forty-eight hours," he is told—Reed argues that there is no choice, since the entire community's safety is at stake. In fact, in a hint of the semidocumentary's social spirit, he advocates a broad definition of community, arguing that New Orleans is just a doorway to the nation, so if the plague goes uncontrolled there, it will rapidly spread across the country. In the face of such a predicament, Dr. Reed becomes, as his wife now recognizes, "the most important guy in this town." Picked out by circumstance, he becomes a representative character, embodying the best social impulse, thinking not of himself, nor even primarily of his own family, but of his society and what must be done to make all its citizens safe. (In pointed contrast, one of the mayor's assistants abandons the search to bring his wife and child upriver to escape the plague's threat.)

In a further link between his character and the focus on appetite here, Reed is the only major figure not shown eating during the emergency. When he returns home to change uniforms, his wife offers him something to eat, but he refuses anything except coffee; and when she prepares a meal anyway, he turns it down. It is a small and perhaps fragile bit of characterization; we might even argue that he would better serve society if he ate something. However, it is narratively consistent, harking back to his initial comments about not being able to pay the grocery bills and setting Reed in clear contrast to those around him who *do* stop to serve the self. His concerns, we see, are consistently other-directed—providing for his family, doing his duty, even denying the self. And in times of emergency, the film hints, the self's needs and desires, even simple appetite, should be deferred in society's interest.

As the film's title implies, the alternative is society's total disruption, its self-consumption after the pattern witnessed in Blackie's gang. "Panic," we should note, takes its common meaning of a widespread fear from its literal definition, a possession by the god Pan and thus a terror brought on by the lonely or isolated places Pan was thought to inhabit. And Pan's name, interestingly, literally translates as "He Who Feeds."[29] In the nexus of isolation and feeding that underlies the term, then, we glimpse a broad outline of the ruinous potential *Panic in the Streets* sketches through this food/eating motif: a social breakdown implicit in the spread not just of a plague but of a driving impulse to self-gratification that leads to a most fundamental human isolation. *Panic* simply sets the culture's emphasis on consumption and self-satisfaction in parallel to the plague and its specifically asocial effects—isolation, panic—to underscore the potentially self-destructive forces subtly at work in this world.

In linking the individual and the cultural, personal, and social problems in this way, *Panic* does compromise the documentary style's radical potential to some extent. But more significant in this regard is its demonstration of how much our sense of the real or the true turns on our structures of belief. This film clearly suggests a veering away from several conventions of realistic representation. For instance, it shifts the weight of truth from such documentary hallmarks as a certifying prologue and voice-of-god narrator to naturalistic imagery and everyday concerns with appetite and food. These concerns and the way in which they are shot argue that what we see accurately reflects reality, the world of everyday experience. In effect, they assume a burden of belief by implying, as Jim Hillier puts it, "an essential faith in the world reproduced and in America's ability to solve its problems."[30]

That "faith" Hillier describes refers not so much to a desire to see our problems and cope with them openly, as to how we accept their formulation and narrative resolution. The problems described here, for example, do little to test such faith. They are less indictments of our culture than flaws in human nature or even *of* nature itself. If topics like juvenile delinquency and police corruption implicitly challenge the social system, the everyday operations of human appetite and desire—or an unusual but natural visitation like an epidemic—do not. In fact, their depiction could even help build a sense of cultural unanimity, afford a path to belief rather than block it. For such problems finally challenge society less than they challenge *difference*. They strike at what threatens unanimity or causes temporary, isolated fissures in its surface. In the process, they reforge our terms of belief by asserting that a social consensus or common voice is indeed possible.

The realistic structure that a film like *Panic* illustrates was, I would suggest, a tenuous one. On the one hand, it incorporates a potential for challenging beliefs and pointing to another version of reality; on the other, it works in a way that resembles the strategy of classical narrative, as it obscures rather than reveals the relationship between viewers and film, especially the sense of how much our point of view, including our notion of what is real, is always conditioned or shaped by various forces—cinematic, cultural, and personal. But as we have seen, the semidocumentary techniques, particularly the form-conscious prologues, newsreel footage, and voice-of-god narration, invoked their own share of obscurantism, rooted in other conventions of belief viewers had been conditioned to bring to the film experience. So we need not view the gradual disappearance of those elements and the semidocumentary's absorption within a narratively simpler, realistic style simply as a regressive turn in keeping with 1950s conservatism, nor even as a great departure from the *noir* spirit. After all, the vision of documentary influence offered by Philip Dunne and others was basically unrealistic; "truthful" and "documentary" were never "synonymous." The sort of realism that we find in a film like *Panic in the Streets* successfully responds to such a naive assumption by using facticity to sketch a *texture* of belief rather than to assert reality itself. In moving from *Boomerang* to *Panic*, Kazan seems to have recognized this problem. His solution was to embrace the tenuous, even paradoxical character of film narrative—a paradox lodged in the inevitably fictive nature of all cinematic reality. In that qualified reality, he found a renewed potential for truth.

We might further assume that in the postwar climate of multiple dissatisfactions and conflicting demands, there could be little true consensus about American "ideals." This explains the shift in focus we see, from particular instances of failure in the system to the broader, commonplace patterns of human behavior. The broader focus that results may have seemed to hold some promise of consensus, of dispelling difference, as *Panic in the Streets* again shows by its ability to locate a message of cultural unanimity even in the broad patterns of human appetite it limns.

While the documentary *noir* appears to have been propelled in part by a desire for a broad perspective, to see ourselves from "outside," with the sort of detached, seemingly objective point of view that *Boomerang*'s opening demonstrates, the remark by Dunne finally points to another, underlying desire, for the sense of meaning that such a view implicitly suggests. Of course, this period saw a myriad of cultural problems that seemed to confound analysis or explanation— problems of inflation, unemployment, changing family structure, cold war politics. And their multiplicity and complexity suggest how very elusive meaning had come to seem. However, a desire for some meaning, or at least for articulating that elusiveness, might help account for the way these films turn toward the everyday and the understandable configurations of human failings. With that sort of subject they could, after a fashion, redeem the promise of their narrative style, letting us confront and perhaps accept a very human truth, wherein we simply appear as complex and contradictory individuals, as human beings who are fated to inhabit a world of contradiction.

NOTES

1. Dunne, "Documentary and Hollywood," p. 165.
2. Bazin, *What Is Cinema?* I.21. A "myth of total cinema," as Bazin terms it, inspired the invention of the cinema; and that myth spurred the development of a technology that could achieve an "integral realism, a realization of the world in its own image, an image unburdened by the freedom of interpretation of the artist or the irreversibility of time."
3. Ibid., II.26.
4. Dunne, "Documentary and Hollywood," p. 165.
5. Agee, *Agee on Film*, I.376.

6. Hirsch, *Dark Side of the Screen*, p. 190.

7. Crowther, "Imitations Unwanted," p. B1.

8. Tyler, "Documentary Technique in Film Fiction," in Jacobs, *Documentary Tradition*, p. 257. Tyler further notes how these films sought to evoke the authority of "history," albeit history with a particular "form—that is, a beginning, middle, end, and a coherent outline" (p. 254). This particular sense of form again reminds us of the strength of classical film narrative.

9. For a detailed discussion of the pattern of melodramatic narrative, see Cawelti's *Adventure, Mystery, and Romance*, pp. 262–63.

10. "Tempest That Brewed in Brooklyn," p. 38. The extent of this toning down remains unclear.

11. For a brief discussion of this case of alteration, see Lucas's entry on *The Sleeping City* in Silver and Ward, *Film Noir*, p. 259.

12. We might consider these areas of evolution in terms of what Robert Ray terms the "formal and thematic paradigms" that structure American film narrative. See *Certain Tendency of the Hollywood Cinema*. In describing the changes that American narrative films underwent in these years, he speaks of "the inflation of standard genres by means of either style or theme" (p. 149).

13. Kozloff, "Humanizing 'The Voice of God,'" p. 43.

14. Crowther, review of *The Naked City*, p. 17.

15. Agee, *Agee on Film*, I.301.

16. Kozloff, "Humanizing 'The Voice of God,'" p. 51.

17. See Malvin Wald's Afterword to Bruccoli's edition of *The Naked City: A Screenplay*, p. 137.

18. Nichols, *Ideology and the Image*, p. 285.

19. See Anthony Wilden's commentary in Lacan's *Speech and Language in Psychoanalysis*, p. 160.

20. See Kawin's *Mindscreen*. He employs this useful term to describe how a cinematic text can "have or imitate mindedness" (p. 3). It might well be argued that all *films noir* have a certain "mindedness," that is, that they all seem, in various fashions, to reflect an awareness of the problems of narration, to be aware of themselves as discursive systems. And indeed, this characteristic may form one of *noir*'s generic markings.

21. MacCabe, "Theory and Film: Principles of Realism and Pleasure," in MacCabe, *Tracking the Signifier*, p. 77.

22. Armes, *Film and Reality*, p. 67. I am indebted to this work for much of my background on neorealism.

23. Zavattini, "Some Ideas on the Cinema," in MacCann, *Film: A Montage of Theories*, p. 219.

24. Bazin, *What Is Cinema?* II.97, 64.

25. Ibid., II.66.

26. Ibid., II.73.

27. Kazan seems to embody precisely the sort of compromise that, it has

been suggested, so often marks the style of the semidocumentaries. The clearly liberal stance we find in a film like *Boomerang* is simply hard to square with his cooperation with HUAC's investigation of possible communist influence in the film industry. In fact, the courageous and isolated stance for justice by *Boomerang*'s protagonist seems, in retrospect, almost to mock Kazan's later position. For background on this situation, see Sklar's *Movie-Made America*, pp. 256–68, and especially Navasky's *Naming Names*, pp. 199–222.

28. Girard, "Plague in Literature and Myth," p. 834.
29. See the entry on "Pan" in *Crowell's Handbook of Classical Mythology*, p. 443.
30. Hillier, "Out of the '40s," p. 16.

The violent world of *film noir*—the shootout in *The Killers* (1946).

Double Indemnity's (1944) strange play of disguise and discovery—like a French farce "gone wrong."

Lost in the fun house: mirror imagery in *The Lady from Shanghai* (1947).

Reenacting the crime, enacting the film, in *Boomerang* (1947).

The telephone as menace and as lifeline in *Sorry, Wrong Number* (1948).

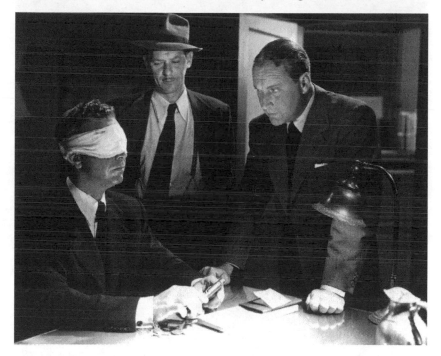

The detective (Dick Powell) with "scorched eyeballs" in *Murder, My Sweet* (1944).

The look of outward regard as menace, *The Lady in the Lake* (1947).

Loss of identity in *Dark Passage* (1947).

Subjectivity and involvement in *Dark Passage* (1947): Bogart and Bacall.

Drama in the "Docudrama," *T-Men* (1947).

An image of the film's own activity—photographing and capturing a "hidden" reality in *Call Northside 777* (1948).

The reporter McNeal interviews the wrongly convicted Frank Wiecek in *Call Northside 777* (1948).

Murder amid a sleazy show-business world in *The City That Never Sleeps* (1953).

Patrolman Johnny Kelly confronts his alter ego, the killer Hayes Stewart, in *The City That Never Sleeps* (1953).

The doctor and the detective, reluctant partners in *Panic in the Streets* (1951).

A discourse at odds: Mike Hammer takes notes from his secretary Velda in *Kiss Me Deadly* (1955).

Gabrielle "speaks" the name of "the Great Whatsit" in *Kiss Me Deadly* (1955).

CHAPTER **10** ———————————————————

Film Noir and the Dangers of Discourse

Be a detective? I could do that; I've seen enough movies.
—*Blackout*

I don't make things happen. All I do is write about them.
—*The Big Carnival*

The comments cited above point to a significant pattern that surfaces in *noir* narratives. They are from films that, like a majority of the works categorized as *films noir*, are highly conventional in both style and narrative technique. But in their own ways, these two films talk revealingly about narrative and our relationship to it. In the first, a man awakes from a night of carousing to find himself accused of murder, and he cannot recall what happened. He is urged, though, to follow a pattern he has seen in many films, to be a detective in the Philip Marlowe mold and prove his innocence. In the second film, a down-on-his-luck reporter finds a man trapped in a cave-in, sees a potential "human interest" story there, and plays up his rescue until it takes on a carnival atmosphere. While the reporter claims to be simply chronicling events, his buildup impedes the rescue and eventually leads to the trapped man's death. Both films present us with a world and characters who are, in effect, shaped by narrative, and while one protagonist recognizes and even draws on that shaping power, the other naively—or dishonestly—denies it. Together, they point up a recurring *noir* pattern, indicating a way in which many *films noir*, while quite conventional in narrative style, pursue the same concern with how we speak or communicate that we have observed in other, less-traditional works. The impulse that produces narrative experimentation in some films surfaces in a different guise here, and in the process suggests a reason for this compelling *noir* concern.

Of course, the varied narrative strategies we have been exploring may have all along seemed like aberrations, divergences from a *noir* mainstream generally marked by classical narrative conventions. But a frequent tendency to see the voice-over/flashback technique as a kind of *noir* norm already cautions otherwise.[1] For critics often take that view, I would suggest, less because that style so dominated than because they perceive how important a sense of speech is to these films, regardless of their narrative mode, as if style and subject were essentially mirror images. Certainly, the classical third-person style appears to approach the world very differently from the other methods discussed here. Its point of view suggests an objective, distanced vantage that disguises the process of narration. As Colin MacCabe puts it, "the camera shows us what happens—it tells the truth,"[2] or seems to, anyway, by effacing all sense of its presence and shaping force. In contrast, the voice-over/flashback and subjective narratives offer explicitly personal, interpretive viewpoints. But the classical style also differs from the seemingly "objective" documentary-style *noirs*. Their vantage, after all, is neither transparent nor direct, but movie-given, filtered through the voice and conventions of a particular style of realist cinema with which we are familiar and whose approach we implicitly accept.

In light of these distinctions, some critics feel there are really two kinds of *film noir*. Foster Hirsch illustrates this attitude when he talks of two main *noir* settings: the "airless studio city" of many early movies and the "real city" backdrops of later ones, that together mark a "distinction between *noir*'s 'private' and 'public' modes, between closed-form stories of festering neurosis on the one hand and the more open-form stories that connect in some way to contemporary social realities on the other."[3] While this distinction essentially rephrases that between *noir*'s expressionistic and realistic styles, it remains useful. In seeing both a private and a public thrust to the form, we can also glimpse a dual perspective at work. In fact, in the classical model *noirs* we can observe how what might seem like two distinct versions of the *noir* formula ultimately come together.

In all of its narrative modes, the *film noir* describes not just alienated, confused, or pathological figures, as much of the criticism suggests, but characters whose voices long to speak in a social sphere, to join with other speaking voices. However, those characters typically encounter a voice different from what they are seeking. They find themselves engaged in a social discourse that, even as it invites participation, also threatens to control or possess those who open up. We have already seen how films like *Double Indemnity*, *Lady from Shanghai*, and *Sorry, Wrong Number*, with their voice-over mechanisms, reflect both a desire and a difficulty that attaches to speaking privately or publicly. In fact, a tension between the narrating voice and the images it generates often seems central to the form's angst-laden atmosphere. Thus one critic argues that this approach generates the pervasive sense of "doom"[4] that is a *noir* hallmark.

More than simply atmospheric, though, this characteristic tension bears an important thematic weight. It reflects and even foregrounds the very context of speech, helping to measure the relationship between human discourse, in all its frequent "confusion," and the conditions under which it operates. Through that foregrounding, we can better gauge how the latter affects the former and *why* the former is marked by a dangerous slippage, as what is said seems to coincide less and less with what is seen or meant. Thus the alluring images of a film like *Lady from Shanghai*, especially Rita Hayworth's movie-siren poses, become more than just images of desire and frustration, projections of a narrator's distanced yet still obsessed commentary; they also represent Orson Welles's efforts at deconstructing the tantalizing spectacle of the movie love goddess that Hayworth had become. Through those images, Welles could express certain reservations he had about the very medium in which he trafficked—reservations that, he seems to suggest, film audiences should share.

Billy Wilder's *noir* efforts further illustrate this pattern. Films like *Double Indemnity* and *Sunset Boulevard* focus respectively on an interior, private discourse and on the movie industry's public discourse, while their respective voice-over narrations attest to a growing anxiety about our ability to find a reliable voice in modern America. With its protagonist's dictaphone confession, *Double Indemnity* models a kind of mediated discourse and illustrates the dangerous distance in human relations that accompanies such mediation. But at the same time, it makes a stab at the personal, as the narrator reaches out to another through that mechanism, almost in spite of all that he knows. *Sunset Boulevard*'s voice-over, provided by the dead screenwriter Joe Gillis, gives this situation a more cynical twist, hinting at a danger in the film industry's own mediated discourse and suggesting how easily and inevitably truth can be corrupted in such circumstances.

The generally jaundiced perspectives of both films point to the sort of duplicity their narrators have met with and, disturbingly, discovered at work even in themselves. Speaking from death or its verge, their voices seem freighted with a weight of anxiety not only about the self, but about modern American culture and the dark potential of human discourse itself. They thus recall the anxiety of which Michel Foucault spoke when he ingenuously asked, "What is so perilous . . .

in the fact that people speak, and that their speech proliferates? Where is the danger in that?" before outlining the "barely imaginable powers and dangers behind this activity."[5] Wilder's films, like other *noir* voice-over narratives, describe our own eroded ingenuousness; that is, a powerful suspicion of both the public and private conditioning at work in our discourse. Yet their insistent, almost compulsive narrating voices work on another level to reassert a level of naivete. As a result, they seem concerned simultaneously with revealing the illusion of autonomous discourse and with describing our persistent desire for it.

This chapter's purpose is to pursue this "perilous" and even contradictory trace of discourse in those *films noir* that take a simpler approach, generally following a classical narrative model. The third-person point of view in such films effectively reduces the image field—and implicitly the sound track as well—to a narrative given, a "truth" that we are simply presented with. But it does not, as we shall see, eliminate an anxiety about our forms of discourse, which just shifts to a thematic level, especially to a concern with the various ways in which our culture communicates and with which it seems so fascinated—the telephone, radio, newspaper, television, dictaphone, and the movies themselves. In fact, we might see this concern as forming a kind of cultural voice-over that speaks about the nature of discourse in modern America. In light of the predicament of most *noir* characters, who seem isolated, deprived of a chance of speaking meaningfully to others, or in a situation where the possibility of communicating any truth seems highly improbable, this other "voice" gains added resonance. It shows how discourse marks a paradoxical potential open to us: on the one hand, a way out of what is often seen as an ideological predicament, a means of speaking a necessary "truth"; but on the other, a possible extension of this predicament, equally conditioning and determining our lives through its already determined—and for Foucault even dangerous—nature.

Certainly, many *noir* titles, and we might especially note *They Won't Believe Me* (1947), *Sorry, Wrong Number, House of Strangers* (1949), *In a Lonely Place* (1950), and *The Glass Web* (1953), immediately suggest this problem. They reflect a concern not just with the personal, if common problem of communication or the anxieties that attend it, but with the social context in which we speak and the elusive manner in which discourse possesses both our public and private lives. *The Glass Web* well illustrates the pattern in its story of a successful television series that reenacts famous crimes. As the show's researcher notes, the key to its success is that "we're selling realism. The people who watch our show every Wednesday night want to eavesdrop on murder; they want to smell the stink of murder. They love it and they watch our show instead of others because they know I give it to them." That discourse, though, also gives him something, namely, the idea for a murder, which he commits and then tries to cover up by turning it into a script for his show and identifying another, competing writer as the killer. He is "written" into that popular discourse by its own lure and his own seeming power over it, but his efforts to write his way out by depicting another as the killer fail, leaving him caught in a "glass web" he has spun for himself. The pattern is common in the *noir* canon, and its details can be glimpsed in such classics as *The Big Carnival* (1951), *Nightmare Alley* (1947), and *In a Lonely Place,* all works that focus on primary forms of public discourse—the newspapers, radio, show business, film.[6]

    The Big Carnival is structured around a dialectic similar to that which Foucault describes: between a persistent will to truth and the forces of power and desire that both drive and conceal discourse's trajectory. Boot, editor of the *Albuquerque Sun-Bulletin,* represents one pole of this pattern, as he prominently displays his paper's motto— "Tell the Truth"—in an outer office for all to see and above his own desk, as a sign of his and the newspaper's guiding ethic. Reporter Chuck Tatum, however, argues his job qualifications with a contrary logic; as he tells Boot, "I'm a pretty good liar. I've done a lot of lying in my time." The implication is that he can adapt his discourse to the situation, that he can even "lie" at telling "the truth," if the job demands it, and he further argues that if no news is available, he will "go out and bite a dog" to create some. The idea that truth might be fashioned so haphazardly and calculatingly, or "dug up," suggests just how arbitrary and elusive it might be here. To Tatum, for instance, truth is whatever increases the paper's circulation and, in the process, adds to his own reputation. While he adopts Boot's emblematic costume of both belt and suspenders—a sign of the editor's commitment to "check and double-check everything I print"—then, it hardly signals a shift from his more pragmatic approach; for Tatum quickly sheds this garb when he gets a chance to align his voice with that of a large New York paper interested only in increasing its readership.

    Underlying an attitude like Tatum's is the idea that the individual can appropriate discourse's power, while staying free of its dangers, especially a potential domination by its public aspect. What quickly becomes clear, though, is how strong this power of appropriation is, as the case of Leo Minosa, a man trapped in a crumbling Indian cliff dwelling, demonstrates. In Leo, Tatum senses a possible "human interest" story and begins shaping its public appeal through the various media. Rather than quickly rescuing Leo, therefore, Tatum stages a drawn-out, unnecessarily complicated, and dangerous effort that will produce maximum publicity. When Leo's wife Lorraine sees this as an opportunity to desert her trapped husband, Tatum argues that leaving him will ruin the story; and her comment, "You'll just have to rewrite me," indicates the facility with which such "truths" might be shaped. She eventually accepts Tatum's contrived scenario—"Your husband's stuck under a mountain; you're worried sick. That's the way the story goes"—only because he backs it with the lure of profits, a promise of what she might gain by letting herself be possessed—or "written"—for a time by this calculated discourse.

We again see the strength of this lure when Tatum, after appropriating the Minosa family's predicament to his own end and turning their private difficulty into a public spectacle, tries to extend his control beyond his subject to discourse itself. He strikes a deal with Sheriff Kretzer to keep out other journalists—"This is my story; I want to keep it mine"—that shows his desire to control the power of discourse, as well as his naive belief that one can do so. For while Tatum wants the story for *his own,* it is only to gain leverage over the large national papers that formerly rejected him; and he measures that leverage by his ability to get a "byline," a sign of his own authorship and control. However, the personal teletype that one paper provides as a mark of his status eventually becomes a comment on that authoring power. The later scenes of his writing on the machine, sending a daily account of the manufactured heroics surrounding Leo's rescue to a national audience, increasingly show Tatum drunk, as he tries to still a troubling conscience and a growing sense of his ephemeral control. Thus when he learns that, due to the delays his publicity has created, Leo cannot be saved, the teletype becomes a mocking image, its droning sound haunting him as he comes to realize how illusory his control has been all along.

Matching this thematic development is a striking narrative shift, as a variety of commentative voices, resembling voice-over narration, occur on the sound track and challenge the film's third-person point of view. This narrative development begins with Lorraine's attempt to leave Leo, as from offscreen we hear the sounds of Tatum typing, "rewriting" her character as Leo's loving and faithful wife, even as she is abandoning that assigned role. Several subsequent scenes more pointedly introduce offscreen, commentative voices to suggest discourse's appropriative and interpretive powers. In one, a long shot shows a drill burrowing down to Leo, while a voice describes and praises the rescue activities; then, the voices of the sheriff and a contractor speak as a chorus of the unselfish efforts being made on Leo's behalf. Emanating from a live radio broadcast from the rescue site, these voices overlay the truth of Leo's situation with the lies of their own concern—lies emphasized by a pan shot that discovers a "Reelect Sheriff Kretzer" sign painted on the cliff where Leo is entombed. In similar fashion, a later scene opens on a high angle shot of crowds thronging to the rescue site, as a song on the sound track lyricizes Leo's plight and the efforts being made to save him. Besides suggesting how easily and quickly the voices of public discourse have inserted Leo into a sort of cultural mythology and in the process created a powerful and widely accepted "truth," this scene points up our common desire to tap discourse's controlling power, as the "voice-over" of the singer and another pan shot show that copies of the song can be bought for only twenty-five cents apiece. While the narrative eventually reveals these voices to be its subjects rather than agents of narration, they inject a metacinematic element to *The Big Carnival* by reminding us of the appropriative and manipulative powers that film also wields, for example, through its voice-over mechanism and musical score. It is precisely such techniques that the movies often use to insert viewers in a realm of public discourse, particularly one of commercialization.

Furthering this effect is a series of other voices that temporarily appropriate part of the narrative. Several voices/characters, for example, lay claim to a share in Leo's story—and the profit Tatum hopes to wring from it. As a result, the narrative advances through various voices that effectively speak appropriation: the barker at a carnival that sets up nearby invokes Leo's name to lure customers ("Proceeds Go To Leo Minosa Rescue Fund," a sign reads); a vacationing insurance agent, interviewed on radio about Leo's plight, dovetails his comments with a sales pitch for his company, Pacific All Risk;[7] and Lorraine bargains with several reporters to sell her "life story." In effect, everyone here seems eager to narrate, to insert his voice into a public discourse, and that readiness helps us measure the great desire for appropriation or capitalization here. However, as the "voices" of Verderber and Lorraine imply, that appropriation has a cost—not just the obvious one of Leo's commercialization, dehumanization, and death, but of the self's distortion, as it is transformed into little more than a function of commercial discourse.

At every level, then, *The Big Carnival* demonstrates a paradoxical play of discourse, showing not just how it might conceal and reveal truth, but also how its power for possession can possess individuals, manipulating them with its inherently elusive or "slippery" nature. Thus the various sorts of discourse dealt with here—newspaper, radio, film—obscure the very desires that drive them, reinterpreting these people's most grasping and self-centered aspects as altruistic, even heroic efforts. In an effort to resurrect his newspaper career, as we see, Tatum causes both his own death and Leo's; in trying to "dig up" a human interest story, he turns Leo into something less than human, an "ace in the hole," as he puts it, and manages to bury his own humanity; and in attempting to grab public attention with headlines, he transforms himself into a sensational and morbid headline, one he offers his New York editor Nagel: "Leo Minosa didn't die. He was murdered! 'Reporter Keeps Man Buried For Six Days.'"[8]

Tatum has reached this end by committing himself to a familiar sort of discourse, one that promises man a profitable place in the world but then strands him there, alone, isolated, and finally unable to communicate at all. This plight is not only Tatum's, whose final, pleading phone call to Nagel goes unanswered, but also Lorraine's, who appears in extreme long shot at the film's end, futilely seeking a ride away, out of that moral desert she inhabits. It is an effective image, hinting at a need to escape a modern wasteland of isolation and human emptiness. But from what we have seen of her character and the ease with which she allowed herself to be "written," we assume that Lorraine will never really escape; and there is no ambiguity at all with Tatum, who is stabbed and left to die alone. His brand of journalism, he earlier noted, hit "not below the belt" but "right in the gut"; appropriately, he is wounded right there, as if the very discourse he embraced had struck the fatal blow.

Edmund Goulding's *Nightmare Alley* gains a similar reflexive dimension through its focus on the lower depths of the entertainment world. It pairs the carnival element of Wilder's film with the subject of mind reading to forge its link between discourse's public and private modes. Like Tatum, carnival pitchman Stan Carlisle wants to reach "the big time," and he sees his chance in a secret "word code" developed by sideshow veterans Pete and Zeena. Their code is basically a way of tricking an audience, deceiving them into thinking that a special communication is going on, and it only naturally attracts Stan, who is not just a hustler, always looking out for the "best trick," but also a skilled user of such skewed discourse. In fact, when they refuse to sell him the code, Stan gains it through his own duplicitous ability, feigning love for Zeena. What Stan turns the code into, though, is hardly the "nest egg" Zeena and Pete term it, a hope for personal security and for their future; for him it is a way to control others and transform himself from a "nobody" into a famous figure, "The Great Stanton," as he styles himself. That word code suggests how nearly magical communication seems in this world, and how an ability to control, or even pervert, it appears a key to power. Thus it points as well to Stan's hubris, since he plans to use it in order to transform himself from a private to a public person and reap the profit such a transformation promises. What Stan, like Tatum, eventually loses sight of, though, is that it is just a trick, an exaggeration but also an emblem of discourse's deceptive capacity, and that oversight eventually leads to his downfall.

As in *The Big Carnival*, then, discourse quickly shows its paradoxical shape, how it can, in the guise of communication, wield a subtly possessive power over those who seem its masters. Stan, we learn, is a "natural" at "working" audiences, and he shows it to good advantage in combining guesswork, platitudes, and a few empty generalizations to convince the sheriff not to close the carnival. As he proudly explains, he acquired this talent—and his cynical attitude toward discourse—at an early age. As an orphan he heard so many salvation lectures that he learned to speak that "language," to "talk salvation," as he puts it, since it could prove "pretty handy when you're in a jam." Thus he boasts to his carnival buddies, "Many's the judge I've good-talked right out of his shirt." Building on this link, Stan finds that his ability for duplicitous discourse and for an evangelistic patter, for combining salvation and show business, holds the key to success. He adds a phony spiritualist angle to a mind-reading act and manages to finagle lucrative club bookings all across the country, the offer of his own tabernacle from a rich society matron, and $150,000 and a radio station with which to carry his message to the masses from millionaire Ezra Grindle. By grounding its analysis in deceptive *religious* communication in this way, in a proto-televangelist, *Nightmare Alley* disturbingly suggests not only discourse's power to shape our beliefs but also, like many other *noirs*, an impoverishment in our deepest cultural beliefs that leaves us eager to embrace any, even an empty, discourse if it reaffirms our fragile faiths. Recognizing this cultural failing, Stan plans to use his discursive manipulations in concert with psychologist Lillian Ritter's recordings of her patients' sessions, to claim the wealth and power he desires.

But just as Chuck Tatum was finally consumed by the story he concocted, so is Stan eventually appropriated by his public role and its manner of discourse. As the Great Stanton, he easily manipulates his high society clientele, but soon finds himself trapped within this persona, unable to divorce his true self from the public one. His increasing lapses into an evangelical style of speech offstage thus seem not simply false but unconscious, as if he were being spoken by his role, taken over by its language, written by a preexistent script. This shift becomes especially obvious when he asks Molly's help in duping Grindle. Larding his speech with platitudes like "a man's faith is trembling in the balance," he describes his task as if it were a difficult religious conversion. Only her reminder that "You're not just talking to one of your chumps; you're talking to your wife, to someone who knows you," reminds him of his audience, one that knows such talk is "just another angle of show business." By this time, though, his life has become just that, a show over which he exercises little real control.

In his relationship with Lillian, Stan's possession by his own spiel shows up even more clearly. While aware that she practices her own racket, he seeks her help in coping with his guilty feelings over Pete's death. Perhaps he turns to her because her sessions seem "private," removed from the "public" arena that Stan identifies with ungenuine communication—with "show business" in its various forms. Adding an irony to his lost perspective is the fact that, despite the different venue, Lillian has her own stage patter, her probing questions and solicitous approach echoing Stan's almost word-for-word. And it is no less powerful, for even after she reveals how she records—and blackmails—her rich clients, he never thinks that she might be recording his confessions as well. That failure returns to haunt him when Lillian blackmails him. In keeping with her own psychological "show," she transforms his discourse from private to public—revealing the recorded, privileged conversation of doctor and patient—to render him helpless, possessed by her possession of his words.

One consequence of such possession, the film suggests, is a loss of identity—a common *noir* theme—as discourse effectively appropriates the individual, swallows him whole, much like Michael in *Lady from Shanghai*. In close-up we view a newspaper headline, "Police Search for Miracle Worker," that ironically recalls Stan's stated desire to "make headlines," even as it illustrates how his identity as "The Great Stanton" has now become a liability that must be exchanged for the safety of anonymity. The only escape Stan can see, though, is one defined by the world of public discourse. He takes a job as a sideshow "geek," effectively abandoning his identity, and along with it his humanity, for "show."

It is a measure of the film's sense of inevitability that this transformation is one we have been looking toward, the end of an inevitable circle the narrative has described in the fashion of Greek tragedy. The film opens, we might recall, on a carnival sideshow that establishes its show business context. A carnival barker directs the crowd's attention to another geek, asking "Is he man or beast?" That question prepares for the link the narrative will forge between a withdrawal from the human and a corresponding withdrawal from discourse. Stan too points to this relationship between discourse and human identity as he remarks, "That geek guy fascinates me," and then goes on to muse about the mysterious slippage from human to animal that the geek represents: "How do you get a guy to be a geek?" A close-up displays his wonder at this mystery; and the same expression recurs several times in the narrative, such as when Pete demonstrates his mind-reading spiel, when Lillian plies her fraudulent psychoanalytic patter on him, and when Stan similarly "works" several gullible characters. This repeated expression reflects the almost mesmerizing power of discourse to control and even transform people through the "truth" it constructs, even as it shows Stan's equal ability and vulnerability, his capacity both to control and to be controlled.

The first geek, we are told, "used to be plenty big," and Stan has similarly aspired to a measure of stature and power. Those ends, he thought, might be achieved by controlling discourse and, with it, people—ultimately by turning the self into a show. With his own fall and transformation into a geek, then, Stan essentially arrives at the fate that has awaited him all along. In effect, his true nature is revealed, his own truth ironically expressed. It is fitting that at the film's end a carnival worker echoes Stan's earlier musing, bringing his words back to haunt him: "How can a guy get so low?" The owner's reply, "You reach too high," strikes a cautionary note of the sort that usually forms a coda for Greek tragedy. It ironically speaks to Foucault's query of what is so "perilous" in our discourse, pointing up how it contains a lure of possession and identity that, once we surrender to it, can possess us and can even deny us the most fundamental identity, our humanity.

Nicholas Ray's *In a Lonely Place* sums up these issues, appropriately by focusing on the movies themselves, a primary channel of public discourse in 1950s America. Like various other films of the period, particularly *Sunset Boulevard* and *The Big Knife* (1955), it focuses on the dark side of cinematic discourse. In fact, seeing the film as a commentary on Hollywood's psychological state just prior to the House Un-American Activities Committee hearings, James Palmer terms it "a critique of Hollywood itself for its bad faith in turning on its own artists, and for its complicity in promoting an atmosphere of paranoia."[9] By reflexively dramatizing how the disturbing effects of discourse can extend from within the movies to those involved in all aspects of the film industry, possessing them just as audiences are, after a fashion, captivated by the cinema's seductive images, *In a Lonely Place* sounds a warning about how "perilous" all of our "speech," including the movies' own, can be.

Significantly, this reflexive stance marks a key shift from the Dorothy B. Hughes novel on which the film is based. In the book, very little attention is given to the film industry; there are only a few references to a character's interest in becoming an actress and hints of the sort of personal compromises she might have to make to achieve that goal. The protagonist, Dixon Steele, is also not a screenwriter as in the film, but an ex-serviceman without any real occupation. While he tells friends he is working on a novel, even that minimal connection to a kind of public discourse is nothing more than a sham, an excuse he has concocted to get support from a rich uncle and to shift attention from his vagrancy.

An equally telling shift occurs in the treatment of the novel's point of view. Hughes employs a third-person vantage, but of a special sort called limited omniscient, a point of view that lets us know all that the protagonist thinks and feels, while withholding similar insight into the other characters. Because of this vantage and the privileged access to Dix's mind it offers, we know from the outset of the narrative that he suffers a psychic disturbance and that he is indeed the killer the police are seeking.[10] Commonly films translate this sort of interior monologue into voice-over reflections, as *noirs* like *Dead Reckoning* (1947) and *The Big Clock* (1948) demonstrate. But that is not the case here, the filmmakers opting instead for a classical third-person approach which treats everyone equally. It seems an appropriate choice, though, for it makes possible a suspense that lingers throughout the narrative, as well as a far more complex and ambiguous central character whose true motivations we can never be sure of. Yet the film still manages the sort of discursive focus we have noted in other *noirs* by shifting the effects of the novel's interior voice to the film's new reflexive dimension, its concern with the movie industry. In effect, the adaptation turns style into subject.

As a result, the film fashions a new context, sketching a broad picture of the film world and those who inhabit it. Dixon Steele becomes a once-successful screenwriter, now unable to work within the Hollywood system, and around him screenwriters Andrew Solt and Edmund North create a variety of industry types: the aging actor

Charley Waterman, the old director Lloyd Barnes, Steele's agent Mel Lippman, the aspiring actress Laurel Gray. Even the everyday characters, like the autograph-seeking kids who haunt Dix's favorite restaurant, the lesbian masseuse who works on the actresses, and the hatcheck girl Mildred Atkinson, who knows precisely how to turn the bestseller *Althea Bruce* into an "epic" film and of whose murder Dix is accused, seem preoccupied with the world of the movies. But even as the film industry moves into the foreground, forming the crucial context of the action, the shift has an ironic effect. As the film's title implies, that glamorous discourse hardly disguises a pervasive and crushing loneliness here. Dix, for instance, seldom answers his telephone, knows none of his neighbors, and physically abuses those around him, especially the women who fall for him. In typical *noir* fashion, then, loneliness, isolation, and a paranoid fear of others seem commonplace, as if ironic correlatives for a world predicated upon a public discourse.

These effects assume their clearest and most antisocial form in Dix, a writer, his career dedicated to communication. As his agent Mel observes, people in Hollywood generally want to *make* headlines, not avoid them, and Dix's long police record demonstrates a certain measure of success in this regard. But what is most significant about his entry into the public sphere through negative headlines is that it also marks a slippage from meaningful discourse. In short, Dix is failing as a writer. As we learn, he frequently gives way to periods of nearly inarticulate rage and violence, vented on those to whom he is closest. At the same time, he has settled into an artistic silence, writing little and turning down what few film assignments have been offered; in fact, he has not written a successful script since before the war. He excuses the stilling of his literary voice by citing a personal code: "I won't work on something I don't like." That stance, though, only cloaks an inner struggle between his public and private voices that is rendering him mute but increasingly violent. Unable to write or even speak his true feelings, he has become a spectacle of sorts, in some ways like the movies themselves: simultaneously fascinating and dangerous. What he thereby demonstrates is something beyond the usual predicament of Nicholas Ray's protagonists, of an individual whose "code" is at odds with his society's "conformist pressures," as one critic puts it.[11] Dix's situation is more complex, because he is also at odds with himself, with an identity that, we suspect, has in some way been distorted or conditioned by the public world of which he is a part.

Dix's latest project suggests one dimension of his problem. He has been commissioned to adapt the murder mystery *Althea Bruce,* a highly successful novel that has already established its own voice in the public discourse. As Mel and the film's producer assume, Dix's task is simple; he just has to frame the story in cinematic terms, subordinate his personal voice to the novel's popular one. From the way Dix approaches this task, it seems clear that he understands the assignment's formulaic nature. But in a hint of his distaste for such work, he refuses to read the book and instead asks Mildred to tell him the story, "just the way you'd tell your Aunt Clara." By thus gleaning those parts of the tale that have proved so appealing to the popular consciousness and combining them with the mystery format in which he is well versed, Dix is promised a most undemanding yet lucrative assignment. However, this seductive promise and the project's repellent aspect both spring from the same source, namely, the notion that Dix's own voice is unnecessary for the film's success—that he does not really have to *say* anything, simply rework several hackneyed formulas.

When Mildred is subsequently murdered and Dix, drawing on his murder mystery background, sketches how it might have happened, the danger of submerging the self in such generic discourse surfaces. As he recounts a probable sequence of events, we see Dix in medium and close-up shots, his face dark except for a strange highlight around his eyes that renders him sinister and frightening, as if he were indeed the murderer whose actions he so precisely and realistically describes. The image also recalls the film's opening, in which we view his eerily lit face in his car's mirror, just before he stops at a traffic light and threatens the driver of a nearby car. This sinister image thus hints at a violent potential in Dix's character, a potential funneling of the self into those violent forms—like the murderous characters he has created for the screen—sanctioned by the film industry's discourse. When his friend Brub actually begins to choke his own wife while acting out Dix's scenario, we see dramatically how easily and unwittingly one can be dominated by the power of this discourse, how one's actions may be patterned by its insinuating voice.

While he never denies his own violent history, Dix sees no connection to his immersion in Hollywood's generic discourse. In fact, like Chuck Tatum and Stan Carlisle, he naively believes that his professional skill—the writer as master of discourse—makes him immune to its conditioning powers. As Dix tells Brub, the police should "look for a man like me, only without my artistic temperament." His argument, that someone who writes stories *about* murder is unlikely to *be* a murderer, assumes that the individual is a totally free agent, unaffected by his environment—unaffected because that world supposedly wields no power, or none to which he is subject. But as Laurel comes to realize, Dix is quite capable of deeds like Mildred's murder. At one point, before she intervenes, he nearly kills a young man who insults him; and the news that someone else has confessed to Mildred's murder comes just as he seems about to kill Laurel. Only a ringing phone brings him out of a murderous rage in which he nearly strangles her. As a result, the fine distinction between guilt and innocence that is drawn here seems almost meaningless, a public determination that simply ignores the private realm, especially the threats and violence felt by Dix's friends. In this context, we should also note the transformation that the public discourse about Dix—the rumors, headlines, police accusations, unspoken beliefs—works on Laurel. These various public "voices" combine to produce an internal discourse of doubt and fear, reflected in Laurel's dream as she hears Captain Lockner's, Martha's, and, in a development suggesting the truly paradoxical way discourse can insinuate its power, even her own voice indicting Dix. The brief voice-over segment that those dominating and transforming voices fashion also reaffirms the link we have suggested between the subjects of these more conventional *films noir* and the narrative techniques of those discussed in the preceding chapters.

What *In a Lonely Place* effectively reveals is both a basic discrepancy between the public and private, between what one seems and what one really is, and the inability of these two voices to harmonize in a humanly satisfying way. This troubling discrepancy is partly due to the sense of distrust or anxiety about the other that marks the whole *noir* world. But we should note that it is more the self than the other which comes under scrutiny here. The film focuses on a person who sees himself as a master of discourse and immune from its effects, someone who is, simply, quite sure about himself. As Brub notes, though, despite their wartime comradery, he has always found it "hard to tell how Dix feels about anything. None of us could ever figure him out." Captain Lockner sees no ambiguities; he judges by appearances and past experience, and he presumes Dix guilty. While that judgment is wrong and he finally apologizes for it, those who believe in Dix's innocence also err after a fashion, their knowledge of his private life proving no more reliable than Lockner's scrutiny of his public image.

This human indecipherability, implying that behind every mysterious figure there might lurk more mystery, is a typical *noir* pattern and a natural accompaniment for what Robert Porfirio describes as a "convoluted" and "incoherent world."[12] In tying this *mise en abime* of human mystery to the problems of discourse, though, films like *In a Lonely Place* reveal a larger scope to this *noir* pattern, locating a possible scheme in this widespread slippage from meaning and harmony. Discourse's paradoxical nature, which Foucault describes as simultaneously "a violence that we do to things . . . a practice we impose upon them," and a "set of relations" that binds us,[13] becomes a model for the mysterious and interrelated problems of man and his world, both of which "speak," after a fashion, even as they find themselves "spoken" or patterned by their speech.

Of course, from within a particular discourse, just as from our normal cinematic point of view, truth seems obvious, meaning hardly questionable, and identity self-evident. Seen through classical narrative's conventions, reality appears manifest, and we generally feel that we have arrived at this judgment on our own. By foregrounding public discourse as it does, though, a film like *In a Lonely Place* strikes a cautionary note. It reminds us that such certitude is just "a practice," a determined "set of relations," in effect, the private self's payoff for accepting a public perspective. On the one hand, then, Ray's film raises the question of how much we can rely on any public discourse, even the movies, for truth. On the other, it also poses an ultimately more unsettling question about our participation in that discourse and our ability to recognize truth when we do see it.

While the *films noir* examined here seem conventional in style, following the pattern of most classical film narrative, their straightforward narratives open onto a complex and unsettling vantage that clearly echoes the more unconventional films we have examined. Persistently they speak of the slippery nature of human discourse, which can leave us alternately grasping for meaning and feeling trapped within a web of overly determined language and significance. It is a slipperiness, moreover, that even affects how we see these films. In calling attention to the paradoxical, deceptive, even dangerous nature of public discourse, they seem reflexively to stake out a basic ground of truth, free from discourse's conditioning force. But even this metadiscursive and, in the case of *In a Lonely Place*, metacinematic turn, even this posture that hints at the special capacity of these films for revelation and self-examination, hides a subtle but disconcerting slippage that recalls Foucault's observation of how discourse's driving "will to truth" only points to a "qualified" or sanctioned truth.[14] *In a Lonely Place*'s ostensible public confession of public fault, of film's manipulative power, for instance, partially dissipates into a study of individual incapacity or psychosis, similar to what we find in many other *noirs,* and indeed in its novel source. Because of that dissipation, we typically see the public and private elements of such films as alternate concerns of the form: not denoting a basic cultural relation of power and domination but simply representing separate focuses for two different *noir* modes, the one dealing with various social realities and the other with individual anxieties and neuroses.

However, the persistent human drive to "speak" and the "danger," as Foucault puts it, attending that speech suggest how intricately these private and public modes are linked and point to a paradoxical amalgam of necessity and jeopardy which, inscribed in the patterns of human discourse, underlies the *film noir*. The dark, intersecting city streets, the crisscrossed purposes of human lives, and the pervasive interplay of desire and violence that we usually associate with the form are in fact congruent with its narrative manner: the cross-purpose narrations, subjective renderings of a seemingly alien world, and efforts to document an elusive reality. And when taken together, these elements point toward a more fundamental intersection the *film noir* reveals: that of a longing, even a need, to participate in a world of human interaction and discourse, which is always being weighed against that world's potential to frustrate and perhaps destroy us.

It is a longing that casts a new light on what Foster Hirsch terms "one of the provocative ideas" of the form, that "a potential criminal is concealed in each of us."[15] A criminal, of course, is defined by his position outside of the law, beyond the bounds established by society; but those laws also seem to create the possibility of an outside. In that longing, then, we might see how much of the criminal potential Hirsch describes arises from necessity, or at least from the constraints of our world, our discourse, and its conditions of articulation. What the *film noir* recognizes through its insistent discursive focus—in the wide variety of its narrative modes—is how the nature of our individual and cultural discourse underlies and informs the other relations in our culture. Although unable to release us, or even, with any certainty, itself, from that deep structure, the *film noir* tries to articulate the ways in which we are bound within a world that is both of our own making and yet already, perilously made.

NOTES

1. For an example of such attribution, see Schrader's "Notes on *Film Noir*," pp. 278–90.
2. MacCabe, *Tracking the Signifier*, p. 37. We might also consider Nichols's comment in his *Ideology and the Image*. Classical narrative, he offers,

works at "minimizing its own status as text, discourse, or signifying system in favor of unmediated representation, a decal, or duplication of everyday appearances" (p. 85).

3. See Hirsch's *Dark Side of the Screen*, p. 17. Also consult Schrader's "Notes on *Film Noir*."

4. Porfirio, "No Way Out: Existential Motifs in the Film Noir," p. 216.

5. Foucault, *Archeology of Knowledge*, p. 216.

6. Certainly, many other films would work as well, and I would particularly note Fritz Lang's "newspaper" films: *The Blue Gardenia* (1953), *While the City Sleeps* (1956), and *Beyond a Reasonable Doubt* (1956), or the little-known Jack Arnold film *The Glass Web*, which I briefly describe here. The films I have chosen, though, clearly emphasize how both individual and public consciousness can seem restricted, conditioned, and even possessed by the very forms created to help us communicate, and thus by the paradoxical pattern of discourse that represents one of *noir's* informing principles and most important contributions to its analysis of our modern culture.

7. With this detail Wilder recalls his *Double Indemnity*, which is practically a model for the paradoxical play of discourse in *noir*, as well as a film that helped establish many of the form's narrative conventions. Walter Neff of *Double Indemnity* also worked for Pacific All Risk; in fact, it is in great part his thorough indoctrination into his company's discourse that precipitates his criminal efforts against it, as our discussion of that film demonstrated.

8. While *The Big Carnival* is the product of an original screenplay, we might note how similar it is to a Jim Thompson novel that appeared a few years later. *The Criminal* (1953) too offers a single individual, a teenager accused of rape and murder, who becomes the focus of a media campaign when a newspaper owner, the Captain, recognizes his story potential; as the paper's editor notes, "it would make a hell of a good story. Yes, sir, a hell of a story! Young love and sex and murder and mystery, and Christ, the color, the human interest! That Captain. You had to hand it to the decadent old buzzard. He didn't have any more principles than those maggots in his brain, but he knew story. He knew what would sell papers." See *The Criminal*, p. 55.

9. Palmer, "*In a Lonely Place*," p. 205.

10. From the first paragraph of the novel, for example, we enter into Dix's mind and learn about his longing to be "a part of the wildness of the air," and that since the war he had been able to find nothing "to take the place of flying wild," as he puts it. Hughes, *In a Lonely Place*, p. 1.

11. Perkins, "Cinema of Nicholas Ray," p. 69. Perkins also recognizes a similarity in the predicaments posed in many of Ray's films that is linked to difficulties of discourse; as he notes, "There are no pure villains in Ray's pictures. There are simply, and more dramatically, failures of communication and understanding" (p. 69).

12. Porfirio, "No Way Out: Existential Motifs in the Film Noir," p. 21.

13. Foucault, *Archeology of Knowledge*, pp. 229, 74.

14. For a discussion of this discursive paradox, see Hayden White's "Michel Foucault," in Sturrock, *Structuralism and Since,* especially his comment, "Discourse wishes to 'speak the truth,' but in order to do this it must mask from itself its service to desire and power, must indeed mask from itself the fact that it is itself a manifestation of the operations of these two forces" (p. 89).

15. Hirsch, *Dark Side of the Screen*, p. 170.

11

Talk and Trouble:
Kiss Me Deadly's Apocalyptic
Discourse

Writing so as not to die . . . or perhaps even speaking so as not
to die is a task undoubtedly as old as the world. The most fateful
decisions are inevitably suspended during the course of a
story. . . . It is quite likely that the approach of death—its
sovereign gesture, its prominence within human memory—
hollows out in the present and in existence the void toward which
and from which we speak.
—Michel Foucault[1]

I have to tell someone. When people are in trouble, they need
to talk.
—*Kiss Me Deadly*

Robert Aldrich's *Kiss Me Deadly* (1955) ends with an image
that, even in the canon of disturbing visuals that characterizes the *film
noir,* is most arresting. A box of stolen atomic matter explodes, destroy-
ing not only the criminals who thought to turn its power into personal
gain but, to all appearances, the detective Mike Hammer and his
secretary Velda who sought to retrieve it.[2] In the series of apocalyptic
explosions that end this film we see reflected not only our culture's
anxieties about the bomb and a nuclear holocaust, fears that surfaced
increasingly in films of the 1950s, but also the image of a world that
seems bent on destruction, thanks to its citizens' grasping, even violent, preoccupation with the self. It is a world whose potential for
avoiding such destruction is metaphorically stated in the film's opening, as Hammer's sports car speeds down a dark highway, as if hurtling
heedlessly toward that cataclysmic end we later witness, only to be
suddenly halted by the appearance of a frightened woman blocking
the road. What this "nut from the looney bin," as Hammer styles her,
introduces is a mystery, one defined not just by her enigmatic presence

in the middle of a highway but by the curious message cited above—really a most sane statement about our need for messages, revelations, communications of a sort that might help avert the "trouble" that seems to impend here both individually and culturally. As we should recognize by now, this pressing need to talk in order to avoid disaster, even death, is a recurrent *noir* motif, and one that finds its most dramatic statement in *Kiss Me Deadly.* Coming near the end of the *noir* cycle, this work articulates a warning implicit in all these films: it depicts an inexorable movement toward destruction resulting from the failure of our talk, from a decreasing ability—individually and culturally—to speak "so as not to die."

The recurrent voice-over narration is probably the *film noir's* most obvious manifestation—a structural one—of this imperative to talk to someone, to locate a receptive audience for some message that urgently needs saying. As we have noted, the narration in films like *Double Indemnity* (1944) and *D.O.A.* (1949) emphasizes this impulse through characters who speak even as they are dying. In their compulsion to leave behind a message, they demonstrate a distinctly human response to the ultimate individual calamity, a means of temporarily suspending "the approach of death" by "hollowing out," as Foucault puts it, "in the present and in existence" a short space of meaning whose boundaries are marked by the very words one speaks. The bloodstain that gradually spreads across the jacket of *Double Indemnity's* Walter Neff as he talks reminds us that his life is, in effect, already spent; however, while he recounts his fatal encounter with Phyllis Dietrichson, he can postpone that inevitable end and even draw some meaning—a cautionary note about the dangers of desire—out of his demise.

D.O.A.'s Frank Bigelow similarly speaks against the clock; "I don't have very much time," he says, as the narrative begins. But in what little time remains to him, he hurriedly tries to sort out the events that have mysteriously led to his poisoning by an unknown assailant. Although he angrily responds to a doctor's diagnosis that he has been fatally poisoned with "You think you can explain my life away in a few words?" he spends his last hours shaping and inhabiting a world of words, explaining for both the police and, we understand, himself how he came to be murdered and what his death might mean. More than simply a last existential retreat from extinction or an assertion of meaning despite all appearance of meaninglessness, though, this film describes a potential we cling to even in the bleakest circumstances. What it points to is the flip side of that possessive and destructive power of discourse described in the previous chapter. It hints at an abiding optimism in communication itself, as it implies a community of speakers and listeners, despite mounting evidence that alienation and isolation are becoming our culture's prevalent characteristics. Amid its dark and apocalyptic overtones, *Kiss Me Deadly* voices this at least minimally hopeful note.

As our prior examination of conventional narratives like *Nightmare Alley, The Big Carnival,* and *In a Lonely Place* suggests, the *noir* world and the characters who inhabit it are haunted not simply by a free-floating anxiety, arising from some postwar malaise, nor by the perceived menace of a criminal underworld that increasingly seems to intrude into the everyday, even forcing its corrupt shape on the normal world. Rather, *noir* films consistently reveal an uncertainty about the various voices that speak throughout our culture, that add a weight of ambiguity and anxiety to all our interactions, and that seem to impinge in almost indeterminate ways on our ability—and, indeed, our need—to speak. Beneath its conventional private-eye mechanism and classical narrative style,[3] *Kiss Me Deadly* is a paradigm of this pattern. While the Mickey Spillane novel on which it is based clearly focuses on the menace of a tangible criminal underworld, the Mafia, and deploys a consistent imagery of body parts to go along with its nickname, "The Black Hand," the film substitutes an unnamed, apparently international, evil at work, dealing not in heroin but in atomic secrets, while it develops as a subtext the various tensions and problems that inform much of our communication. By linking a persistent human need to talk with the manifestly widespread "trouble" afflicting modern society, it provides probably the most revealing *noir* assessment of both the problems and the lingering hope bound up in our individual and cultural discourse.

As its backdrop, *Kiss Me Deadly* evokes a world not quite reduced to silence; in fact, this world is often cacophonous, filled with the noises of car horns, blaring radios, even people whose talk is nothing more than sound effects. But that noise tends to drown out or stand in for real communication, and most forms of human discourse seem suspect, threatening, or simply pointless. The film's theme song, "I'd Rather Have the Blues," heard on Hammer's car radio as he stops to pick up the mysterious Christina in the opening sequence, quickly establishes this atmosphere, telling us that "the night is mighty chilly and conversation seems so silly." If the ensuing conversation between Mike and Christina is not quite "silly," it does reveal how difficult communication is here by showing how little these two have in common and thus the barriers of experience that their talk must surmount. Along with that difficulty, though, we also glimpse a general reluctance to speak—or fear of speaking—that marks almost every character in the film. Despite her curious message about the necessity of talk, for example, Christina seems unable to speak straightforwardly about the trouble she is in, mainly because she is unsure whom she can trust. As we learn, she has already refused to talk to government agents and later, even under torture by the criminals seeking it, refuses to talk about the missing atomic matter. And while she seems to size Mike up quite accurately, commenting on his vanity and self-concern, she hesitates to confide in him too.

In great part because he is a detective, accustomed to dealing with a dark and unpredictable world, Mike is similarly suspicious and reluctant to talk. But as a detective, he is supposed to ask questions, to be able to probe an enigmatic and unforthcoming world. His silence, consequently, hints at some compromise in his ability to ask "why," and it represents a marked shift from the novel, in which he is self-assured and aggressive in seeking out the truth. Here, though, he delegates much of that important interrogative function to his secretary Velda, who must gather the information he seems unwilling—perhaps even unable—to solicit for himself. Indeed, Mike prides himself on his ability to *withhold* information—from the police, from gangsters like Carl Evello, even from his friends—not simply because it is important to do so but as a working principle, a habit of silence his work and experience of the world have fostered. Thus when first his detective friend Pat Murphy and then several government agents question him about Christina, Hammer simply remains silent. In response to Pat's plea to "tell us what you know," he offers his own query, "What's in it for me?"—a remark cleverly calculated to stop any further questioning by suggesting that he might be as corrupt as he is suspected of being. It is a characteristically strategic withholding of the self, further demonstrated by his use of a telephone-answering machine and tape recorder to screen his calls and allow him to answer only when he chooses. In this way, of course, he can keep a personal distance and maintain some power over the entanglements human discourse almost inevitably brings.

This stance already hints at both positive and negative potentials in Hammer's character. His answering machine, for instance, suggests a suspicion of how communication works in his culture and his desire for a measure of control over it. And the fact that Christina, who also can withhold information when it is necessary, confides an enigmatic, even poetic message to Mike—who does not read poetry—implies that she sees her own concern with meaningful talk, with truth, reflected in him. But at the same time, this trait links Hammer to the negative, degenerative forces at work in his society, forces shown here as repressing, conditioning, or distorting discourse. In fact, we might see Hammer's tendency to silence as reformulating the classical detective's ambiguous coloring, his ability to seem allied alternately with the world of laws and with a criminal underworld, in order to suggest how nearly Hammer's professional reticence verges on the negative, talk-distorting forces in this world.

Pat Murphy's response to Hammer's silence—"Who do you think you are?"—is especially significant in this context. The previous chapter considered the significance of classical narrative's point of view but gave slight attention to the importance of character and identity in that style. Through character we are usually placed in the classical text, given an identity we can embrace and find some meaning in. And that character is, as David Bordwell explains, created according to certain ground rules. Typically he is a "psychologically-defined, goal-oriented" figure who assumes the burden of causality for the narrative;[4] simply put, he is consistent and knowable. With this point in mind, we can read Murphy's question in two ways. It is, first, a rhetorical remark, simply asserting that Hammer has no right to interfere with things, especially since he knows how dangerous and even deadly that knowledge may be. But second, it suggests an unusually unstable character, hinting that Hammer literally does not know "who" he really is. We might well take Murphy's question quite seriously, therefore, as indicating a link between Mike's refusal to talk and his sense of self, and implying that a person's character might be measured by his ability or willingness to open the self up and talk.

A later incident, when Hammer investigates Carl Evello's involvement in Christina's murder and encounters the gangster's half sister Friday, subtly restates this connection. On meeting her for the first time, he asks if he can be her friend, intending, we suppose, to use her, much like he uses Velda, to gain access to her brother. Friday's curious reply, "If you want to be a close friend, ask me something," has the ring of a seductive come-on. But her remark too resonates tellingly in the context of Christina's plea for someone to talk to and of Velda's comment about being "glad" when Mike is in trouble, "because then you come to me," to suggest both the deep-felt need for communication that marks this world and how one's humanness might be fundamentally defined in terms of a willingness to talk, to ask the appropriate and even necessary questions of others.[5] In Hammer's quixotic identity, especially his reluctance to talk even as he seems committed to asking the sort of questions that will reveal the reasons behind Christina's death, then, *Kiss Me Deadly* most dramatically presents this world's enigmatic and dangerous aspect.

Hammer's reticence gains added significance when we notice that this world's larger pattern, one of the cultural landscape's basic traits, is a general retreat from human discourse. It is a retreat that shows up most obviously in a reluctance or fear of talking to anyone, which throughout the narrative produces awkward silences and opportunities for communication that typically issue in only the most banal or enigmatic dialogue. As a result, even when Mike does ask the right questions of those he encounters, he often meets only with silence or more mystery. Fight trainer Eddie Yeager, for instance, assures him he does not "know anything," but he obliquely adds that his silence is due to two of Carl Evello's thugs who promised to "make it worth my while; they said they'd let me breathe." Following this principle, Hammer shows his own thuglike nature as he forces amateur opera singer Carmen Trivago to talk by smashing his original Caruso recording. In the process, Hammer demonstrates an inherent contempt for the beautiful and the artistic that reinforces our negative conceptions of him, and he gains little, since what he hears is just a replication of the enigma he already faces, as Trivago describes the melancholy of his dead friend Nicholas Raymondo and his mysterious allusion to "a riddle without an answer."

That phrase, in fact, sends Hammer back to the realm of art and its mysterious ability to communicate by recalling Christina's last words, "Remember me." It is a riddle that he puzzles over for much of the narrative, and one whose only clue he finds in a volume of her namesake Christina Rossetti's poems. When he searches her apartment, Mike finds that Christina has left one large legacy, a room of books; and one of them is left open to the sonnet "Remember," which speaks prominently of the "silent land" where she has now gone, the land of the dead. But for much of the narrative that clue remains beyond him, mainly because Mike does not read—or cannot understand—poetry. It is especially fitting, therefore, that when he searches the room her books are being packed away, a legacy of words being stored until someone who properly values words, understands poetry, prizes communication—an envoy from a land of talk, not silence— might come to claim it.

Carmen Trivago helps us see another way in which the human capacity for communication seems "packed away" here. In the novel a generally nondescript character, a tenement landlord who provides Hammer with some key information, Trivago here becomes a model of the withdrawn, aspiring artist. Occupying a small, dingy tenement apartment, oblivious to a world that finds his love of classical music eccentric and bothersome, he surrounds himself with his records and sheet music, singing to and for himself. And in an act that Hammer puzzles over, we learn how Ray Diker, writer and science editor of a local newspaper, has similarly withdrawn, walking away from his editorial post and locking himself within his small apartment, where he seems afraid to talk to anyone. Mike remarks in some amazement about how "the science editor of a newspaper drops out of sight and no one knows why"; but what makes this reversion to silence, like the others noted here, go almost unnoticed is its rather frequent occurrence. Indeed, its real significance rests in the fact that in this culture practically no one any longer bothers to ask "why" because it hardly seems unusual.

In this context, Hammer's status as what Jack Shadoian observantly terms a "mythical quester"[6] is most revealing, for the world *Kiss Me Deadly* describes appears very much in need of a modern-day Perceval, someone who by his ability to ask the right questions might help restore life to this modern wasteland. We might recall, however, that the mythic Perceval initially holds his tongue and by keeping silent leaves the land in distress. Hammer's frequent lapses into silence and his failure to ask the right questions combine with his one-sided approach to communication to link him to this pattern in a most fundamental way, in the process suggesting both his potential and his limitations. Mike clearly uses people, as he does Friday to gain access to her brother, his friend Nick whom he tells to "ask around" about the bombing of his new car, and especially Velda—and in every case he seems little concerned with the consequences of that employment. This trait leads Alain Silver to suggest that "deception, not detection, is Hammer's trade," and that seems an accurate assessment of his activities, although we should qualify it with a mindfulness of how pervasive deception is here.[7] By using Velda to ferret information and encouraging her to use her sexual attractions to manipulate men, however, Mike points up his darker potential. For in this practice he clearly resembles Dr. Soberin, Carl Evello's employer, who similarly employs Gabrielle, masquerading as Christina's roommate Lilly Carver, to get information from Hammer by trading on her sexuality.

The impetus behind using such human "filters" certainly seems similar, since both Hammer and Soberin want to get information while staying apart, avoiding the consequences—of feeling or vulnerability—that go with all human communication. Largely because of this attitude Mike's relationship to Velda remains ambiguous for much of the film, as it does not in the novel: is she simply a human tool he uses effectively in his trade or does she represent something more, something personal to him, a path out of silence, a grail worth seeking when that atomic one proves unworthy?[8] His embraces and kisses, though, provide no satisfactory clue, for in a disturbing but apparently characteristic disjunction between words and actions, Mike always seems to talk business, even when making love to Velda; between kisses he discusses his job, the police, or her progress on the assignments he has given her. It is as if he can give her only a small portion of the self, and even that not the true self which he has to hold aloof to digest and assess the information she provides. Gabrielle's later taunting of Hammer before she shoots him reiterates this point and suggests how, like Perceval, Mike fails as a quester. Her description of "the liar's kiss that says I love you but means something else. You're good at giving such kisses," strikes right to the point. It emphasizes how he typically holds himself apart, even in the most humanly intimate situations, and how he uses discourse not so much to close the gaps between people but defensively, to maintain those gaps or profit from them. Consequently, it is most fitting that, in a major change from Spillane's novel, the film's Hammer is a divorce detective, someone who specializes in separation. Shadoian's description of him as "an image of his world—cold, cynical, unprincipled, callous, emotionally repressed,"[9] well sums up this failing Hammer shares even with those he ranks himself against, a failure rooted in his reluctance to talk and thereby counter the trouble that clearly impends here.

Hammer's weakness as a proper quester, in fact, derives from the discursive failings he shares with a world that is almost at odds with itself and with a people who are similarly torn or, as R. D. Laing would describe it, "disintegrated"—disjointed from the self and its proper environment.[10] This problem of disintegration is behind one of the film's most distinctive stylistic traits, as the narrative links the way people use language with how they are visually framed—or to be more precise, omitted from the frame. When in the opening sequence Hammer and Christina are waylaid and then tortured by some unknown figures, we glimpse only parts of human bodies—legs, feet, torsos—while the sound track plays the voices of these partially pictured people—voices effectively sundered from identities. First of all, such fragmentation suggests that these are people somehow not whole, beings not just lacking identity for the moment because we cannot see their faces but figures wanting in or denied a full humanity, and in the case of the torturers easily given over to violence and inhuman action. Moreover, this technique implies a reason for that incompleteness, by emphasizing a discourse that seems fundamentally divorced from the human source which remains offscreen. As an example, we might recall how Dr. Soberin's menace through most of the narrative is underscored by his appearance as a dispassionate, disembodied voice, speaking anonymously on a phone, through a semiconscious daze, or into Hammer's drug-induced sleep, and surreptitiously working through both a sinister gangster like Evello and the seemingly innocent Gabrielle. At times we do see his feet, legs, a hand, but these are not really clues of any sort; we are given nothing to link them to an identity. They are just signs of his enigmatic, partial presence—which is all the more menacing because of that very partialness. What he demonstrates so disconcertingly is how easily and variously discourse and the violence it unleashes can be divorced from the self, at least as long as the individual perceives communication as nothing more than a filter or medium for extending one's power and remaining aloof from the impingements of others. It is an attitude that shows up particularly in Soberin's effort to elicit the secret of Christina's final words—"Remember me"—by injecting Hammer with sodium pentathol. Again seen only partially—fancy shoes, an arm, a hand holding a syringe—Soberin simply asserts a fact. He informs Mike, "You will cry out what it is you must remember." Clearly, he sees the drug as ensuring a divorce of voice from consciousness, separating truth from Hammer's compunctions about speaking what he knows.

Disconcertingly, Mike's own methods of gaining information differ mainly in degree. It is obvious that he takes some pleasure in roughing up Dr. Kennedy at the morgue and the attendant at the Hollywood Athletic Club to get them to talk. And behind his strong-arm tactics, we can see the common impulse to force speech, to wrest it from the individual, to see it not so much as a natural communication between people but as a thing or commodity to be extracted. Mike too tends to defer the self and to see the world as composed of isolated selves, not so much linked as insulated by discourse—as he is by his answering machine, Velda, and even Nick. But filtered through such a perspective, human discourse quickly loses its special ability, as Foucault puts it, to "suspend" or defer the catastrophic. Deployed in this way, it only propels these people, like lemmings, all the more precipitously toward some fearful end—as less a basic "task" of life than the ironic "gesture" of a cultural death impulse that seems to afflict Hammer as much as it does his opposition.

The corruption of that opposition, of Carl Evello and his henchmen, is fittingly shown not just in the unnatural leisure implied by their lounging about the pool and drinking in midday or their concern with the horse races reported on the radio, although all are common methods of suggesting corruption or criminality in Hollywood narratives. Equally telling is a pattern of disjunctive discourse used to introduce them. As Hammer comes to investigate Evello's links to Christina, we hear horse races being announced on the radio. Besides inserting the world of gambling into this scene, the radio, like the one that also drones on in Soberin's beach house when Mike is later being drugged and beaten, points to the distancing effect that discourse has for these people. Evello's thugs, Sugar Smallhouse and Charley Max, are bothered by the talk and embraces of their female companions, who distract them from the more important message of the race results. When Evello himself interrupts, sending them to beat up Hammer in the bathhouse, the blaring radio commentary assumes another distancing function by providing a noise to drown out the sounds of the ensuing fight. The radio works throughout this scene to disguise violence, both the physical forms promised by Sugar and Charley and the subtler forms implicit in how these people hold each other at a distance, isolate or simply ignore one another.

This effect becomes particularly obvious in the later beach house sequence when Evello and Soberin drug Hammer, for in this case it also paints the consequences of such an attitude toward human exchange. In this sequence, in which they try to force Hammer to talk, the primary discourse is actually one of violence: dominating the sound track is a radio report of a prizefight that Evello, Sugar, and Charley raptly listen to. That violent discourse is appropriate here, though, since it stands in for the violence they intend to do to Hammer, who is drugged and tied to a bed in the next room, as they try to extract information before killing him. In fact, the description of the fight that plays throughout this sequence corresponds point by point with Hammer's predicament, as it describes an underdog who is being beaten and is "on the ropes," but who surprisingly comes back to beat his adversary. The scene's primary function, though, seems to be to emphasize how easily a discourse of distance and disguise can backfire and work its implicitly violent potential on those who use it so casually. First, the fight sounds drown out the noise of Mike's escape from his bonds and his subduing of Evello. Then its blaring lets him disguise his voice to call Sugar and muffle the sounds of the struggle in which he kills Evello and Sugar. When discussing Hammer's special talent for violence, Evello had earlier told him, "Maybe you *can* speak my language," and this scene shows how correct that surmise was, even as it further links the particular kinds of discourse that seem preeminent in this world with a capacity for violence. Through his own violent capacity, Hammer has turned these gangsters' corrupt discourse against them, evoking that deceptive potential, appropriately, to separate his adversaries so that he might deal with them one at a time, in the sort of violent "language" they best understand.

Of course, Hammer has shown that he knows how to use various sorts of discourse with facility, and to use them while staying aloof from their manipulations or impingements. In fact, it is this ability that signals his potential for aiding this world—or for failing it. The way in which he uses Velda, Nick, and other informants suggests one side of this ability, while its darker manifestations surface in the violence he so readily, and almost pleasurably, unleashes on others. But precisely because they too closely mirror those of Evello and his men, Hammer's discursive talents ultimately prove unavailing, backfiring just as they did for his criminal opponents. As we see, he can effectively "talk" his way out of that beach house trap once by drawing on his violent skills—which he, in fact, defines as a kind of language; but at the film's end Mike and Velda are both caught there and to all appearances consumed in the apocalyptic destruction that occurs. A key to this failing, I would suggest, shows up in a peculiar inversion that Hammer offers, as he describes his judo skills with a lexical metaphor: "I think it's a good idea to speak a lot of languages. Any country you go to, you can handle yourself." As this remark emphasizes, Hammer simply sees his violent skills as another language, one in which both he and the people with whom he must deal are fluent. At the same time, his comment hints at how he, like many others here, tends to see discourse as a potentially dangerous thing, an impingement or weapon over which one must exercise careful control. By equating language and violence in this way, of course, he loses sight of language's fundamental ability to link people together, to forge a kind of community. On a larger scale there results a general avoidance of human communication, as we have already noted, as well as a sort of paranoia about it, such as the writer Ray Diker manifests: "Make it sound good," he tells Mike, fearing that even in his apartment every word he says is being monitored by some unknown enemy to be used against him.

How well Mike can really "handle" himself linguistically, given this attitude and the troubled world in which he moves, is crucial to the narrative's resolution. In the film's final sequence, the nature of the physical threat that he must deal with—and that finally seems just beyond his understanding—is pointedly framed in a lexical context that casts a revealing light on Hammer's abilities and weaknesses. In what seems like a lecture on the nature of language and the importance of its proper use for communication, Pat Murphy explains that Christina held the key to a stolen atomic device: "Now listen, Mike. Listen carefully. I'm going to pronounce a few words. They're harmless words, just a bunch of letters scrambled together, but their meaning is very important. Try to understand what they mean: Manhattan Project, Los Alamos, Trinity." Ironically, Pat never clearly states what he is referring to; he simply marks this enigma off with a series of allusive, referential terms, code words that suggest his own reluctance to speak about such a thing. What his elliptic approach further implies is how much this atomic device fundamentally violates our usual categories of understanding, even our language of description. It seems, in this context, a telling comment on the perceived dangers of atomic power/weaponry in this period. How could we hope to control that which we are reluctant even to name and cannot speak straightforwardly about?

Perhaps even more to the point, this lecture drives home a fundamental failing that Mike has in common with many other characters here. If Murphy seems to talk down to Hammer, as if he were a child— and the shot composition, with the camera first looking down from Pat's vantage, then up from Mike's, suggests such an interpretation[11]—it is to underscore what clearly remains beyond the detective's understanding or outside his lexicon of violence. While Mike has been confident of his ability to decipher whatever remains to be understood, and has even demonstrated a deeper understanding of the workings of discourse than many of the people he encounters, he has also clearly bungled things: both Christina and Nick have been killed, the latter because Mike used him to get information; Velda has been kidnapped in an effort to control Mike; and the missing atomic matter has been practically handed over to Soberin. Because of these failures, Mike is forced to examine just how much remains omitted from that lexicon, resulting not only in his failure to "listen" and talk but even to understand what he does hear. The kind of "language" he speaks well, a language of violence and ego protection, has proved nearly useless to his friends and seems almost pointless in the context of the sort of calamitous violence and destruction that might be unleashed as a result of not speaking a more humane language. Velda's earlier mocking comment, that Hammer's investigation is nothing more than a search for "the great whatsit," thus refers to more than, as one critic offers, "the vagaries of chance or destiny" operating here.[12] That phrase denotes an empty lexical marker and the sundered relationship between meaning and thing that defines Hammer's personal limitations, characterizes the problematic understanding that plagues his world, and helps explain its gradual slide toward meaninglessness and self-destruction, as its inhabitants increasingly lose their human capacity to speak "so as not to die."

Yet *Kiss Me Deadly* does hold out some potential for salvation, for the sort of redemption from a "silent land" that an ability to talk about, to communicate, and thus to share this human predicament might afford. It is a possibility iconically suggested at the start when, with arms outstretched in a Christ-like pose, Christina (the name literally translates, after all, as "resembling Christ") forces Mike to stop and listen to her message. Her haunting injunction, "Remember me," continues this motif by recalling Christ's commandment to his apostles, "Do this in memory of me," and suggesting a level on which she is trying to pass on her ministry of communication to Mike as a kind of disciple. Strengthening such redemptive allusions, as well as our expectations of what they might mean here, is an observation early in the film that, after being unconscious for three days, Mike seems to have "returned from the dead." But rather than a resurrected redeemer, Mike is more, as his friend Nick styles him, "like Lazarus, rose out from the grave." In fact, the redeemer allusions work almost ironically, dovetailing with the quest motif and our usual expectations of the private eye to underscore the slippage that marks this world, as expectation and reality fail to coincide. *Kiss Me Deadly*, in effect, intertwines the religious and the mythic, Christ, Lazarus, and the legend of Perceval and the wasteland, in order to describe both the hope and the failure of human communication in this world. Because of his limitations, Mike has only partially grasped the portent of Christina's gospel of the necessity for "talk" in a world of trouble. When he comes to, therefore, it is fitting that he lapses into a dead silence, refusing to answer the questions put to him. His egocentric question at that point, "What's in it for me?" suggests not only the failure of her message, but also Mike's abiding desire to determine what is said and when, thereby making the self the sole focus of discourse and its only profiteer.

This pattern also links *Kiss Me Deadly*'s opening with its apocalyptic conclusion, wherein a similarly missed message leads to death and destruction. Just as Hammer fails to fully grasp Christina's message of the need for talk and embarks on his egocentric quest for "the great whatsit," so too does Gabrielle, in the film's final sequence, ignore Dr. Soberin's warnings about the mysterious box for which so many people have already died. Her simple assertion, "I want it," defines her character at this point much as does Mike's "What's in it for me." And another shift from the novel drives this characterization home, for here it is not Mike who kills Soberin; rather, Gabrielle shoots her former employer so she can have the box all to herself and thereby satisfy her curiosity and compelling desire. Emphasizing the parallel between this sequence and the opening is a preceding scene in which Pat acerbically dismisses Hammer's halfhearted apology for his silence and overriding self-interest: "You didn't know. Do you think you'd have done any differently if you had known?" Echoing this remark and thus further linking Hammer to Gabrielle is Soberin's comment that she "should have been called Pandora" on account of her equally stubborn curiosity: "Of course you wouldn't believe me. You'd have to see for yourself, wouldn't you?" But like the other warnings and messages sounded throughout this story, his last one to her—and the one that seems to carry the film's crucial warning against the Pandora-like nature of our human curiosity—simply goes unheeded: "Listen to me, as if I were Cerberus with all his heads, barking at the gates of hell. I'll tell you where to take it, but don't open that box."[13]

Of course, Soberin's windy rhetoric and his recourse to myths that are as meaningless to his listener as Trivago's Caruso recordings are to Hammer are partly to blame here, but the sense that these people speak almost different languages and that the common cultural referents have been lost—the lexical markers rendered empty or meaningless—suggests the problem's larger dimensions. It seems that because no one is quite able to listen or talk in a meaningful way about the troubles afflicting them this world is practically brought to "the gates of hell"—as the film's fiery conclusion evokes—rather than redeemed at the last moment from the atomic holocaust that impends.

What *Kiss Me Deadly*'s destructive conclusion thrusts home, then, is the disconcerting but seemingly inevitable consequence of a self-centering that has been measured throughout the narrative by a focus on human discourse and its recurrent failure. Hammer, our modern grail quester, is presented from the start as fundamentally selfish and inarticulate, unwilling and unable to put himself out, to talk meaningfully to others, or to stop in his headlong rush to oblivion. But then he is like so many others here who cannot or will not talk, or simply see it as a pointless, profitless activity. Of course, we invest more hope in Mike because of how we conventionally "read" the private eye in such films. In defying our expectations for Hammer's success, though, *Kiss Me Deadly* puts us on warning, suggests that we should examine such received cultural wisdom—and cultural heroes—more closely.

Mike's friend Nick, one of the film's more sympathetic characters, helps to give us this perspective. Unlike many others here, he is eager to talk and ready to help; in fact, he puts himself out for his friend and, in an addition to the novel, is killed for his efforts. Mike tends to use Nick, just as he does Velda, to get information, yet he pays little heed to Nick's warnings of trouble, partly because Mike is so pig-headed, but also because of the way Nick talks. His efforts at conversation typically come out translated in the language of the fast cars that he worships. His most expressive articulations are "Va va voom" and "pretty pow"—terms that suggest both the allure of that speeding, powerful, modern world and also its danger, in fact, terms that hint of the big "pow" on which the film ends. Nick, I would suggest, is simply a product of his culture, conditioned, like Hammer, by what it holds valuable and, also like Mike, finally unable to deal with this world on its own, life-denying terms.

Even beyond a simple inability to talk or to ask the right questions, then, we can see how what one knows or needs to know is redefined here in terms of self-interest and personal possession. In such a context, talk, with its implicit giving or opening up of the self, seldom seems to be in an individual's best, that is, self-, interest. While the film repeatedly emphasizes that what people truly need to survive, both individually and culturally, is an openness to others and to human interrelationships, that message seems lost on most of these characters nearly from the start. In fact, as Christina demonstrates, that message can hardly even be articulated in circumstances where every speech act seems conditioned and perilous, where the very language used seems incommensurate or unintelligible, and where some surrender or threatening exposure of the ego always seems involved. Still, as Foucault explains, "speaking so as not to die" is a most basic human impulse and an appropriate gesture for a world that, like Soberin's beach house or Mike's car after Christina stops him in the opening scene, appears precariously perched on the edge of an abyss. It is an alternative to destruction, however, that is simply overlooked by these people. Yet their oversight and its explosive consequences help us see how our common discourse all too easily slips from a form of communion to, as the previous chapter illustrated, a tool of appropriation and self-satisfaction—a tool that promises to appropriate and perhaps eventually destroy us.

Analogous themes, such as a general cultural alienation, individual isolation, and the destructive workings of desire, are, of course, the common hallmarks of the *film noir*. But their inscription here within a consistent motif of communication and its failings suggests an important development which bears out Shadoian's contention that *Kiss Me Deadly* is "the film the genre has been winding up to."[14] It points toward a clear awareness, largely implicit or formative in the films we have previously discussed, of how the forms of our individual and

cultural discourse underlie and even structure the oth
our society, shaping them for good or ill as our own ho]
worst instincts take voice—or become garbled. In its at
of" these problems articulately, *Kiss Me Deadly* man
revealing light on the darkness of the *noir* world. For it provides not
just a necessary commentary on the state of human discourse but also
a cinematic paradigm for the sort of "talk" we need to engage in if we
are to avert the apocalyptic "trouble" toward which our culture even
now seems to be hurtling.

NOTES

An earlier version of this chapter appeared in the *Journal of Popular Film and Television* 13.2 (1985): 69–79. Reprinted with permission of the Helen Dwight Reid Educational Foundation. Published by Heldref Publications, 4000 Albemarle St., N.W., Washington, D.C. 20016. Copyright © 1985.

1. Foucault, *Language, Counter-Memory, Practice*, p. 53.
2. I must qualify this point because there is, among the commentaries on this film, some disagreement about what happens to Mike and Velda at the conclusion. *Kiss Me Deadly* ends with an interior shot of Soberin's burning beachhouse, as the wounded Mike frees Velda from a locked room, followed by a long shot of the beachhouse and shoreline, as the house goes up in flames and explosions. Several accounts of this last scene suggest that Mike and Velda escape this conflagration and can be seen running along the beach. Whether such accounts indicate the existence of an alternate ending for the film or simply represent the kind of creative recollection—prodded by wish fulfillment—that often marks film commentary, though, I am unable to say with certainty. The narrative does set out visual and thematic clues that would justify either ending. Because of its first-person point of view, the novel obviously requires Hammer's survival. By opting instead for the third-person vantage, however, Robert Aldrich and screenwriter A. I. Bezzerides eliminated the necessity for Mike's escape; in fact, the shift in narration, especially in light of the *film noir*'s frequent use of the voice-over technique, is itself most telling. I see it as a stylistic signal of Hammer's demise, since its effect is to devalue the character of Hammer somewhat, presenting him as another—and perhaps equally expendable—player in this larger drama. In any case, the various prints of this film I have viewed all end similarly, with no visual evidence that Mike and Velda escape the apocalyptic finale.
3. I want to qualify the notion of "classical narrative" here, for while *Kiss Me Deadly* uses a third-person point of view typical of classical film

style, it does so with a telling difference. Note, for instance, its recurrent use of various "Brechtian" estrangement techniques, most notably the opening credits that scroll in reverse, the mismatched shots of Christina running down the highway at the film's opening, shots of a neon clock behind Hammer that indicate great gaps of time during a continuous action, a number of disorienting reverse-angle shots, and even the camera's shadow appearing in a late scene. These effects, along with a number of others throughout the narrative, serve to undermine our normal immersion in the narrative and force us to look at it from a rather different perspective; in effect, they suggest an alternate approach to a pattern we have noted in many other *noirs,* as they call into question our normal perspective, especially our usual *cinematic* point of view.

4. Bordwell, "Art Cinema as a Mode of Film Practice," p. 57. See also the more extended discussion of character in classical narration in Bordwell, Staiger, and Thompson, *Classical Hollywood Cinema,* pp. 13–18.

5. A further suggestion of the similarity between Christina and Velda, and thus of a similar redemptive possibility they might hold out, can be seen in Velda's appropriation of Christina's haunting enjoinder, "Remember me," to mark her skewed relationship with Mike. "Hey, you remember me?" Velda asks on two occasions, one as they embrace and he questions her about her inquiries for him, as if that were the only reason he might have for such intimate contact.

6. Shadoian, *Dreams and Dead-Ends,* p. 273.

7. Silver, "*Kiss Me Deadly:* Evidence of a Style," p. 25. Silver further suggests that "deception is the key to this world," and he links that characteristic to "a subject-object split" here which we might do well to see in the context of the disjunction between the self and others— and analogously, the disjunction between words and meaning—detailed in this chapter.

8. In this context, the characters' names seem especially telling. Velda's last name, "Wakeman," suggests her warning potential, to awaken Mike to a new life. It should be noted that this evocative last name does not occur in the Spillane novel and seems a significant addition that argues for the attention to detail in this film.

9. Shadoian, *Dreams and Dead-Ends,* p. 271.

10. See Laing's study of such individual and cultural disjunctions, *Divided Self: An Existential Study in Sanity and Madness,* p. 23.

11. For a detailed description of this visual pattern, see Silver's "*Kiss Me Deadly:* Evidence of a Style," p. 30.

12. Ibid., p. 26.

13. The various classical references that mark the film's conclusion seem clearly to work in contrast to the Christian allusions of the earlier sequences, the former speaking primarily of death, the latter of life and a redemptive possibility. Of course, since Gabrielle does not share Soberin's learning, his allusions are lost on her, just as much of

what Christina says seems lost on Mike. On the one hand, these allusions represent a further level of failed communication, a level on which language becomes empty markers, unintelligible and nearly meaningless. On the other, they have a specifically cultural thrust, suggesting how so many of our Western cultural myths have become largely unavailing in the face of the contemporary world's problems.

14. Shadoian, *Dreams and Dead-Ends,* p. 267.

12 ———————————

Conclusion:
Noir's Dark Voice

> From morning till evening, unceasingly, streets and buildings are
> haunted by narratives. They articulate our existences by teaching
> us what they should be. They "cover the event," i.e. they *make*
> our legends. . . . Seized from the moment of awakening by the
> radio (the voice is the law), the listener walks all day through
> a forest of narrativities, journalistic, advertising and televised,
> which, at night, slip a few final messages under the door of sleep.
> —Michel de Certeau[1]

As Michel de Certeau dramatically describes, discourse in its
various forms seems to condition much of modern life. Even as we
dream, he suggests, a "forest of narrativities" haunts the unconscious,
invading the psyche with a kind of preformed cultural speech and, in
the process, blurring the distinction between how much we narrate
and how much we are narrated by the world we inhabit. But still, we
go on dreaming, and in that dreaming attest to a fundamental desire
or need for other narratives than those that seem commonly sanctioned and subtly insinuated into our daily lives.

As this study has suggested, the *film noir* reflects this pattern in
various ways. Its dark images and often nightmarish events mirror the
sort of tension Certeau describes, suggesting by turns how much we
are bound by patterns not of our own design, and by a desire, however
blunted or distorted, to give an alternate and personal shape to the
narrative of our life. It does so, moreover, "at night," that is, within a
darkness of mood and setting that seems especially conducive to
alternate visions or different perspectives. In fact, the context it
creates almost demands an altered perspective, after the fashion
glimpsed in the shifting focal points of *Murder, My Sweet,* the interplay
between stage and backstage in *City That Never Sleeps,* or in Walter
Neff's remark to Barton Keyes in *Double Indemnity,* "I just wanted to set
you right about something you couldn't see because it was right smack

up against your nose." What the *film noir* does so effectively is to recognize what we "couldn't see" normally, and then shift focus to that which is, disconcertingly, too close to be seen, too much a part of our personal and cultural lives for us to view and assess clearly.

Of course, a similar impulse propelled the social problem films of an earlier era, resulting in works like *I Am a Fugitive from a Chain Gang* (1932), *Wild Boys of the Road* (1933), and *Dead End* (1937). Those films also sought to raise consciousness, to make us more aware of societal ills. What we often overlook in examining the *film noir*'s visual style or cataloguing its disturbing subjects, though, is that it goes a step further, speaking of the difficulties involved in "racking focus," as it were. For unlike earlier reflections of our cultural failings, especially the Depression-era films noted above, it lays bare the more fundamental problem of talking about, making sense of, or giving formulation to our world. The *film noir* thus not only depicts certain problems but also explores the terms under which we perceive and respond to them. In effect, it helps us see why we must "slip" those messages in "at night."

Certeau's commentary also points up how these films operate against a background of the "forest of narrativities" we commonly traverse. In fact, the *film noir* finds in our common stories and their received forms the context of its alterity. For this reason it often seems like the flip or darker side of melodrama, but melodrama without the final restoration of social order, the sense of a world made right, that we expect from that form. But through them—through those narratives of how we normally act, what we commonly think, what we should be—*noir* refocuses attention on what much of our discourse leaves out, even on what that discourse appears incapable of fully articulating. And that may ultimately be the form's most disturbing aspect—its revelation of our difficulty in ever seeing or speaking the truth of our human situation. When he describes the *film noir* as "a nightmarish world of American mannerism,"[2] Paul Schrader thus strikes right to its core, if not precisely as he intended. For these films do rely on a certain "mannerism," one that typifies how we traditionally tell our American stories, as well as how we construct our film narratives, but they do so to show how that manner is part of the larger human puzzle, contributing to our nightmares, haunting our waking lives with a shaping power that threatens to bind us in its coils.

What that mannerism ultimately suggests is that a great part of the *noir* story *is* the *noir* story, that is, the curious shapes its narratives take as they set about revealing the curious shapes both our lives and our world have assumed. Undeniably there moves in these films a strange, often disturbing, impulse, one that seems to suggest a determinism, a locked-in-ness, that is reflected in the fatalism of so many *noir* characters and the inevitability of their situations. Yet these elements represent less an older, naturalistic sense of determinism than a very modern awareness of the various systems, including language itself, that construct our lives and often seem, on close scrutiny, bent on frustrating our hopes for order, certainty, or control. But at the same time, and almost contrarily, the films do speak a hope, even if it often seems a forlorn one, lodged in that ability for speaking or formulating the human situation. In general, their voice constantly echoes *The Maltese Falcon*'s Sam Spade, as he tells Brigid O'Shaughnessy, "Listen. This won't do any good. You'll never understand me, but I'll try once and then give it up." The remark sounds despairing, but it is nevertheless an effort at speech, at making something dark and obscure understandable, despite all obstacles. Appropriately, it is a remark that leads into the film's most forthright assertion of ethics, of what one *must* do, simply because it is "right." That effort to speak, as well as the ethic prompting it, is central to the *film noir;* for it points to a persistent, driving, and finally *human* force that qualifies the form's otherwise fatalistic bent, and that can help us understand why such a dark form would have proved so popular.

We have been able to see these patterns clearly by following a path staked out by Michel Foucault, one that involves "isolating a . . . body of procedures and inverting its obscure content into a spotlight."[3] In this case, I began by categorizing the amorphous body of *films noir* into groups of discrete narrative practices and then, by examining typical samples of each practice, exploring the implications of the different strategies. However, my aim was never to pursue the full implications of each narrative approach. To do justice to the voice-over/flashback technique alone, for instance, would require a far longer and more sophisticated study than this one. The value to this approach is that it "inverts" how we normally see the *film noir,* and thus sheds light on what the form's darkness, as well as those narrative practices that we might take for granted, too often obscures from view. When seen from a different angle, the *film noir* reveals a fascination with narration and a desire to speak of discourse's problems and potentials. And that will to speak, I would suggest, reflects the form's larger concern with our longing to see clearly and make some sense of the modern human situation. This longing, in the face of the manifest dangers that seem to accompany and qualify all discourse, finally shows forth as the "obscure content" of *noir*'s various narrative "procedures."

In describing these mechanisms and speculating on their implications, I have tried to go beyond the stylistic or thematic focus of earlier *noir* criticism and follow a loosely ideological model. However, that approach too, I have found, constrains an adequate accounting for the *noir* phenomenon. Most ideological studies, after all, treat narrative structures reductively, disavow desire as other than a controlling effect of a capitalist system, and advance what Christopher Lasch calls the widespread "ideological assault on the ego"[4] that devalues the self and reinterprets it as little more than a helpless construct of various cultural and historical forces. The *film noir*, though, directly addresses the self and lays bare the various "assaults" it must withstand in the modern world, including those that surge from within, and I have tried to mirror this strategy. Of course, in foregrounding the forms of *noir* narrative, I run a risk of seeming almost ahistorical, of making the series of violations—of classical form and of cultural practice—that these films describe appear almost causeless. However, the alternative is to devalue the intense subjective emphasis of the form, its insistent concern with presenting a quite "other" view of reality, what I earlier termed the "private I" perspective. Thus this study has privileged desire as a kind of basic force underlying even our ideological structures. But that privileging lets us embrace rather than exorcise the threatened ego advertised so prominently in such *noir* titles as *I Wake Up Screaming* (1948), *I Walk Alone* (1948), and *I Died a Thousand Times* (1955), and more important, to recognize the appeal which that sovereign self holds.

This approach is also indebted to the response of Gilles Deleuze and Felix Guattari to traditional ideological models. In introducing their *Anti-Oedipus: Capitalism and Schizophrenia,* Foucault describes how they have outlined a new kind of "ethics" in trying to reveal "the fascism in us all . . . that causes us to love power, to desire the very thing that dominates and exploits us."[5] They call man a "desiring-machine" and argue "that the social field is immediately invested by desire, that it is the historically determined product of desire" rather than vice versa.[6] Thus, even as they outline how ideological mechanisms typically work, they also describe a precarious, at times unpredictable, foundation for these mechanisms, as well as a level on which they can easily subvert themselves by libidinously speaking the individual's desires, even as those desires are supposedly being channeled in a proper social direction. In this way desire invariably escapes the ideological system. As Elizabeth Wright explains it, "Desire refuses a final embodiment in a particular power-machine; it will always find a way out."[7]

One such "way out" may well be the *film noir*—a strangely dichotomous form that can seem by turns to support and to undermine the status quo. At times, it clearly articulates desires that no social system would seem to sanction. And as my narrative focus suggests, it speaks in some uncharacteristic ways for American film. Yet we often see it resorting to recuperative strategies that qualify its disconcerting message, as if it were searching for a compromise with conventional film practices and the viewing habits of American filmgoers, both "power-machines" in their own fashion. Both these multiple thrusts and the efforts at recuperation, though, indicate a desire at work in the *film noir* that might generically define it and that determines its nature every bit as much as its visual styling and disconcerting themes do.

The particular pattern of desire we find in *noir* is for a kind of communication—or to be more accurate, for a way of formulating our place in the cultural landscape and articulating that formulation for others. Thus we find the form simultaneously embracing subjective, voice-over narrators and detached, documentary-style voices as alternate hopes for speaking some elusive truth. Of course, given how much seemed displaced or lost in the postwar era, how much of our sense of cultural purpose, identity, and common values seemed blasted away with the war's wide destruction, we should be far more surprised if we could not detect in our films a casting about for reassurance and answers. But the shape of this searching is itself significant. For what the *film noir* seems especially intent on is finding a language in which to speak and understanding the difficulties inherent in such a discourse.

This argument, that the *film noir* is fundamentally concerned with the problems of giving formulation to the modern American environment, may well be just a symptomatic reading. That is, it might only reflect the very striving for articulation and the anxiety about expression that resulted when these films tried to describe or narrate an amorphous, essentially unformulable human and cultural predicament. Certainly America and Americans in the post–World War II era did not "feel right," and part of that wrong feeling was due to what we could not see or well understand. With the war, much had apparently been won, but we also seemed to have lost a great amount. At the same time, we had no satisfying *sign* either way: we were victorious but felt little like victors, given the rapid drawing of the cold war's lines; and any sense of loss we felt was unsupported by the visible scars of sacrifice and endurance, particularly of physical devastation, that most of the world then sported. This absence made our postwar cultural situation all the more difficult to chronicle.

Mirroring this situation, the *film noir* describes a culture that might well have suffered a physical rather than spiritual devastation, as it chronicles our common anomie and points to several contributing causes: the breakdown of traditional family structures, woman's shifting role in society, corruption in office, a perceived failure of the American Dream itself. But like its diversity of narrative shapes, the very variety of these causal conditions is telling, for it suggests a groping about, a reaching for something, as our films presented us with persistent and troubling shadows rather than a clear point of attack, more absence than presence—the ghosts that haunt our cultural and individual psyches. What proves constant is this sense of groping, of an urgent need for expressing something that seems frustratingly ineffable.

The focus on narrative strategies taken here brings that consistency to light. By forcing us to confront the various mechanisms *film noir* uses to tell its stories, this vantage eventually begs a question—that we consider *why* those multiple castings about were needed. One answer immediately suggests itself, that we had come to feel that the conventional patterns of film narrative were inadequate for taking the measure of things in postwar America. Classical narrative, after all, appears to place viewers in a position of coherence, even omniscience, from which they view and judge the filmed world against a set of implicit norms. But *noir*'s typical subjects—sudden murders, illicit desires, official corruption—cut deeply into that coherence, questioning whether such a privileged and truthful position is possible, whether there are any such reliable norms. The deep thrust of these films, then, is to underscore the need for other vantages and alternate ways of understanding our world.

Yet this answer still stops short, for the narrative strategies that emerge and help identify the whole *noir* project had a relatively brief vogue, as we have noted. The subjective camera experiments, for example, largely cluster around 1947 and thereafter find only limited narrative application. The documentary style's popularity also wanes rather rapidly, with only isolated elements of its mechanism lingering into the 1950s, although it would later resurface in such popular—and *noir*-influenced—television series as *The Naked City* and *The Untouchables*. Even the intense subjectivity of the voice-over/flashback technique appears far less popular after the 1940s; a film like *Sunset Boulevard* (1950)—its corpse narrator perhaps the ultimate application of the strategy—represents one of its last major *noir* uses. But the appearance and disappearance of these techniques, their measurable success and their passing from vogue, tell us much. They indicate a pattern of narrative desire and frustration at work—efforts at communication, failures, and perhaps attempts that work too well, showing or telling more than we could commonly or comfortably accept about our culture or ourselves. In any case, the answer must account for the desire and felt need for speaking our human situation that these various strategies attest to.

On both the individual and cultural levels, we usually look for—and cling to—patterns of order, systems of continuity. They provide us with a defense against both the contradictions in our culture and ourselves and those sudden upwellings of desire in each. Of course, they never vanquish disorder or the discontinuous; they just give us a temporary refuge against those forces that are always there, eating away at our sense of cultural coherence or secure self-identity. But simply embracing that refuge can be dangerous; as Certeau offers, "To be spoken without knowing it is to be caught dead unawares; it is to proclaim death, believing all the while it is conquered; it is to bear witness to the opposite of what one affirms."[8] Our best hope against the chaotic or the discontinuous, then, rests paradoxically in our ability to testify to it, to speak of its inevitable place in our individual and cultural lives.

The *film noir*, I would suggest, offers just such a testimony, a speaking of, but also against, death, in order to preserve what we had come to see as a most fragile human order. In fact, it is a discourse partly *about* our need for such speaking in a world that seems already narrated, bound within and to a certain pattern of order. As a film like *Kiss Me Deadly* (1955) climactically demonstrates, these works speak even in our "spokenness," even as the very world they chronicle seems to embrace—to "kiss" if not to "proclaim"—death. Yet I do not want to suggest that they represent a kind of *liebestod* in the American cinema, for by speaking in this way, *noir* films enact what we might term a talking cure. In discussing the relation between language and psychoanalytic practice, Jacques Lacan notes that verbalization might hold a "cure" for hysteria and similar psychic ills. As he puts it, a patient can begin to overcome his pathology by making it "pass into the *verbe*, or, more precisely, into the *epos* by which he brings back into present time the origins of his own person."[9] In trying to articulate our personal and cultural anxieties, the *film noir* similarly works out such a "cure," offering us a better sense of ourselves, or at least a clearer notion of who we are individually and socially.

Because of the bonds of convention, such a curative speech almost requires a special cinematic voice, an unconventional way of speaking. What the *film noir* developed was a variety of such voices, each speaking in a dark, experimental, and even approximate language about the discontinuities and uncertainties of our modern experience. Of course, those voices differ greatly from other film forms, especially from the norms of classical film narrative; however, through them *noir* could effectively let difference speak, give voice even to death itself, and in the process, like a kind of vital talisman, perhaps even stay that threat. Hardly a morbid or pathological form, as some would see it, then, the *film noir,* especially in the ways it speaks of and to our human darkness, is essentially a genre of life.

NOTES

1. Certeau, "Jabbering of Social Life," p. 152.
2. Schrader, "Notes on *Film Noir,*" p. 290.
3. Certeau, *Heterologies: Discourse on the Other,* p. 172.
4. Lasch, *Minimal Self,* p. 224.
5. Foucault, Preface to Deleuze and Guattari, *Anti-Oedipus,* p. xiii.
6. Deleuze and Guattari, *Anti-Oedipus,* p. 29.
7. Wright, *Psychoanalytic Criticism,* p. 169.
8. Certeau, *Heterologies,* p. 181.
9. Lacan, *Ecrits,* pp. 46–47. What Lacan is speaking of here is the sort of narrative that we compose of our lives, a kind of personal epic (*epos*) that is then articulated, put into the patterns of speech (*verbe*)—and conditioned by those patterns—within the psychoanalytic experience.

Appendix:
A *Noir* Filmography

The following list of films indicates those works that were consulted in the course of this study. It includes most of the major and a large number of the minor, seldom-seen *films noir*. However, it should be taken as broadly representative of the form, not as an exhaustive catalogue.

The Accused. Paramount (1949). Dir.: William Dieterle. Prod.: Hal B. Wallis. Script: Ketti Frings, from the June Truesdell novel *Be Still, My Love*. Photog.: Milton Krasner. Ed.: Warren Low. Cast: Loretta Young, Robert Cummings, Wendell Corey. Running time: 101 min.

Angel Face. RKO (1953). Dir. and Prod.: Otto Preminger. Script: Frank Nugent. Photog.: Harry Stradling. Ed.: Frederic Knudtson. Cast: Robert Mitchum, Jean Simmons. Running time: 91 min.

Appointment with Danger. Paramount (1951). Dir.: Lewis Allen. Prod.: Robert Fellows. Script: Richard Breen and Warren Duff. Photog.: John F. Seitz. Ed.: LeRoy Stone. Cast: Alan Ladd, Paul Stewart, Phyllis Calvert. Running time: 89 min.

The Asphalt Jungle. MGM (1950). Dir.: John Huston. Prod.: Arthur Hornblow, Jr. Script: Ben Maddow and Huston, from the W. R. Burnett novel. Photog.: Harold Rosson. Ed.: George Boemler. Cast: Sterling Hayden, Jean Hagen, Sam Jaffe. Running time: 112 min.

Beware, My Lovely. RKO (1952). Dir.: Harry Horner. Prod.: Collier Young. Script: Mel Dinelli, from his play *The Man*. Photog.: George E. Diskant. Ed.: Paul Weatherwax. Cast: Robert Ryan, Ida Lupino. Running time: 76 min.

Beyond a Reasonable Doubt. RKO (1956). Dir.: Fritz Lang. Prod.: Bert Friedlob. Script: Douglas Morrow. Photog.: William Snyder. Ed.: Gene Fowler, Jr. Cast: Dana Andrews, Joan Fontaine. Running time: 80 min.

The Big Carnival (*Ace in the Hole*). Paramount (1951). Dir. and Prod.: Billy Wilder. Script: Wilder, Lesser Samuels, and Walter Newman. Photog.: Charles B. Lang. Ed.: Arthur Schmidt. Cast: Kirk Douglas, Jan Sterling. Running time: 119 min.

The Big Clock. Paramount (1948). Dir.: John Farrow. Prod.: Richard Maibaum. Script: Jonathan Latimer, from the Kenneth Fearing novel. Photog.: John F. Seitz. Ed.: Gene Ruggiero. Cast: Ray Milland, Charles Laughton, Maureen O'Sullivan. Running time: 93 min.

The Big Combo. Allied Artists (1955). Dir.: Joseph H. Lewis. Prod.: Sidney Harmon. Script: Philip Yordan. Photog.: John Alton. Ed.: Robert Eisen. Cast: Cornell Wilde, Richard Conte, Brian Donleavy. Running time: 89 min.

The Big Frame. RKO (1953). Dir.: David Macdonald. Script: Steve Fisher and John Gilling. Photog.: Monty Berman. Cast: Mark Stevens, Jean Kent, John Bentley. Running time: 85 min.

The Big Heat. Columbia (1953). Dir.: Fritz Lang. Prod.: Robert Arthur. Script: Sydney Boehm, from the William P. McGivern novel. Photog.: Charles Lang. Ed.: Charles Nelson. Cast: Glenn Ford, Lee Marvin, Gloria Grahame. Running time: 90 min.

The Big Knife. United Artists (1955). Dir. and Prod.: Robert Aldrich. Script: James Poe, from the Clifford Odets play. Photog.: Ernest Laszlo. Ed.: Michael Luciano. Cast: Jack Palance, Ida Lupino, Rod Steiger. Running time: 111 min.

The Big Sleep. Warner Brothers (1946). Dir. and Prod.: Howard Hawks. Script: William Faulkner, Leigh Brackett, and Jules Furthman, from the Raymond Chandler novel. Photog.: Sid Hickox. Ed.: Christian Nyby. Cast: Humphrey Bogart, Lauren Bacall. Running time: 118 min.

Blackout. Lippert Pictures (1954). Dir.: Terence Fisher. Prod.: Michael Carreras. Script: Richard Landau. Photog.: Jimmy Harvey. Ed.: Maurice Rootes. Cast: Dane Clark, Belinda Lee. Running time: 87 min.

The Blue Dahlia. Paramount (1946). Dir.: George Marshall. Prod.: John Houseman. Script: Raymond Chandler. Photog.: Lionel Lindon. Ed.: Arthur Schmidt. Cast: Alan Ladd, Veronica Lake, William Bendix. Running time: 98 min.

The Blue Gardenia. Warner Brothers (1953). Dir.: Fritz Lang. Prod.: Alex Gottlieb. Script: Charles Hoffman, from Vera Caspary's story "Gardenia." Photog.: Nicholas Musuraca. Ed.: Edward Mann. Cast: Anne Baxter, Richard Conte, Ann Sothern, Raymond Burr. Running time: 90 min.

Body and Soul. United Artists (1947). Dir.: Robert Rossen. Prod.: Bob Roberts. Script: Abraham Polonsky. Photog.: James Wong Howe. Ed.: Robert Parrish. Cast: John Garfield, Lilli Palmer. Running time: 105 min.

Boomerang. 20th Century-Fox (1947). Dir.: Elia Kazan. Prod.: Louis de Rochemont. Script: Richard Murphy. Photog.: Norbert Brodine. Ed.: Harmon Jones. Cast: Dana Andrews, Lee J. Cobb, Arthur Kennedy. Running time: 88 min.

The Brasher Doubloon. 20th Century-Fox (1947). Dir.: John Brahm. Prod.: Robert Bassler. Script: Dorothy Hannah, from Raymond Chandler's novel *The High Window.* Photog.: Lloyd Ahern. Ed.: Harry Reynolds. Cast: George Montgomery, Nancy Guild. Running time: 72 min.

The Bribe. MGM (1949). Dir.: Robert Z. Leonard. Prod.: Pandro S. Berman. Script: Marguerite Roberts, from a Frederick Nebel story. Photog.: Joseph Ruttenberg. Ed.: Gene Ruggiero. Cast: Robert Taylor, Ava Gardner, Charles Laughton. Running time: 98 min.

The Brothers Rico. Columbia (1957). Dir.: Phil Karlson. Prod.: Lewis J. Rachmil. Script: Lewis Meltzer and Ben Perry, from Georges Simenon's *Les Freres Rico.* Photog.: Burnett Guffey. Ed.: Charles Nelson. Cast: Richard Conte, Dianne Foster. Running time: 92 min.

Brute Force. Universal-International (1947). Dir.: Jules Dassin. Prod.: Mark Hellinger. Script: Richard Brooks. Photog.: William Daniels. Ed.: Edward Curtiss. Cast: Burt Lancaster, Hume Cronyn, Yvonne DeCarlo. Running time: 95 min.

Caged. Warner Brothers (1950). Dir.: John Cromwell. Prod.: Jerry Walk. Script: Virginia Kellogg and Bernard C. Schoenfeld. Photog.: Carl Guthrie. Ed.: Owen Marks. Cast: Eleanor Parker, Agnes Moorehead, Hope Emerson. Running time: 97 min.

Call Northside 777. 20th Century-Fox (1948). Dir.: Henry Hathaway. Prod.: Otto Land. Script: Jerome Cady and Jay Dratler, from James P. McGuire's *Chicago Times* articles. Photog.: Joe MacDonald. Ed.: J. Watson Webb, Jr. Cast: James Stewart, Richard Conte, Lee J. Cobb. Running time: 111 min.

Champion. United Artists (1949). Dir.: Mark Robson. Prod.: Stanley Kramer. Script: Carl Foreman. Photog.: Frank Planer. Ed.: Harry Gerstad. Cast: Kirk Douglas, Arthur Kennedy, Ruth Roman. Running time: 90 min.

Christmas Holiday. Universal (1944). Dir.: Robert Siodmak. Prod.: Frank Shaw. Script: Herman J. Mankiewicz, from the W. Somerset Maugham novel. Photog.: Woody Bredell. Ed.: Ted Kent. Cast: Deanna Durbin, Gene Kelly. Running time: 93 min.

City across the River. Universal-International (1949). Dir. and Prod.: Maxwell Shane. Script: Shane and Dennis Cooper. Photog.: Maury Gertsman. Ed.: Ted Kent. Cast: Stephen McNally, Sue England, Jeff Corey. Running time: 90 min.

City That Never Sleeps. Republic (1953). Dir.: John H. Auer. Prod.: Herbert J. Yates. Script: Steve Fisher. Photog.: John L. Russell, Jr. Ed.: Fred Allen. Cast: Gig Young, Mala Powers, Edward Arnold. Running time: 90 min.

Clash by Night. RKO (1952). Dir.: Fritz Lang. Prod.: Harriet Parsons. Script: Alfred Hayes, from the Clifford Odets play. Photog.: Nicholas Musuraca. Ed.: George J. Amy. Cast: Barbara Stanwyck, Paul Douglas, Robert Ryan. Running time: 104 min.

Conflict. Warner Brothers (1945). Dir.: Curtis Bernhardt. Prod.: William Jacobs. Script: Arthur T. Horman and Dwight Taylor. Photog.: Merritt Gerstad. Ed.: David Weisbart. Cast: Humphrey Bogart, Alexis Smith, Sydney Greenstreet. Running time: 86 min.

Convicted. Columbia (1950). Dir.: Henry Levin. Prod.: Jerry Bresler. Script: William Bowers, Fred Niblo, Jr., and Seton I. Miller, from Martin Flavin's play *Criminal Code.* Photog.: Burnett Guffey. Ed.: Al Clark. Cast: Glenn Ford, Broderick Crawford, Dorothy Malone. Running time: 91 min.

Cornered. RKO (1945). Dir.: Edward Dmytryk. Prod.: Adrian Scott. Script: John Paxton. Photog.: Harry J. Wild. Ed.: Joseph Noriega. Cast: Dick Powell, Walter Slezak. Running time: 102 min.

Crack-Up. RKO (1946). Dir.: Irving Reis. Prod.: Jack J. Gross. Script: John Paxton, Ben Bengal, and Ray Spencer, from Fredric Brown's story "Madman's Holiday." Photog.: Robert de Grasse. Ed.: Frederick Knudtson. Cast: Pat O'Brien, Claire Trevor. Running time: 93 min.

Criss Cross. Universal-International (1949). Dir.: Robert Siodmak. Prod.: Michel Kraike. Script: Daniel Fuchs, from the Don Tracy novel. Photog.: Franz Planer. Ed.: Ted J. Kent. Cast: Burt Lancaster, Yvonne DeCarlo, Dan Duryea. Running time: 88 min.

Crossfire. RKO (1947). Dir.: Edward Dmytryk. Prod.: Adrian Scott. Script: John Paxton, from Richard Brooks's novel *The Brick Foxhole.* Photog.: J. Roy Hunt. Ed.: Harry Gerstad. Cast: Robert Young, Gloria Grahame, Robert Ryan. Running time: 85 min.

Cry Danger. RKO (1951). Dir.: Robert Parrish. Prod.: Sam Wiesenthal and W. R. Frank. Script: William Bowers. Photog.: Joseph F. Biroc. Ed.: Bernard W. Burton. Cast: Dick Powell, Rhonda Fleming, William Conrad. Running time: 79 min.

Cry of the City. 20th Century-Fox (1948). Dir.: Robert Siodmak. Prod.: Sol Siegel. Script: Richard Murphy, from Henry Edward Helseth's novel *The Chair for Martin Rome.* Photog.: Lloyd Ahern. Ed.: Harmon Jones. Cast: Victor Mature, Richard Conte, Hope Emerson. Running time: 96 min.

D.O.A. United Artists (1950). Dir.: Rudolph Mate. Prod.: Leo C. Popkin. Script: Russell Rouse and Clarence Green. Photog.: Ernest Laszlo. Ed.: Arthur H. Nadel. Cast: Edmond O'Brien, Pamela Britton, Luther Adler. Running time: 83 min.

Dark City. Paramount (1950). Dir.: William Dieterle. Prod.: Hal Wallis. Script: John Meredyth Lucas and Larry Marcus. Photog.: Victor Milner. Ed.: Warren Low. Cast: Charlton Heston, Lizabeth Scott, Dean Jagger. Running time: 98 min.

The Dark Corner. 20th Century-Fox (1946). Dir.: Henry Hathaway. Prod.: Fred Kohlmar. Script: Jay Dratler and Bernard Schoenfeld, from Leo Rosten's story. Photog.: Joe MacDonald. Ed.: J. Watson Webb. Cast: Mark Stevens, Lucille Ball, Clifton Webb. Running time: 99 min.

The Dark Mirror. Universal-International (1946). Dir.: Robert Siodmak. Prod. and Script: Nunnally Johnson. Photog.: Milton Krasner. Ed.: Ernest Nims. Cast: Olivia De Haviland, Lew Ayres, Thomas Mitchell. Running time: 85 min.

Dark Passage. Warner Brothers (1947). Dir.: Delmer Daves. Prod.: Jerry Wald. Script: Daves, from David Goodis's novel. Photog.: Sid Hickox. Ed.:

David Weisbart. Cast: Humphrey Bogart, Lauren Bacall, Agnes Moorehead. Running time: 106 min.

The Dark Past. Columbia (1948). Dir.: Rudolph Maté. Prod.: Buddy Adler. Script: Philip MacDonald, Michael Blankfort, and Albert Duffy, from James Warwick's play *Blind Alley.* Photog.: Joseph Walker. Ed.: Viola Lawrence. Cast: William Holden, Nina Foch. Running time: 74 min.

Dead Reckoning. Columbia (1947). Dir.: John Cromwell. Prod.: Sidney Biddell. Script: Oliver Garrett and Steve Fisher. Photog.: Leo Tover. Ed.: Gene Havlick. Cast: Humphrey Bogart, Lizabeth Scott, Morris Carnovsky. Running time: 100 min.

Detective Story. Paramount (1951). Dir. and Prod.: William Wyler. Script: Philip Yordan and Robert Wyler, from the Sidney Kingsley play. Photog.: Lee Garmes. Ed.: Robert Swink. Cast: Kirk Douglas, Eleanor Parker, George Macready. Running time: 103 min.

Detour. PRC (1945). Dir.: Edgar G. Ulmer. Prod.: Leon Fromkess. Script: Martin Goldsmith. Photog.: Benjamin Kline. Ed.: George McGuire. Cast: Tom Neal, Ann Savage. Running time: 68 min.

Double Indemnity. Paramount (1944). Dir.: Billy Wilder. Prod.: Joseph Sistrom. Script: Raymond Chandler and Wilder, from the James M. Cain novel. Photog.: John F. Seitz. Ed.: Doane Harrison. Cast: Barbara Stanwyck, Fred MacMurray, Edward G. Robinson. Running time: 106 min.

A Double Life. Universal-International (1948). Dir.: George Cukor. Prod.: Michael Kanin. Script: Ruth Gordon and Garson Kanin. Photog.: Milton Krasner. Ed.: Robert Parrish. Cast: Ronald Colman, Edmond O'Brien, Shelley Winters. Running time: 103 min.

The Enforcer. Warner Brothers (1951). Dir.: Bretaigne Windust and Raoul Walsh. Prod.: Milton Sperling. Script: Martin Rackin. Photog.: Robert Burks. Ed.: Fred Allen. Cast: Humphrey Bogart, Zero Mostel, Everett Sloane. Running time: 88 min.

Fallen Angel. 20th Century-Fox (1946). Dir. and Prod.: Otto Preminger. Script: Harry Kleiner, from Marty Holland's novel. Photog.: Joseph La Shelle. Ed.: Harry Reynolds. Cast: Alice Faye, Dana Andrews, Linda Darnell. Running time: 98 min.

The File on Thelma Jordan. Paramount (1950). Dir.: Robert Siodmak. Prod.: Hal B. Wallis. Script: Ketti Frings. Photog.: George Barns. Ed.: Warren Low. Cast: Barbara Stanwyck, Wendell Corey, Paul Kelly. Running time: 100 min.

Framed. Columbia (1947). Dir.: Richard Wallace. Prod.: Jules Schermer. Script: Ben Maddow. Photog.: Burnett Guffey. Ed.: Richard Fantl. Cast: Glenn Ford, Janis Carter, Barry Sullivan. Running time: 82 min.

Gilda. Columbia (1946). Dir.: Charles Vidor. Prod.: Virginia Van Upp. Script: Marion Parsonnet. Photog.: Rudolph Maté. Ed.: Charles Nelson. Cast: Glenn Ford, Rita Hayworth, George Macready. Running time: 110 min.

The Glass Key. Paramount (1942). Dir.: Stuart Heisler. Prod.: B. G. DeSylva. Script: Jonathan Latimer, from the Dashiell Hammett novel. Photog.:

Theodor Sparkuhl. Ed.: Archie Marshek. Cast: Alan Ladd, Veronica Lake, Brian Donleavy. Running time: 85 min.

The Glass Web. Universal-International (1953). Dir.: Jack Arnold. Prod.: Albert J. Cohen. Script: Robert Blees and Leonard Lee. Photog.: Maury Gertsman. Ed.: Ted J. Kent. Cast: Edward G. Robinson, John Forsythe, Kathleen Hughes. Running time: 81 min.

The Harder They Fall. Columbia (1956). Dir.: Mark Robson. Prod. and Script: Philip Yordan, from the Budd Schulberg novel. Photog.: Burnett Guffey. Ed.: Jerome Thoms. Cast: Humphrey Bogart, Rod Steiger, Jan Sterling. Running time: 108 min.

He Walked by Night. Eagle-Lion (1949). Dir.: Alfred Werker. Prod.: Robert Kane. Script: John C. Higgins and Crane Wilbur. Photog.: John Alton. Ed.: Alfred DeGaetano. Cast: Richard Basehart, Scott Brady. Running time: 79 min.

High Sierra. Warner Brothers (1941). Dir.: Raoul Walsh. Prod.: Hal B. Wallis. Script: John Huston and W. R. Burnett, from Burnett's novel. Photog.: Tony Gaudio. Ed.: Jack Killifer. Cast: Humphrey Bogart, Ida Lupino, Arthur Kennedy. Running time: 100 min.

The High Wall. MGM (1947). Dir.: Curtis Bernhardt. Prod.: Robert Lord. Script: Sydney Boehm and Lester Cole, from the Alan Clark and Bradbury Foote novel. Photog.: Paul Vogel. Ed.: Conrad A. Nervig. Cast: Robert Taylor, Audrey Totter, Herbert Marshall. Running time: 100 min.

House of Strangers. 20th Century-Fox (1949). Dir.: Joseph L. Mankiewicz. Prod.: Sol C. Siegel. Script: Philip Yordan, from Jerome Weidman novel *I'll Never Go There Again*. Photog.: Milton Krasner. Ed.: Harmon Jones. Cast: Edward G. Robinson, Susan Hayward, Richard Conte. Running time: 101 min.

The House on 92nd Street. 20th Century-Fox (1945). Dir.: Henry Hathaway. Prod.: Louis de Rochemont. Script: Barre Lyndon, Charles G. Booth, and John Monks, Jr. Photog.: Norbert Brodine. Ed.: Harmon Jones. Cast: William Eythe, Lloyd Nolan, Signe Hasso. Running time: 89 min.

Human Desire. Columbia (1954). Dir.: Fritz Lang. Prod.: Lewis J. Rachmil. Script: Alfred Hayes, from the Emile Zola novel *La Bête Humaine*. Photog.: Burnett Guffey. Ed.: William A. Lyon. Cast: Glenn Ford, Gloria Grahame, Broderick Crawford. Running time: 90 min.

I Died a Thousand Times. Warner Brothers (1955). Dir.: Stuart Heisler. Prod.: Willis Goldbeck. Script: W. R. Burnett, from Burnett's novel *High Sierra*. Photog.: Ted McCord. Ed.: Clarence Kolster. Cast: Jack Palance, Shelley Winters, Lee Marvin. Running time: 109 min.

I, the Jury. United Artists (1953). Dir.: Harry Essex. Prod.: Victor Saville. Script: Harry Essex, from the Mickey Spillane novel. Photog.: John Alton. Ed.: Fredrick Y. Smith. Cast: Biff Elliot, Preston Foster, Peggie Castle. Running time: 88 min.

I Walk Alone. Paramount (1948). Dir.: Byron Haskin. Prod.: Hal B. Wallis. Script: Charles Schnee, from Theodore Reeves's play *Beggars Are Coming to Town.* Photog.: Leo Tover. Ed.: Arthur Schmidt. Cast: Burt Lancaster, Lizabeth Scott, Kirk Douglas. Running time: 98 min.

In a Lonely Place. Columbia (1950). Dir.: Nicholas Ray. Prod.: Robert Lord. Script: Andrew Solt, from the Dorothy B. Hughes novel. Photog.: Burnett Guffey. Ed.: Viola Lawrence. Cast: Humphrey Bogart, Gloria Grahame, Frank Lovejoy. Running time: 94 min.

Johnny O'Clock. Columbia (1947). Dir.: Robert Rossen. Prod.: Edward G. Nealis. Script: Rossen. Photog.: Burnett Guffey. Ed.: Warren Low and Al Clark. Cast: Dick Powell, Evelyn Keyes, Lee J. Cobb. Running time: 95 min.

Journey into Fear. RKO (1943). Dir.: Norman Foster and Orson Welles. Prod.: Welles. Script: Joseph Cotton and Welles, from the Eric Ambler novel. Photog.: Karl Struss. Ed.: Mark Robson. Cast: Cotton, Welles, Dolores Del Rio. Running time: 71 min.

Key Largo. Warner Brothers (1948). Dir.: John Huston. Prod.: Jerry Wald. Script: Huston and Richard Brooks, from the Maxwell Anderson play. Photog.: Karl Freund. Ed.: Rudi Fehr. Cast: Humphrey Bogart, Lauren Bacall, Edward G. Robinson. Running time: 100 min.

The Killers. Universal (1946). Dir.: Robert Siodmak. Prod.: Mark Hellinger. Script: Anthony Veiller, from the Ernest Hemingway story. Photog.: Woody Bredell. Ed.: Arthur Hilton. Cast: Burt Lancaster, Edmond O'Brien, Ava Gardner, Albert Dekker. Running time: 105 min.

Killer's Kiss. United Artists (1955). Dir.: Stanley Kubrick. Prod.: Kubrick and Morris Bousel. Script and Photog.: Kubrick. Ed.: Kubrick. Cast: Frank Silvera, Jamie Smith, Irene Kane. Running time: 67 min.

The Killing. United Artists (1956). Dir.: Stanley Kubrick. Prod.: James B. Harris. Script: Kubrick and Jim Thompson, from Lionel White's novel *The Clean Break.* Photog.: Lucien Ballard. Ed.: Betty Steinberg. Cast: Sterling Hayden, Coleen Gray, Vince Edwards. Running time: 84 min.

Kiss Me Deadly. United Artists (1955). Dir. and Prod.: Robert Aldrich. Script: A. I. Bezzerides, from the Mickey Spillane novel. Photog.: Ernest Laszlo. Ed.: Michael Luciano. Cast: Ralph Meeker, Albert Dekker, Maxine Cooper. Running time: 105 min.

Kiss of Death. 20th Century-Fox (1947). Dir.: Henry Hathaway. Prod.: Fred Kohlmar. Script: Ben Hecht and Charles Lederer. Photog.: Norbert Brodine. Ed.: J. Watson Webb, Jr. Cast: Victor Mature, Brian Donleavy, Richard Widmark. Running time: 98 min.

Kiss the Blood Off My Hands. Universal-International (1948). Dir.: Norman Foster. Prod.: Richard Vernon. Script: Leonardo Bercovici and Hugh Gray, from the Gerald Butler novel. Photog.: Russell Metty. Ed.: Milton Carruth. Cast: Joan Fontaine, Burt Lancaster, Robert Newton. Running time: 79 min.

The Lady from Shanghai. Columbia (1948). Dir. and Prod.: Orson Welles. Script: Welles, from Sherwood King's novel *Before I Die.* Photog.: Charles Lawton, Jr. Ed.: Viola Lawrence. Cast: Welles, Rita Hayworth, Everett Sloane. Running time: 86 min.

Lady in the Lake. MGM (1947). Dir.: Robert Montgomery. Prod.: George Haight. Script: Steve Fisher, from the Raymond Chandler novel. Photog.: Paul C. Vogel. Ed.: Gene Ruggiero. Cast: Montgomery, Audrey Totter, Lloyd Nolan. Running time: 105 min.

Laura. 20th Century-Fox (1944). Dir. and Prod.: Otto Preminger. Script: Jay Dratler, Samuel Hoffenstein, and Betty Reinhardt, from the Vera Caspary novel. Photog.: Joseph La Shelle. Ed.: Louis Loeffler. Cast: Gene Tierney, Dana Andrews, Clifton Webb. Running time: 88 min.

The Locket. RKO (1947). Dir.: John Brahm. Prod.: Jack J. Gross. Script: Sheridan Gibney. Photog.: Nicholas Musuraca. Ed.: J. R. Whittredge. Cast: Laraine Day, Brian Aherne, Robert Mitchum. Running time: 85 min.

The Long Wait. United Artists (1954). Dir.: Victor Saville. Prod.: Lesser Samuels. Script: Alan Green and Samuels, from the Mickey Spillane novel. Photog.: Franz Planer. Ed.: Ronald Sinclair. Cast: Anthony Quinn, Peggie Castle. Running time: 94 min.

The Maltese Falcon. Warner Brothers (1941). Dir.: John Huston. Prod.: Hal B. Wallis. Script: Huston, from the Dashiell Hammett novel. Photog.: Arthur Edeson. Ed.: Thomas Richards. Cast: Humphrey Bogart, Mary Astor, Sydney Greenstreet, Peter Lorre. Running time: 100 min.

The Mask of Dimitrios. Warner Brothers (1944). Dir.: Jean Negulesco. Prod.: Henry Blanke. Script: Frank Gruber, from Eric Ambler's novel *A Coffin for Dimitrios.* Photog.: Arthur Edeson. Ed.: Frederick Richards. Cast: Sydney Greenstreet, Zachary Scott, Faye Emerson, Peter Lorre. Running time: 95 min.

Mildred Pierce. Warner Brothers (1945). Dir.: Michael Curtiz. Prod.: Jerry Wald. Script: Ranald MacDougall, from the James M. Cain novel. Photog.: Ernest Haller. Ed.: David Weisbart. Cast: Joan Crawford, Zachary Scott, Ann Blythe, Jack Carson. Running time: 113 min.

Ministry of Fear. Paramount (1945). Dir.: Fritz Lang. Prod.: B G. DeSylva. Script: Seton I. Miller, from the Graham Greene novel. Photog.: Henry Sharp. Ed.: Archie Marshek. Cast: Ray Milland, Marjorie Reynolds, Dan Duryea. Running time: 86 min.

Mr. Arkadin. M & A Alexander Productions (1955). Dir.: Orson Welles. Prod.: Louis Dolivet. Script: Welles, from Welles's novel. Photog.: Jean Bourgoin. Ed.: Renzo Lucidi. Cast: Welles, Paola Mori, Robert Arden. Running time: 100 min.

The Mob. Columbia (1951). Dir.: Robert Parrish. Prod.: Jerry Bresler. Script: William Bowers, from Ferguson Findley's novel *Waterfront.* Photog.: Joseph Walker. Ed.: Charles Nelson. Cast: Broderick Crawford, Betty Buehler. Running time: 87 min.

Murder, My Sweet. RKO (1944). Dir.: Edward Dmytryk. Prod.: Adrian Scott. Script: John Paxton, from the Raymond Chandler novel *Farewell, My Lovely.* Photog.: Harry J. Wild. Ed.: Joseph Noriega. Cast: Dick Powell, Claire Trevor, Anne Shirley, Mike Mazurki. Running time: 95 min.

The Naked City. Universal-International (1947). Dir.: Jules Dassin. Prod.: Mark Hellinger. Script: Albert Maltz and Malvin Wald. Photog.: William Daniels. Ed.: Paul Weatherwax. Cast: Barry Fitzgerald, Dorothy Hart, Don Taylor. Running time: 96 min.

Niagara. 20th Century-Fox (1953). Dir.: Henry Hathaway. Prod.: Charles Brackett. Script: Brackett, Walter Reisch, and Richard Breen. Photog.: Joe MacDonald. Ed.: Barbara McLean. Cast: Marilyn Monroe, Joseph Cotton, Jean Peters. Running time: 92 min.

Night and the City. 20th Century-Fox (1950). Dir.: Jules Dassin. Prod.: Samuel G. Engel. Script: Jo Eisinger, from the Gerald Kersh novel. Photog.: Max Greene. Ed.: Nick De Maggio and Sidney Stone. Cast: Richard Widmark, Gene Tierney, Googie Withers. Running time: 95 min.

The Night Has a Thousand Eyes. Paramount (1948). Dir.: John Farrow. Prod.: Endre Bohem. Script: Barre Lyndon and Jonathan Latimer, from the Cornell Woolrich novel. Photog.: John F. Seitz. Ed.: Eda Warren. Cast: Edward G. Robinson, Gail Russell, John Lund. Running time: 81 min.

Nightmare. United Artists (1956). Dir.: Maxwell Shane. Prod.: William C. Pine and William C. Thomas. Script: Maxwell Shane, from the William Irish (pseudonym of Cornell Woolrich) story. Photog.: Joe Biroc. Ed.: George Gittens. Cast: Kevin McCarthy, Edward G. Robinson. Running time: 89 min.

Nightmare Alley. 20th Century-Fox (1947). Dir.: Edmund Goulding. Prod.: George Jessel. Script: Jules Furthman, from the William Lindsay Gresham novel. Photog.: Lee Garmes. Ed.: Barbara McLean. Cast: Tyrone Power, Joan Blondell, Colleen Gray. Running time: 110 min.

Notorious. RKO (1946). Dir. and Prod.: Alfred Hitchcock. Script: Ben Hecht. Photog.: Ted Tetzlaff. Ed.: Theron Warth. Cast: Cary Grant, Ingrid Bergman, Claude Rains. Running time: 101 min.

On Dangerous Ground. RKO (1952). Dir.: Nicholas Ray. Prod.: John Houseman. Script: A. I. Bezzerides, from Gerald Butler's novel *Mad with Much Heart*. Photog.: George E. Diskant. Ed.: Roland Gross. Cast: Robert Ryan, Ida Lupino, Ward Bond. Running time: 82 min.

Out of the Past. RKO (1947). Dir.: Jacques Tourneur. Prod.: Warren Duff. Script: Geoffrey Homes (pseudonym of Daniel Mainwaring), from his novel *Build My Gallows High*. Photog.: Nicholas Musuraca. Ed.: Samuel E. Beetley. Cast: Robert Mitchum, Jane Greer, Kirk Douglas. Running time: 96 min.

Panic in the Streets. 20th Century-Fox (1950). Dir.: Elia Kazan. Prod.: Sol C. Siegel. Script: Richard Murphy. Photog.: Joe MacDonald. Ed.: Harmon Jones. Cast: Richard Widmark, Jack Palance, Paul Douglas, Barbara Bel Geddes. Running time: 96 min.

Phantom Lady. Universal (1944). Dir.: Robert Siodmak. Prod.: Milton Feld and Joan Harrison. Script: Bernard C. Schoenfeld, from the William Irish (pseudonym of Cornell Woolrich) novel. Photog.: Woody Bredell. Ed.: Arthur Hilton. Cast: Ella Raines, Franchot Tone, Alan Curtis. Running time: 87 min.

Pickup on South Street. 20th Century-Fox (1953). Dir.: Samuel Fuller. Prod.: Jules Schermer. Script: Fuller. Photog.: Joe MacDonald. Ed.: Nick De

Maggio. Cast: Richard Widmark, Jean Peters, Thelma Ritter. Running time: 83 min.

Possessed. Warner Brothers (1947). Dir.: Curtis Bernhardt. Prod.: Jerry Wald. Script: Sylvia Richards and Ranald MacDougall, from Rita Weiman's *One Man's Secret.* Photog.: Joseph Valentine. Ed.: Rudi Fehr. Cast: Joan Crawford, Van Heflin, Raymond Massey. Running time: 108 min.

The Postman Always Rings Twice. MGM (1946). Dir.: Tay Garnett. Prod.: Carey Wilson. Script: Harry Ruskin and Niven Busch, from the James M. Cain novel. Photog.: Sidney Wagner. Ed.: George White. Cast: John Garfield, Lana Turner, Cecil Kellaway. Running time: 113 min.

The Prowler. United Artists (1951). Dir.: Joseph Losey. Prod.: S. P. Eagle. Script: Hugo Butler. Photog.: Arthur Miller. Ed.: Paul Weatherwax. Cast: Van Heflin, Evelyn Keyes. Running time: 92 min.

Railroaded. PRC (1947). Dir.: Anthony Mann. Prod.: Charles F. Riesner. Script: John C. Higgins, from a Gertrude Walker story. Photog.: Guy Roe. Ed.: Louis H. Sackin. Cast: John Ireland, Hugh Beaumont, Jane Randolph. Running time: 71 min.

Ride the Pink Horse. Universal-International (1947). Dir.: Robert Montgomery. Prod.: Joan Harrison. Script: Ben Hecht and Charles Lederer, from the Dorothy B. Hughes novel. Photog.: Russell Metty. Ed.: Ralph Dawson. Cast: Montgomery, Thomas Gomez, Wanda Hendrix. Running time: 101 min.

Road House. 20th Century-Fox (1948). Dir.: Jean Negulesco. Prod. and Script: Edward Chodorov. Photog.: Joseph La Shelle. Ed.: James B. Clark. Cast: Ida Lupino, Cornell Wilde, Celeste Holm, Richard Widmark. Running time: 95 min.

Scarlet Street. Diana-Universal (1945). Dir. and Prod.: Fritz Lang. Script: Dudley Nichols, from Georges de la Fouchardiere's novel *La Chienne.* Photog.: Milton Krasner. Ed.: Arthur Hilton. Cast: Edward G. Robinson, Joan Bennett, Dan Duryea. Running time: 102 min.

The Set-Up. RKO (1949). Dir.: Robert Wise. Prod.: Richard Goldstone. Script: Art Cohn, from Joseph Moncure March's poem. Photog.: Milton Krasner. Ed.: Roland Gross. Cast: Robert Ryan, Audrey Totter, George Tobias. Running time: 72 min.

711 Ocean Drive. Columbia (1950). Dir.: Joseph M. Newman. Prod.: Frank N. Seltzer. Script: Richard English and Francis Swan. Photog.: Franz F. Planer. Ed.: Bert Jordan. Cast: Edmond O'Brien, Joanne Dru, Sammy White. Running time: 102 min.

Shadow of a Doubt. Universal (1943). Dir.: Alfred Hitchcock. Prod.: Jack H. Skirball. Script: Thornton Wilder, Sally Benson, and Alma Reville, from a Gordon McDonell story. Photog.: Joseph Valentine. Ed.: Milton Carruth. Cast: Joseph Cotton, Teresa Wright, Macdonald Carey. Running time: 108 min.

The Sleeping City. Universal-International (1950). Dir.: George Sherman. Prod.: Leonard Goldstein. Script: Jo Eisinger. Photog.: William Miller. Ed.: Frank Gross. Cast: Richard Conte, Coleen Gray, Peggy Dow. Running time: 85 min.

Sorry, Wrong Number. Paramount (1948). Dir.: Anatole Litvak. Prod.: Hal B. Wallis and Litvak. Script: Lucille Fletcher, from her radio drama. Photog.: Sol Polito. Ed.: Warren Low. Cast: Barbara Stanwyck, Burt Lancaster, Ann Richards. Running time: 89 min.

The Strange Love of Martha Ivers. Paramount (1946). Dir.: Lewis Milestone. Prod.: Hal B. Wallis. Script: Robert Rossen. Photog.: Victor Milner. Ed.: Archie Marshek. Cast: Van Heflin, Barbara Stanwyck, Lizabeth Scott, Kirk Douglas. Running time: 115 min.

The Stranger. RKO (1946). Dir.: Orson Welles. Prod.: S. P. Eagle. Script: Anthony Veiller, from a Victor Trivas story. Photog.: Russell Metty. Ed.: Ernest Nims. Cast: Welles, Edward G. Robinson, Loretta Young. Running time: 95 min.

Strangers on a Train. Warner Brothers (1951). Dir. and Prod.: Alfred Hitchcock. Script: Raymond Chandler and Czenzi Ormonde, from the Patricia Highsmith novel. Photog.: Robert Burks. Ed.: William H. Ziegler. Cast: Farley Granger, Ruth Roman, Robert Walker. Running time: 101 min.

Sunset Boulevard. Paramount (1950). Dir.: Billy Wilder. Prod.: Charles Brackett. Script: Brackett, Wilder, and D. M. Marshman, Jr. Photog.: John F. Seitz. Ed.: Arthur Schmidt. Cast: William Holden, Gloria Swanson, Erich von Stroheim. Running time: 115 min.

Suspense. Monogram (1946). Dir.: Frank Tuttle. Prod.: Maurice and Frank King. Script: Philip Yordan. Photog.: Karl Struss. Ed.: Dick Heermance. Cast: Belita, Barry Sullivan, Albert Dekker. Running time: 101 min.

T-Men. Eagle-Lion (1948). Dir.: Anthony Mann. Prod.: Aubrey Schenck. Script: John C. Higgins. Photog.: John Alton. Ed.: Fred Allen. Cast: Dennis O'Keefe, Alfred Ryder, Wallace Ford. Running time: 92 min.

They Live by Night. RKO (1948). Dir.: Nicholas Ray. Prod.: John Houseman. Script: Charles Schnee, from Edward Anderson's novel *Thieves like Us.* Photog.: George E. Diskant. Ed.: Sherman Todd. Cast: Cathy O'Donnell, Farley Granger, Howard Da Silva, Jay C. Flippen. Running time: 95 min.

They Won't Believe Me. RKO (1947). Dir.: Irving Pichel. Prod.: Joan Harrison. Script: Jonathan Latimer. Photog.: Harry J. Wild. Ed.: Elmo Williams. Cast: Robert Young, Susan Hayward, Jane Greer. Running time: 95 min.

This Gun for Hire. Paramount (1942). Dir.: Frank Tuttle. Prod.: Richard M. Blumenthal. Script: Albert Maltz and W. R. Burnett, from the Graham Greene novel. Photog.: John Seitz. Ed.: Archie Marshek. Cast: Alan Ladd, Veronica Lake, Robert Preston. Running time: 80 min.

Touch of Evil. Universal-International (1958). Dir.: Orson Welles. Prod.: Albert Zugsmith. Script: Welles, from Whit Masterson's novel *Badge of Evil.* Photog.: Russell Metty. Ed.: Virgil M. Vogel and Aaron Stell. Cast: Welles, Charlton Heston, Janet Leigh. Running time: 105 min.

Uncle Harry. Universal (1945). Dir.: Robert Siodmak. Prod.: Joan Harrison. Script: Stephen Longstreet, from the Thomas Job play. Photog.: Paul Ivano. Ed.: Arthur Hilton. Cast: George Sanders, Ella Raines, Geraldine Fitzgerald. Running time: 80 min.

The Undercover Man. Columbia (1949). Dir.: Joseph H. Lewis. Prod.: Robert Rossen. Script: Sydney Boehm and Malvin Wald, from a Frank J. Wilson article. Photog.: Burnett Guffey. Ed.: Al Clark. Cast: Glenn Ford, Nina Foch, James Whitmore. Running time: 85 min.

Union Station. Paramount (1950). Dir.: Rudolph Maté. Prod.: Jules Schermer. Script: Sydney Boehm. Photog.: Daniel L. Fapp. Ed.: Ellsworth Hoagland. Cast: William Holden, Nancy Olson, Lyle Bettger. Running time: 80 min.

The Web. Universal-International (1947). Dir.: Michael Gordon. Prod.: Jerry Bresler. Script: William Bowers and Bertram Millhauser. Photog.: Irving Glassberg. Cast: Edmond O'Brien, Vincent Price, Ella Raines. Running time: 87 min.

Where Danger Lives. RKO (1950). Dir.: John Farrow. Prod.: Irving Cummings, Jr. Script: Charles Bennett. Photog.: Nicholas Musuraca. Ed.: Eda Warren. Cast: Robert Mitchum, Faith Domergue, Claude Rains. Running time: 82 min.

Where the Sidewalk Ends. 20th Century-Fox (1950). Dir. and Prod.: Otto Preminger. Script: Ben Hecht, from William L. Stuart's novel *Night Cry*. Photog.: Joseph La Shelle. Ed.: Louis Loeffler. Cast: Dana Andrews, Gene Tierney, Gary Merrill. Running time: 95 min.

While the City Sleeps. RKO (1956). Dir.: Fritz Lang. Prod.: Bert Friedlob. Script: Casey Robinson, from Charles Einstein's novel *The Bloody Spur*. Photog.: Ernest Laszlo. Ed.: Gene Fowler, Jr. Cast: Dana Andrews, Rhonda Fleming, George Sanders. Running time: 99 min.

White Heat. Warner Brothers (1949). Dir.: Raoul Walsh. Prod.: Lou Edelman. Script: Ivan Goff and Ben Roberts, from a Virginia Kellogg story. Photog.: Sid Hickox. Ed.: Owen Marks. Cast: James Cagney, Virginia Mayo, Edmond O'Brien. Running time: 114 min.

The Window. RKO (1949). Dir.: Ted Tetzlaff. Prod.: Frederic Ullman, Jr. Script: Mel Dinelli, from Cornell Woolrich's *The Boy Cried Murder*. Photog.: William Steiner. Ed.: Frederic Knudtson. Cast: Barbara Hale, Bobby Driscoll, Arthur Kennedy, Paul Stewart. Running time: 73 min.

The Woman in the Window. RKO (1945). Dir.: Fritz Lang. Prod. and Script: Nunnally Johnson, from J. H. Wallis's novel *Once Off Guard*. Photog.: Milton Krasner. Ed.: Marjorie Johnson and Gene Fowler, Jr. Cast: Edward G. Robinson, Joan Bennett, Raymond Massey. Running time: 99 min.

Woman on the Run. Universal-International (1950). Dir.: Norman Foster. Prod.: Howard Welsch. Script: Alan Campbell and Foster, from a story by Sylvia Tate. Photog.: Hal Mohr. Ed.: Otto Ludwig. Cast: Ann Sheridan, Dennis O'Keefe, Robert Keith. Running time: 77 min.

The Wrong Man. Warner Brothers (1956). Dir. and Prod.: Alfred Hitchcock. Script: Maxwell Anderson and Angus MacPhail, from Maxwell Anderson's "The True Story of Christopher Emmanuel Balestrero." Photog.: Robert Burks. Ed.: George Tomasini. Cast: Henry Fonda, Vera Miles, Anthony Quayle. Running time: 105 min.

Bibliography

Agee, James. *Agee on Film*. Vol. 1. New York: Grosset & Dunlap, 1969.

Althusser, Louis. *Lenin and Philosophy and Other Essays*. Trans. Ben Brewster. London: New Left Books, 1971.

Anon. Review of *The Lady in the Lake*. *New York Times*, 24 Jan. 1947: 18.

———. "A Tempest That Brewed in Brooklyn Blew 'Disparaging' Words from Movie Foreword." *New York Times*, 12 Apr. 1949: 38.

Archer, Eugene. "Elia Kazan—The Genesis of a Style," *Film Culture* 2.2 (1956), 5–7, 21–24.

Armes, Roy. *Film and Reality*. Baltimore: Penguin, 1974.

Baxter, John. "Something More than Night," *Film Journal* 2.4 (1975), 4–9.

Bazin, André. *Orson Welles: A Critical View*. Trans. Jonathan Rosenbaum. New York: Harper & Row, 1978.

———. *What Is Cinema?* 2 vols. Trans. Hugh Gray. Berkeley: U of California P, 1967, 1971.

Bogdanovich, Peter. *Fritz Lang in America*. New York: Praeger, 1967.

Bonitzer, Pascal. "Partial Vision: Film and the Labyrinth." Trans. Fabrice Ziolkowski. *Wide Angle* 4.4 (1981), 56–63.

Borde, Raymond, and Etienne Chaumeton. *Panorama du Film Noir Americain (1941–1953)*. Paris: Editions de Minuit, 1955.

———. "The Sources of *Film Noir*." Trans. Bill Horrigan. In *Film Reader 3*, ed. Bruce Jenkins. Evanston: Northwestern UP, 1978. Pp. 58–66.

Bordwell, David. "The Art Cinema as a Mode of Film Practice," *Film Criticism* 4.1 (1979), 56–64.

Bordwell, David, Janet Staiger, and Kristin Thompson. *The Classical Hollywood Cinema: Film Style and Mode of Production to 1960*. New York: Columbia UP, 1985.

Brinton, Joseph P., III. "Subjective Camera or Subjective Audience?" *Hollywood Quarterly* 2 (1947), 359–66.

Brody, Meredith. "Killer Instinct: Jim Thompson," *Film Comment* 20.5 (1984), 46–47.

———. "Missing Persons: David Goodis," *Film Comment* 20.5 (1984), 42–43.

Browne, Nick. "Introduction: Point of View." In *Film Reader 4*, ed. Blaine Allan et al. Evanston: Northwestern UP, 1979. Pp. 105–7.

Bruccoli, Matthew J., ed. *The Naked City: A Screenplay.* Carbondale: Southern Illinois UP, 1979.

Cain, James M. *Double Indemnity.* New York: Random House, 1936, 1978.

———. *Mildred Pierce.* New York: Random House, 1941, 1978.

———. *The Postman Always Rings Twice.* New York: Random House, 1934, 1978.

———. *Three of a Kind.* New York: Knopf, 1944.

Carringer, Robert. *The Making of "Citizen Kane."* Berkeley: U of California P, 1985.

———. "Orson Welles and Gregg Toland: Their Collaboration on *Citizen Kane*," *Critical Inquiry* 8 (1982), 651–74.

———. "Rosebud, Dead or Alive: Narrative and Symbolic Structure in *Citizen Kane*," *PMLA* 91 (1976), 185–93.

Cawelti, John G. *Adventure, Mystery, and Romance: Formula Stories as Art and Popular Culture.* Chicago: U of Chicago P, 1976.

———. "*Chinatown* and Generic Transformation." In *Film Theory and Criticism*, 3d ed., ed. Gerald Mast and Marshall Cohen. New York: Oxford UP, 1985. Pp. 503–20.

Certeau, Michel de. *Heterologies: Discourse on the Other.* Trans. Brian Massumi. Minneapolis: U of Minnesota P, 1986.

———. "The Jabbering of Social Life." Trans. Richard Miller and Edward Schneider. In *On Signs*, ed. Marshall Blonsky. Baltimore: The Johns Hopkins UP, 1985.

Chandler, Raymond. *The Big Sleep.* New York: Random House, 1939, 1976.

———. *Farewell, My Lovely.* New York: Random House, 1940, 1976.

———. *The Lady in the Lake.* New York: Random House, 1943, 1976.

———. *The Long Goodbye.* New York: Ballantine, 1953, 1971.

———. *The Simple Art of Murder.* New York: Ballantine, 1972.

Clarens, Carlos. *Crime Movies: From Griffith to "The Godfather" and Beyond.* New York: Norton, 1980.

Coburn, Marcia Froelke. "And the Enemy Is Us: Patricia Highsmith," *Film Comment* 20.5 (1984), 44–45.

Cohen, Mitchell S. "Villains and Victims," *Film Comment* 10.6 (1974), 27–29.

Comolli, Jean-Louis. "Machines of the Visible." In *Film Theory and Criticism*, 3d ed., ed. Gerald Mast and Marshall Cohen. New York: Oxford UP, 1985. Pp. 741–60.

Cook, David. *A History of Narrative Film.* New York: Norton, 1981.

Crowell's Handbook of Classical Mythology. Ed. Edward Tripp. New York: Crowell, 1970.

Crowther, Bosley. "Imitations Unwanted." *New York Times,* 22 Feb. 1948: B1.

————. Review of *Call Northside 777*. *New York Times*, 19 Feb. 1948: 29.

————. Review of *Dark Passage*. *New York Times*, 6 Sept. 1947: 11.

————. Review of *The Naked City*. *New York Times*, 5 Mar. 1948: 17.

Culler, Jonathan. *The Pursuit of Signs*. Ithaca: Cornell UP, 1981.

Damico, James. "Film Noir: A Modest Proposal." In *Film Reader 3*, ed. Bruce Jenkins. Evanston: Northwestern UP, 1978. Pp. 48–57.

Deleuze, Gilles, and Felix Guattari. *Anti-Oedipus: Capitalism and Schizophrenia*. Trans. Robert Hurley, Mark Seem, and Helen R. Lane. Minneapolis: U of Minnesota P, 1983.

Deming, Barbara. *Running Away from Myself: A Dream Portrait of America Drawn from the Films of the Forties*. New York: Grossman, 1969.

Derrida, Jacques. *Speech and Phenomena and Other Essays on Husserl's Theory of Signs*. Trans. David B. Allison. Evanston: Northwestern UP, 1973.

————. *Spurs: Nietzsche's Styles*. Chicago: U of Chicago P, 1979.

Dick, Bernard F. *Anatomy of Film*. New York: St. Martin's, 1978.

Dowdy, Andrew. *The Films of the Fifties: The American State of Mind*. New York: Morrow, 1973.

Dreyfus, Hubert L., and Paul Rabinow. *Michel Foucault: Beyond Structuralism and Hermeneutics*. 2d ed. Chicago: U of Chicago P, 1983.

Dunne, Philip. "The Documentary and Hollywood." In *Nonfiction Film Theory and Criticism*, ed. Richard Meran Barsam. New York: Dutton, 1976. Pp. 158–66.

Durgnat, Raymond. "The Family Tree of Film Noir," *Film Comment* 10.6 (1974), 6–7.

Eisner, Lotte H. *The Haunted Screen*. Berkeley: U of California P, 1969.

Everson, William K. *The Detective in Film*. Seacaucus: Citadel, 1972.

Farber, Stephen. "Violence and the Bitch Goddess," *Film Comment* 10.6 (1974), 8–11.

Foucault, Michel. *The Archeology of Knowledge and The Discourse on Language*. Trans. A. M. Sheridan Smith. New York: Harper & Row, 1972.

————. *The History of Sexuality*. Trans. Robert Hurley. New York: Random House, 1980.

————. *Language, Counter-Memory, Practice: Selected Essays and Interviews*. Ed. Donald F. Bouchard. Ithaca: Cornell UP, 1977.

————. *Madness and Civilization: A History of Insanity in the Age of Reason*. Trans. Richard Howard. New York: Random House, 1965.

————. *Power/Knowledge: Selected Interviews and Other Writings*. Ed. Colin Gordon. New York: Pantheon, 1980.

————. "What Is an Author?" In *Textual Strategies*, ed. Josué V. Harari. Ithaca: Cornell UP, 1979. Pp. 41–60.

Fox, Terry Curtis. "City Knights," *Film Comment* 20.5 (1984), 30–36.

Frank, Nino. "Un Nouveau Genre 'Policier': L'aventure Criminelle," *L'Ecran Français* 61 (1946), 8–9, 14.

Freud, Sigmund. *Beyond the Pleasure Principle*. Trans. James Strachey. New York: Bantam, 1961.

Furness, R. S. *Expressionism*. London: Methuen, 1973.

Gehr, Richard. "The Atomic Gun: Mickey Spillane," *Film Comment* 20.5 (1984), 38–39.

Girard, René. *Deceit, Desire, and the Novel.* Trans. Yvonne Freccero. Baltimore: The Johns Hopkins UP, 1965.

———. "The Plague in Literature and Myth," *Texas Studies in Literature and Language* 15 (1974), 833–50.

———. *Violence and the Sacred.* Trans. Patrick Gregory. Baltimore: The Johns Hopkins UP, 1977.

Gomery, Douglas. *The Hollywood Studio System.* New York: St. Martin's, 1986.

Goodis, David. *Nightfall.* Berkeley: Creative Arts, 1947, 1987.

Graham, Mark. "The Inaccessibility of *The Lady from Shanghai*," *Film Criticism* 5.2 (1981), 21–37.

Grant, Barry Keith, ed. *Film Genre Reader.* Austin: U of Texas P, 1986.

Gross, Larry. "Film Après Noir," *Film Comment* 12.4 (1976), 44–49.

Hammett, Dashiell. *The Maltese Falcon.* New York: Random House, 1930, 1984.

———. *Red Harvest.* New York: Random House, 1929, 1972.

Hankoff, Peter. "Film Noir, Life Noir," *Film Comment* 12.4 (1976), 35.

Heath, Stephen. *Questions of Cinema.* Bloomington: Indiana UP, 1981.

Higham, Charles. *The Films of Orson Welles.* Berkeley: U of California P, 1970.

Higham, Charles, and Joel Greenberg. *Hollywood in the Forties.* Cranbury: Barnes, 1968.

Hillier, Jim. "Out of the '40s," *Movie* 19 (1971), 14–16.

Hirsch, Foster. *The Dark Side of the Screen: Film Noir.* New York: Barnes, 1981.

Hughes, Dorothy B. *In a Lonely Place.* Bantam, 1947, 1979.

———. *Ride the Pink Horse.* Bantam, 1946, 1979.

Jacobs, Lewis, ed. *The Documentary Tradition.* New York: Hopkinson and Blake, 1971.

Jameson, Fredric. *The Prison-House of Language.* Princeton: Princeton UP, 1972.

Jameson, Richard T. "Son of Noir," *Film Comment* 10.6 (1974), 30–33.

Jenkins, Stephen, ed. *Fritz Lang: The Image and the Look.* London: BFI, 1981.

Jensen, Paul. "Raymond Chandler and the World You Live In," *Film Comment* 10.6 (1974), 18–26.

Kaminsky, Stuart. *American Film Genres.* New York: Dell, 1974.

Kaplan, E. Ann, ed. *Women in Film Noir.* London: BFI, 1980.

Kawin, Bruce F. *The Mind of the Novel: Reflexive Fiction and the Ineffable.* Princeton: Princeton UP, 1982.

———. *Mindscreen: Bergman, Godard, and First-Person Film.* Princeton: Princeton UP, 1978.

Kerr, Paul. "Out of What Past? Notes on the B Film Noir," *Screen Education* 32–33 (1979/80), 45–65.

Kozloff, Sarah. "Humanizing 'The Voice of God': Narration in *The Naked City*," *Cinema Journal* 23.4 (1984), 41–53.

Kracauer, Siegfried. "Hollywood's Terror Films," *Commentary* 2 (Aug. 1946), 132–36.

Krohn, Bill. "King of the B's," *Film Comment* 19.4 (1983), 60–64.

Krutnik, Frank. "Desire, Transgression and James M. Cain: Fiction into *Film Noir*," *Screen* 23.1 (1982), 31–44.

Lacan, Jacques. *Ecrits: A Selection.* Trans. Alan Sheridan. New York: Norton, 1977.

———. *Speech and Language in Psychoanalysis.* Trans. Anthony Wilden. Baltimore: The Johns Hopkins UP, 1968.

Lafferty, William. "A Reappraisal of the Semi-Documentary in Hollywood, 1945–1948," *Velvet Light Trap* 20 (1983), 22–26.

Laing, R. D. *The Divided Self: An Existential Study in Sanity and Madness.* Baltimore: Penguin, 1965.

Lasch, Christopher. *The Minimal Self: Psychic Survival in Troubled Times.* New York: Norton, 1984.

LaValley, Albert J., ed. *Mildred Pierce.* Wisconsin/Warner Bros. Screenplay Series. Madison: U of Wisconsin P, 1980.

Lavery, David. "The Eye of Longing," *ReVision* 6.1 (1983), 22–33.

Leaming, Barbara. *Orson Welles: A Biography.* New York: Viking, 1985.

Luhr, William. *Raymond Chandler and Film.* New York: Ungar, 1982.

———. "Raymond Chandler and *The Lady in the Lake*," *Wide Angle* 6.1 (1984), 28–33.

MacCabe, Colin. *Tracking the Signifier.* Minneapolis: U of Minnesota P, 1985.

Madden, David. "James M. Cain and the Movies of the Thirties and Forties," *Film Heritage* 2.4 (1972), 9–25.

Marshall, Stuart. "*Lady in the Lake:* Identification and the Drives," *Film Form* 1.2 (1977), 34–50.

McArthur, Colin. *Underworld USA.* New York: Viking, 1972.

McCarthy, Todd, and Charles Flynn, eds. *Kings of the B's: Working within the Hollywood System.* New York: Dutton, 1975.

Melville, Herman. *Moby Dick.* Ed. Charles Feidelson, Jr. Indianapolis: Bobbs-Merrill, 1964.

Merleau-Ponty, Maurice. *The Visible and the Invisible.* Trans. Alphonso Lingis. Evanston: Northwestern UP, 1968.

Metz, Christian. *The Imaginary Signifier.* Trans. Celia Britton et al. Bloomington: Indiana UP, 1982.

Michaels, Lloyd. "Elia Kazan: A Retrospective," *Film Criticism* 10.1 (1985), 32–46.

Miller, J. Hillis. "Ariadne's Thread: Repetition and the Narrative Line," *Critical Inquiry* 3 (1976), 57–77.

———. "Narrative Middles: A Preliminary Outline," *Genre* 9 (1978), 375–87.

Moreno, Julio. "Subjective Camera: And the Problem of Film in the First Person," *Quarterly of Film, Radio, and Television* 7 (1953), 341–58.

Naremore, James. *The Magic World of Orson Welles.* New York: Oxford UP, 1978.

Navasky, Victor S. *Naming Names.* New York: Viking, 1980.

Nichols, Bill. *Ideology and the Image.* Bloomington: Indiana UP, 1981.

Ottoson, Robert. *A Reference Guide to the American Film Noir.* Metuchen: Scarecrow, 1981.

Palmer, James W. *"In a Lonely Place:* Paranoia in the Dream Factory," *Literature/ Film Quarterly* 13.3 (1985), 200–207.

Percy, Walker. *Love in the Ruins.* New York: Farrar, Straus, 1971.

———. *The Message in the Bottle.* New York: Farrar, Straus, 1975.

Perkins, V. F. "The Cinema of Nicholas Ray." In *Movie Reader,* ed. Ian Cameron. New York: Praeger, 1972. Pp. 64–70.

Phillips, Gene D. "Kubrick, *Killer's Kiss, The Killing,* and Film Noir," *American Classic Screen* 4.3 (1980), 13–18.

Place, J. A., and L. S. Peterson. "Some Visual Motifs of *Film Noir,*" *Film Comment* 10.1 (1974), 30–35.

Polan, Dana B. "Blind Insights and Dark Passages: The Problem of Placement in Forties Film," *Velvet Light Trap* 20 (1983), 27–33.

Porfirio, Robert G. "No Way Out: Existential Motifs in the Film Noir," *Sight and Sound* 45.4 (1976), 212–17.

Ray, Robert B. *A Certain Tendency of the Hollywood Cinema, 1930–1980.* Princeton: Princeton UP, 1985.

Renov, Michael. *"Raw Deal:* The Woman in the Text," *Wide Angle* 6.2 (1984), 18–22.

Rosenbaum, Jonathan. "Black Widow: Cornell Woolrich," *Film Comment* 20.5 (1984), 36–38.

———. "The Voice and the Eye: A Commentary on the *Heart of Darkness* Script," *Film Comment* 8.4 (1972), 27–32.

Salt, Barry. *Film Style and Technology: History and Analysis.* London: Starword, 1983.

Sartre, Jean-Paul. *"No Exit" and Three Other Plays.* New York: Random House, 1948.

Sattin, Richard. "Joseph H. Lewis: Assessing an (Occasionally) Brilliant Career," *American Classic Screen* 7.5–6 (1983), 51–55.

Schatz, Thomas. *Hollywood Genres: Formulas, Filmmaking, and the Studio System.* Philadelphia: Temple UP, 1981.

Schrader, Paul. "Notes on *Film Noir.*" In *Awake in the Dark,* ed. David Denby. New York: Random House, 1977. Pp. 278–90.

Shadoian, Jack. *Dreams and Dead-Ends: The American Gangster/Crime Film.* Cambridge: MIT, 1977.

Shindler, Colin. *Hollywood Goes to War: Films and American Society, 1939–1952.* London: Routledge & Kegan Paul, 1979.

Silver, Alain. *"Kiss Me Deadly:* Evidence of a Style," *Film Comment* 11.2 (1975), 24–30.

Silver, Alain, and Elizabeth Ward, eds. *Film Noir: An Encyclopedic Reference to the American Style.* Woodstock: Overlook Press, 1979.

Sklar, Robert. *Movie-Made America: A Cultural History of American Movies.* New York: Random House, 1975.

Smoodin, Eric. "The Image and the Voice in the Film with Spoken Narration," *Quarterly Review of Film Studies* 8.4 (1983), 19–32.

Sturrock, John, ed. *Structuralism and Since: From Lévi-Strauss to Derrida.* New York: Oxford UP, 1979.

Thompson, Jim. *The Criminal*. Berkeley: Creative Arts, 1953, 1986.
———. *A Hell of a Woman*. Berkeley: Creative Arts, 1954. 1984.
———. *Nothing More than Murder*. Berkeley: Creative Arts, 1959, 1985.
———. *Pop. 1280*. Berkeley: Creative Arts, 1964, 1984.
———. *Savage Night*. Berkeley: Creative Arts, 1953, 1985.
Thompson, Kristin. "Closure within a Dream: Point-of-View in *Laura*." In *Film Reader 3*, ed. Bruce Jenkins. Evanston: Northwestern UP, 1978. Pp. 90–105.
Thomson, David. *America in the Dark: Hollywood and the Gift of Unreality*. New York: William Morrow, 1977.
Tripp, Edward, ed. *Crowell's Handbook of Classical Mythology*. New York: Crowell, 1970.
Tuska, Jon. *Dark Cinema: American Film Noir in Cultural Perspective*. Westport: Greenwood Press, 1984.
Vernet, Marc. "The Filmic Transaction: On the Openings of Film Noirs." Trans. David Rodowick. *Velvet Light Trap* 20 (1983), 2–9.
Wead, George. "Towards a Definition of Filmnoia," *Velvet Light Trap* 13 (1974), 2–6.
Welsh, James M. "Knockout in Paradise: An Appraisal of *The Set Up*," *American Classic Screen* 2.6 (1978), 14–16.
Whitney, J. S. "A Filmography of *Film Noir*," *Journal of Popular Film* 5.3–4 (1976), 321–71.
Williams, Alan. "Is a Radical Genre Criticism Possible?" *Quarterly Review of Film Studies* 9.2 (1984), 121–25.
Wood, Michael. *America in the Movies*. New York: Basic Books, 1975.
Wright, Elizabeth. *Psychoanalytic Criticism: Theory in Practice*. London: Methuen, 1984.
Zavattini, Cesare. "Some Ideas on the Cinema." In *Film: A Montage of Theories*, ed. Richard Dyer MacCann. New York: Dutton, 1966. Pp. 216–28.
Zolotow, Maurice. "Through a Shot Glass Darkly: How Raymond Chandler Screwed Hollywood," *Action* 2.4 (1978), 52–57.

Index

Agee, James, 139, 155, 158
Aldrich, Robert: director of *Kiss Me Deadly*, 198, 213n
Althusser, Louis: on ideological structures, 33, 137
Appointment with Danger (film), 27
As I Lay Dying (novel), 89
Asphalt Jungle, The (film): and film realism, 2, 26, 87n, 168

B-film, 10, 18, 136
Barth, John: and modernist narrative, 107
Bazin, André: theories of film realism, 24, 154, 168–69, 176n
Beyond a Reasonable Doubt (film), 27, 29, 196n
Bezzerides, A. I.: screenwriter for *Kiss Me Deadly*, 213n
Bicycle Thieves (film): and neorealist narrative, 168–69
Big Carnival, The (film), 27, 179, 182–87, 196n, 200
Big Clock, The (film), 15, 27, 190
Big Heat, The (film), 94
Big Knife, The (film), 27, 34, 189
Big Sleep, The (novel), 6; (film), 30, 94
Blackout (film), 179
Blood Simple (film): as modern *film noir*, 3
Blue Gardenia, The (film), 27, 196n
Body Heat (film): as modern *film noir*, 3
Bogart, Humphrey, 100, 121, 131
Bonitzer, Pascal, 20, 106, 123

Boomerang (film), 10, 13, 24, 26, 92, 134–36, 138–45, 148, 150–51, 155–56, 158, 161, 170, 175–76
Borde, Raymond: defines the *film noir*, 5
Bordwell, David: on classical narrative, 202
Borges, Jorge Luis: and modernist narrative, 89, 107
Brasher Doubloon, The (film), 16
Browne, Nick: on cinematic point of view, 20
Burnett, W. R.: and hard-boiled fiction, 5

Cain, James M., 5–8, 16, 43, 45, 49–50, 53, 86
Call Northside 777 (film), 22, 24–25, 134, 136, 138–39, 145–52, 155–56, 158, 161, 167
Capra, Frank: the director's wartime experience, 22–23
Carringer, Robert: on the making of *Citizen Kane*, 59, 104
Casablanca (film), 131
Cawelti, John: on the detective genre, 113, 116, 118; on melodrama, 150
Certeau, Michel de, 216–17, 222
Chandler, Raymond: his novels, 5–8, 16, 18–19, 88, 92, 100, 103–4; his screenplays, 45, 51, 114
Chaumeton, Etienne: defines the *film noir*, 5
Chinatown (film): as modern *film noir*, 3
Circular narrative, 58, 60–61, 63 65, 67–68, 71

Citizen Kane (film), 14, 15, 42, 59–61, 70–71, 74–77, 144. *See also* Welles, Orson
City across the River (film), 25, 155–56, 160
City That Never Sleeps, The (film), 160–68, 216
Clarens, Carlos, 88
Classical film narrative, 12, 14, 17, 18, 24, 26–28, 30, 54, 93, 113, 126, 130, 136, 140, 158, 162, 171, 180, 182, 194, 200, 223; characteristics of, 3, 92, 148, 161; point of view in, 16, 19, 21, 43, 75–76, 89–92, 97, 100, 103, 110, 122, 146, 175, 180, 202, 213n, 221; function of character in, 20, 99, 106, 123, 143, 146–47, 202; distinction from modernist narrative, 36n; linear structure of, 58, 60; resolution in, 71; and ideology, 130; and realism, 135, 155, 168. See also *Film noir*
Comolli, Jean-Louis: on the cinematic apparatus, 134–35, 151
Coupe de Torchon (film), 8
Criminal, The (novel), 8, 196n
Crowther, Bosley, 121, 130, 135, 149, 156, 158
Cry of the City (film), 2

Damico, James: on defining *film noir*, 10, 11
Dark Mirror, The (film), 88
Dark Passage (film), 19, 21, 40, 92, 100, 117–18, 120–33
Dark Past, The (film), 10, 19, 117
Daves, Delmer: director of *Dark Passage*, 121
Dead End (film), 217
Dead Reckoning (film), 53, 190
Deconstruction: and voice-over narration, 56n
Deleuze, Gilles: on the limits of ideological criticism, 219
DeMille, William: pioneer filmmaker, 3
Discourse: public and private modes, 27–28, 78, 91, 180, 182–83, 186, 188–95, 200, 212–13; its threatening power, 45, 182, 185–87, 199, 206–8, 218; desire as discourse, 46, 49–51, 54, 183; uncertainties in, 47–48; and truth, 49, 189; of the other, 49, 193; and the unconscious, 51, 188, 216; paradoxical

character of, 52–53, 84, 163, 185–86, 193–95, 196n; and its limits, 53–54, 78, 107, 181, 211; of film, 55, 181, 185, 187, 192, 217; authorship of, 85–86, 184, 192; autonomy in, 181–84, 187, 205; source of, 205–7. See also *Film noir;* Foucault, Michel
D.O.A.: film (1949), 54, 199; film (1988), 3
Documentary film, 22–23, 135–36, 138, 140, 143, 150, 154–56, 158–60, 168, 174–75
Double Indemnity (film), 13, 15, 31, 40–54, 75, 83–84, 86, 92, 155, 180–81, 196n, 199, 216; and homosexuality, 51
Double Indemnity (novel), 6, 16, 43, 45; characters in, 50; and romanticism, 51; language in, 55n; difference from film, 55n
Douglas, Paul, 169
Dunne, Philip: on film realism, 154–55, 157, 175–76

Enforcer, The (film), 12
Expressionism, 10, 34, 69, 104, 136; characteristics of, 17–18; influence on *film noir,* 17, 32, 93

Fallen Angel (film), 30
Fantasy, 161–62
Farewell, My Lovely (novel), 19, 92
Faulkner, William, 89
Fellini, Federico: as neorealist director, 154
Film noir, 32–33, 35; defined, 2, 5, 10–11, 220; narrative voice of, 2, 68, 71, 78, 144, 158–59, 182, 222; as genre, 3, 5, 9, 31, 37n, 90, 94, 217, 223; narrative experimentation in, 3, 14, 104, 131, 179, 222; its literary sources, 5–9, 16, 18, 89, 100, 103–4, 190, 194, 196n, 200–201, 203, 205, 210–11; visual style of, 10, 12, 31–32, 88, 103, 108–9, 136, 173, 198, 205, 217, 220; subjective camera in, 12–13, 17–21, 58, 88–94, 96, 98–101, 102n, 103–13, 117–18, 120–25, 127–32, 134, 180, 220–21; documentary mode, 12–13, 22–26, 134–39, 142–45, 148–52, 154–62, 166–70, 173–76, 180, 220–21; flashbacks in, 12–16, 25, 40–42, 53–54, 57–62, 72, 74–77, 79, 83–86, 90, 92,

95, 134, 137, 141–42, 180, 218, 221;
voice-over in, 12–16, 25, 40–42, 44,
49–50, 52–54, 57–62, 66, 68, 70, 72,
74–77, 79, 83–86, 88, 90, 92, 96, 98–
99, 134–35, 137, 140–41, 145–46, 158,
160–63, 167–68, 180–81, 184–85, 190,
193, 199, 218, 220–21; and classical
narrative, 26–28, 30, 54, 58, 60, 71, 75,
89–93, 99–100, 103, 110, 113, 122, 130,
135, 143, 146–47, 155, 158, 161–62, 168,
171, 175, 180, 182, 190, 194, 200, 202,
221, 223; and public discourse, 27–28,
78, 91, 184–86, 188, 190–95, 212–13;
and desire, 29, 57, 59–61, 66–70, 74,
112, 129, 137, 160, 170–75, 199, 212, 216,
219–20, 222; and ideology, 31, 33–34,
84, 90, 96, 104, 130, 137–39, 145, 151,
159, 182, 219; its image of woman, 33,
44, 50, 51, 68, 77, 97, 109, 111, 115, 119n,
165; as paradoxical form, 34–36, 77,
87, 98, 128, 137–39, 150–51, 157, 162–
63, 167, 176, 186, 195, 196n, 218, 222;
its period of popularity, 36n, 218, 221;
as existential tale, 53, 127, 199; ironic
character of, 54–55, 128, 165, 188, 191;
narrative patterns in, 57–58, 66–67,
70–71, 72n, 149, 160, 179, 217–18; and
the double, 61, 67, 69, 111–12, 125,
165–66, 193, 195; and violence, 68–69,
191–92, 198, 206–9; environment of,
74, 193, 195, 200–201, 203; multiple
narrators in, 74–75, 79, 83–87; and
paranoia, 86, 129–30, 190–91, 208; as
subversive text, 90, 92–93, 113, 115–17,
132, 137, 162, 220; as reflexive form,
90–91, 95, 97, 99–101, 103, 107, 111–12,
117, 126, 131, 134, 138–39, 142, 146–48,
158, 161–64, 167, 185–86, 189–92, 194;
recuperative strategies in, 91–93, 95,
99–101, 105, 113–16, 118, 127, 130, 166,
220; and realism, 105, 107, 110, 113,
134–39, 145, 147–48, 151–52, 154, 157–
60, 162–63, 168–69, 172, 174–75, 180;
social thrust of, 136, 151, 155, 157–60,
166, 170, 172–75, 182, 195, 217; its
evolution, 154, 157–60, 168–69, 175.
See also Classical film narrative;
Discourse
Ford, John: the director's wartime
experience, 22

Foucault, Michel: on madness, 11; critical
method, 11–12, 218; on paradox in
discourse, 14, 25, 28, 36, 38n, 152n,
194; on language, 35, 54; on the
dangers of discourse, 44–46, 77, 181–
83, 189, 195; on authorship, 85; and
truth in discourse, 138; on speech,
198–99, 206, 212; on fascism, 219. See
also Discourse
Fox, Terry Curtis, 6, 16
Framed (film), 27
Frank, Nino, 9
Frenzy (film), 19
Freud, Sigmund: on repetition
compulsion, 58, 71
Friday the Thirteenth (film), 19

Genre criticism, 31, 39n, 177n
Getaway, The (film), 8
Girard, Rene: and mimetic desire, 67; on
the plague as metaphor, 173
Glass Web, The (film), 27, 182, 196n
Gledhill, Christine, 15, 75
Goodis, David: hard-boiled novelist, 5
Graham, Mark, 64
Grant, Barry, 31
Greek tragedy, 189
Greene, Graham, 5
Griffith, D. W.: and narrative
experimentation, 2, 3
Guattari, Felix: on the limits of
ideological criticism, 219

Halloween (film), 19
Hammett, Dashiell: and the hard-boiled
tradition, 5–6, 8, 45
Harvey, Sylvia, 30
Hathaway, Henry: as director of
semidocumentaries, 22, 134–36
Hayworth, Rita: as sex goddess, 67, 181
Heath, Stephen, 21, 27
Hell of a Woman, A (novel), 8
Hellinger, Mark: producer of The Naked
City, 25, 138, 158–60
High Noon (film), 167
High Wall, The (film), 19
Hillier, Jim, 175
Hirsch, Foster, 10, 12, 26, 155, 195; on
voice-over/flashback, 40, 42; on noir
settings, 180

Hitchcock, Alfred, 19, 143
House of Strangers (film), 182
House on 92nd Street, The (film), 22, 24–25, 134–39, 161
House Un-American Activities Committee: effects on Hollywood films, 170, 189
Hughes, Dorothy B., 5, 190
Huston, John: the director's wartime experience, 22

I Am a Fugitive from a Chain Gang (film): and social problem films, 217
I Died a Thousand Times (film), 219
I Wake Up Screaming (film), 219
I Walk Alone (film), 219
Ideological criticism, 31, 33–34, 219
In a Lonely Place (film), 13, 27, 34, 182–83, 189–94, 200
In a Lonely Place (novel), 190, 196n
Ince, Thomas: as film pioneer, 3
Invasion of the Body Snatchers (film), 167
It's a Wonderful Life (film): and film fantasy, 161

Jacobs, Lewis: on the documentary, 22
Johnny Guitar (film), 12
Judge Priest (film): and early use of flashback, 14

Kawin, Bruce, 16, 75, 88; mindscreens, 37n, 41, 52, 177n; on reflexivity, 90–91; on subjectivity, 91
Kazan, Elia: director of semidocumentaries, 26, 135, 170, 175; as HUAC witness, 177–78n
Key Largo (film), 40
Killers, The (film), 15, 75, 77
Killer's Kiss (film), 40
Killing, The (film), 7
Kiss Me Deadly (film), 13, 26, 30, 94, 198–215, 222; its debated conclusion, 198, 213n; wasteland motif in, 204–5, 210–11; redeemer motif in, 210; classical allusions in, 211, 214n; Brechtian devices in, 214n
Kiss Me Deadly (novel), 200–201, 203, 205, 210–11, 214n
Kiss of Death (film), 2, 134, 160

Kozloff, Sarah: on voice-of-god narration, 158–59
Kracauer, Siegfried: on crime films, 4, 5, 151
Krutnik, Frank: on voice-over narration in *Double Indemnity*, 44, 51, 83; on adaptation, 49
Kubrick, Stanley: the director's work with Jim Thompson, 7

Lacan, Jacques: on the unconscious, 28; on speech, 49, 52, 222, 223n; on desire, 51; his concept of the mirror stage, 146, 162
Lady from Shanghai, The (film), 15, 57–72, 74–75, 84, 86, 155, 158, 162, 170, 180–81, 188; storytelling in, 62–63
Lady in the Lake, The (film), 13, 18–21, 92, 100–101, 103–18, 121, 130, 132; reviewed, 105; identity in, 111–13, 123
Lady in the Lake, The (novel), 103
Lafferty, William, 24
Laing, R. D.: on disintegration, 205
Lang, Fritz, 17, 29, 32, 196n
Lasch, Christopher: on ideology and the ego, 219
Laura (film), 18
Lavery, David, 129
Litvak, Anatole: director of *Sorry, Wrong Number,* 76
Luhr, William, 92, 114

MacCabe, Colin: on conventions of film realism, 135, 168, 180
Magnificent Ambersons, The (film), 58–60. *See also* Welles, Orson
Maltese Falcon, The (film), 6, 13, 18, 94, 218
March of Time, The (film): origins, 23–24; its formula, 135–36. *See also* Rochemont, Louis de
Marshall, Stuart, 112
Mask of Dimitrios, The (film), 75
Melodrama: as narrative mode, 150–51, 156, 166–67, 173, 217
Melville, Herman: influence on *Lady from Shanghai,* 64–66
Merleau-Ponty, Maurice: on perception, 89, 91, 94

MGM Studios: and postwar profits, 104, 119n
Mildred Pierce (film), 40, 171
Mildred Pierce (novel), 7, 16
Miller, J. Hillis, 72
Moby Dick (novel): resonances in *Lady from Shanghai*, 64, 66
Modernist narrative: its distinction from classical style, 36n; its characteristics, 89
Montgomery, Robert: director of *Lady in the Lake*, 13, 103–4, 106, 114
Moreno, Julio: on subjective camera, 20, 107
Murder, My Sweet (film), 10, 18–19, 88–101, 103–5, 108, 113, 130, 132, 216
Murder, My Sweet (novel), 16
Murnau, F. W.: as expressionist director, 17
Musketeers of Pig Alley (film), 2

Naked City, The: as film, 10, 13, 24–25, 134, 138–39, 156, 158–61; as television series, 221
Naremore, James: on Rita Hayworth, 67
Neorealism, 10, 25, 170; characteristics of, 24, 155, 168–69; influence on the *film noir*, 135, 168, 172; its evolution, 154
Newsreels: influence on *film noir*, 23–24, 135–36
Nichols, Bill: on narrative and ideology, 25, 34, 84, 101, 131, 162
Night and the City (film), 26
Nightmare (film), 162
Nightmare Alley (film), 27, 182, 186–89, 200
North, Edmund: screenwriter for *In a Lonely Place*, 190
Notorious (film), 27

O'Brien, Geoffrey, 8
Open City (film), 24, 168
Out of the Past (film), 15, 31, 33

Pabst, G. W.: as expressionist director, 17
Paisan (film): and Italian neorealism, 24, 168
Panic in the Streets (film), 10, 26, 160, 168–76; and the god Pan, 174

Pearson, Drew: his introduction to *City across the River*, 157
Peeping Tom (film), 112
Percy, Walker: on the function of language, 1, 32
Peterson, L. S., 10, 11
Phantom Lady (film), 30
Place, J. A., 10, 11, 33, 97
Polan, Dana, 126, 132n
Pop. 1280 (novel), 8
Porfirio, Robert, 13, 53, 127
Possessed (film): and subjective camera, 19, 117
Postman Always Rings Twice, The (film), 15, 40, 57, 86, 92, 158, 171
Postman Always Rings Twice, The (novel), 7, 53
Powell, Dick, 92
Power and the Glory, The (film): multiple narrators in, 14
Preminger, Otto: and the German impact on American film, 32
Production Code: its influence on *film noir*, 51
Psycho (film), 19
Pynchon, Thomas, 107

Rancho Notorious (film), 12
Ray, Nicholas: director of *In a Lonely Place*, 189, 191, 196n
Rear Window (film), 112
Rebecca (film): and voice-over/flashback narration, 14
Red Harvest (novel), 6
Renov, Michael, 115
Repetition mechanism, 58, 71. *See also* Freud, Sigmund
Repression mechanism, 28, 39; *film noir* as repressive text, 39n. *See also* Freud, Sigmund
Rochemont, Louis de: producer of semidocumentaries, 135–36, 145. *See also March of Time*

Salt, Barry: on technological developments in film, 18
Sartre, Jean-Paul: and *No Exit* (play), 126
Savage Night (novel), 8–9
Schrader, Paul, 9, 10, 11, 12, 24, 25, 31, 217

Serie Noire, 9
Serres, Michel, 110
Shadoian, Jack, 204–5, 212
Shepherd of the Hills (film), 22
Shindler, Colin, 4
Silver, Alain, 5, 10, 204
Siodmak, Robert: and the German
  influence on *film noir*, 32
Sleeping City, The (film), 155, 157
Smoodin, Eric: on voice-over narration,
  41
Social problem film, 33, 217
Solt, Andrew: screenwriter for *In a
  Lonely Place*, 190
Sorry, Wrong Number (film), 12, 14, 15, 74–
  87, 155, 180, 182; as radio play, 76;
  possession motif in, 77–83, 85; and the
  pastoral, 87n
Spellbound (film), 10
Spillane, Mickey, 200, 205
Stewart, Jimmy, 146–47
Sunset Boulevard (film), 8, 16, 34, 42, 181,
  189, 221
Sweet Smell of Success, The (film), 27

T-Men (film), 24, 134, 138–39
Technological development: in filming
  equipment, 18, 23, 104, 169; and
  effects on *noir* style, 38n, 118n; as
  metaphor, 148–49, 162
They Won't Believe Me (film), 182
Thin Man, The (film), 100
13 Rue Madeleine (film), 22, 135
Thompson, Jim: and the crime novel, 5,
  7–9, 89, 196n
Totter, Audrey, 105
Trail of the Lonesome Pine (film), 22
Tuska, John: on the *noir* visual style, 136
Twentieth Century-Fox, 135
Tyler, Parker, 23, 156, 177n

Union Station (film), 168
Untouchables, The (television series), 221

Vernet, Marc, 34, 57, 107, 113, 118
Visconti, Luchino: as neorealist director,
  154
Voice-of-god narration: 24–26, 137–38,
  151, 155–59, 161, 167–68, 174–75;
  characteristics of, 38n

Wald, Jerry: and voice-over/flashback
  narration, 40
Wald, Malvin: screenwriter for *The Naked
  City*, 159
Ward, Elizabeth, 5, 10
Welles, Orson: his influence on American
  film, 14, 181; his *Heart of Darkness*
  experiment, 58, 64, 104; and the
  Mercury Theatre, 58, 72n; and *Lady
  from Shanghai*, 58–59, 64, 66–67, 71,
  72n; and *Citizen Kane*, 74–76
While the City Sleeps (film), 196n
Whitney, John S., 10
Widmark, Richard, 169
Wild Boys of the Road (film): and the social
  problem film, 33, 217
Wilder, Billy: director, 17, 51; his view of
  public discourse, 181–82; his linking of
  The Big Carnival and *Double Indemnity*,
  196n
Wills, Chill, 161
Window, The (film), 88
Wing and a Prayer, A (film), 22
Woman in the Window, The (film), 88, 92
Wood, Michael, 89
Woolrich, Cornell: and the crime novel, 5
World War II: influence on *film noir*, 4,
  23, 220; as spur to technological
  development, 18, 104; and the
  documentary, 22–23, 135, 154
Wright, Elizabeth, 219
Wrong Man, The (film), 143
Wyler, William: the director's wartime
  experience, 22

Zavattini, Cesare: and neorealism, 168

A Note on the Author

J. P. Telotte is an associate professor of English at Georgia Institute of Technology, where he has taught since 1979. He received his B.S. from Loyola University of the South, an M.A. from the University of New Orleans, and the Ph.D. from the University of Florida. He has previously published in such journals as *Film Quarterly, Genre, South Atlantic Review, Journal of Popular Film and Television,* and *Southern Quarterly,* and is the author of *Dreams of Darkness: Fantasy and the Films of Val Lewton.*